Letters
to the Next President

Letters
to the Next President

What We Can Do About the Real Crisis
in Public Education

2008 ELECTION EDITION

Edited by Carl Glickman
Foreword by Bill Cosby

Teachers College, Columbia University
New York and London

Published by Teachers College Press, 1234 Amsterdam Avenue, New York, NY 10027

Library of Congress Cataloging-in-Publication Data

Glickman, Carl D.
    Letters to the next President : what we can do about the real crisis
in public education / edited by Carl Glickman ; foreword by Bill Cosby.
— 2008 election ed.
      p. cm.
    Includes bibliographical references.
    ISBN 978-0-8077-4809-1 (pbk. : alk. paper)
    1. Public schools—United States. 2. Educational change—United
· States. 3. Education and state—United States. I. Glickman, Carl D.
LA217.2.L48 2007
371.010973—dc22   2007023714

ISBN 978-0-8077-4809-1 (paper)

Printed on acid-free paper
Manufactured in the United States of America

14   13   12   11   10   09   08   07   8   7   6   5   4   3   2   1

To *all* children,
who deserve an education
steeped in wisdom, engagement,
and public purpose.

Contents

PART ONE
SCHOOLS FOR ALL

PART TWO
LEARNING FOR ALL

PART THREE
TEACHING FOR ALL

PART FOUR
STANDARDS FOR ALL

PART FIVE
EDUCATION FOR ALL

NOTE ON THE
2008 ELECTION EDITION

"The most important office in our democracy is that of citizen." —*Supreme Court Justice Louis Brandeis*

This special 2008 election edition of *Letters to the Next President* aims to open the discussion about what truly can be done to promote an education system that works for all students. There is a new introduction, some of the letters have been updated, a new letter from Elizabeth DeBray-Pelot has been added, and a new resources section for parents, educators, and activists has been included at the back of the book.

Why a new edition? Because we are beginning a new era of possibilities about what it means to be a well-educated American and because no issue is more important to America's future than the quality of education for its next generation of citizens. Only an informed and engaged citizenry can revitalize American democracy, so this time we have to get it right.

—Carl Glickman

WHERE DO WE START TO SWEEP?

Bill Cosby

Dear Mr./Madame President

I'm looking at a room. I've got a mop and a broom and a rag and some detergent. It's the junkiest room I've ever seen. A child did not make this room junky; this room was made junky and left junky by grown people: generations of litterers. Educated people—legislators, school board members, superintendents, principals, taxpayers, teachers, and presidents—have entered this room and added their mess to the mess that was already there. For all those who added to the junk, there are some of us who left and, knowing how junky it is, never went back. Some of us may even be those legislators, taxpayers, superintendents, teachers, principals, and presidents who have now forgotten and pile in more junk.

Turn around and examine what you took away from the junky room called school. Look at it and think about why there is so little sympathy, clarity, and support for those students and teachers who must live in the mess that we all helped make. Today, it is a wonder that our schools are able to do even as well as they do. I think we must be grateful that there always have been talented and determined teachers with hands on their hips and a certain strength of character who look the junkman in the eye and say, "You aren't going to put that trash in my room!" They find their way through the maze of rules and special interests and just do what they became teachers to do—help their students shine.

Is there no one to clean that room?

Why have we made it so hard and so discouraging for those who have to live in the mess we have made for them? We know what is needed to grow strong children. We raise money—millions of dollars—to find a cure for polio. We raise money—millions of dollars—to research and find immunizations for smallpox, typhoid, tetanus, and measles. We raise money—millions of dollars—to aid businesses, build prisons, strengthen homeland defense, and provide security for our elderly. Yet our neighborhood public school, particularly in places of poverty, is left in terrible condition. It doesn't matter how or where the school began—from marble, brick, stone, cement, or glass. That school, that room, is cluttered and crumbling and doesn't function as it should because legislators, taxpayers, teachers, superintendents, and principals all keep adding to the junky room. What is it that these children, these victims, have done to deserve this?

Of course, I'm assuming that the president of the United States probably never went to a poor and neglected public school—where books have missing pages, walls have peeling paint, children have nothing to draw or write with, and where there is no library for reading a story or doing homework. These are the junkiest rooms: the poorest public schools where every year there are more cutbacks, where there's less money all the time.

This time, on top of the mess is a new mess—a slew of new directives stretching budgets for more tests, more requirements, more unfunded programs—creating even more gaps in the education given to our wealthiest kids compared to our poorest kids.

Wealthy people drive by the junky school and comfort themselves by thinking that money is not the issue. But nothing that is dear to America was ever maintained without it, from our nation's security to our communications systems, from our airlines to our highways. Believe this: The poor performance of schools and the lack of achievement among many of our students is indeed about money. We need money to secure great teachers, money to update teaching methods, money for technology and supplies, and money for time. Time is a precious commodity and teachers need it to meet and plan with students, parents, principals, and citizens about how to take back their schools so that they can teach and kids can learn.

This is a book about how we can sweep up all of this mess and get back to what education comes down to: caring, intelligent, trustworthy, and knowledgeable adults who will ensure that every student can learn. For when the junk is cleaned out of that junky room, its structure is sound: Public education is a good foundation on which to build a better life for each of us, for our families and society. If we want to prove that education is worth the trouble to these children who never made the mess in the first place, our schools have to inspire and advance them so they can do what they ought to do.

The power of the letters in this book underscores the urgency of the clean-up mission to save our public schools. I have lived a good part of my life as a public figure with a strong commitment to education. I receive letters all the time, and I know they can make a difference. Here is a small piece of one to help you begin the journey. It comes to me from a young woman, a teacher returning to graduate school to improve her craft. Her name is Sheena Oommen and she attends Teachers College, Columbia University. She writes to us about poor urban schools, but the message is universal. The plight of our most vulnerable children is all around us—in the inner city and the poorest rural and suburban communities as well—from preschool to high school and beyond. This junk is found in classrooms, schools, and neighborhoods across America. Listen to her eloquent words:

> In my heart, I always knew that I would become an educator, but I never thought that I would want to teach in the urban world. I asked myself, as well as others such as family and friends, "Why do I want to teach in the city? Why do I want

to teach children who do not have a safe environment to learn in and who lack resources and support from administrators and family? Why do I want to put the time and effort in to teach these children, knowing that in return the only certain thing I will get is stress?" These questions run through my head over and over again. I sometimes think that I will wake up one day and say to myself that I do not want to teach in the urban world. But this never occurs and I am glad to say that I am thankful that it never occurs. Through my experiences teaching in cities such as New York and Philadelphia I saw through the innocent eyes of my students that they need people who will love them and support them through the good and bad times. My heart and mind are dedicated to urban youths. I believe I can make a difference.

What do we owe this young woman and those just like her who refuse to give up and who continue to work amid the poverty, the violence, and the junk? If she will not turn her back, can you?

I INVITE YOU TO LOOK INTO THIS ROOM. You have these letters to point the way, to keep you going as you sweep and mop and dust and even do some of the heavier work. You can say to our nation, "We must begin, we cannot wait for someone else to clear out the mess." My hope is that 30 years from now this book will no longer matter because kids will have the public schools that they deserve. And for a start, let's give them back recess.

Respectfully
Bill Cosby

ACKNOWLEDGMENTS

I would like to express my gratitude to all the people who made this 2008 election edition a reality. The staff at Teachers College Press was once again superb. I wish to thank my colleagues—faculty, students, and administrators—in the Educational Administration and Policy Studies program at the University of Georgia's College of Education for so graciously welcoming me back and for providing support for my work on this edition. Also, I'd like to offer my sincere appreciation to my former colleagues at Texas State University–San Marcos and the Mitte Family for their steadfast help during the first edition of this book.

I wish to acknowledge the influence of my fellow board members at the Forum for Education and Democracy (www.forumforeducation. org), as well as the many other educators, parents, students, and citizens who continue to reinforce in word and deed the fact that public education belongs to all of us.

Finally, I cannot say enough in praise of the wonderful array of authors who wrote letters for this book. They donated all royalties to nonprofit organizations working on behalf of children and better schools. This was clearly a labor of mutual care, wisdom, and commitment. It is our highest desire that these updated, heartfelt, and reasoned letters will be read, discussed, and used in the revitalization of democracy through an educated citizenry.

I WISH IT WASN'T SO . . .
NOW MAKE US PROUD

Carl Glickman

Dear Reader,

I wish it wasn't so! I wish we did not need another edition of *Letters to the Next President*. The first edition came out in early spring of 2004, just as the presidential primaries were being contested. I wrote then: "These letters from students; great elementary, middle, and secondary school teachers; principals who lead some of the most outstanding schools in the country; parents who organize for their local public schools; education scholars, reformers, and activists on the leading edge of what is possible for all students; and current and former elected officials point us in a better and healthier direction for improving education, our schools, and our democracy."

So why, nearly four years later, is there a need for a second edition of this book? As you are well aware, there is a morass in our land about the future of our country and the future of American democracy. Most of us think that participatory democracy in America today is a sham, that it is not based on the reality of what actually happens, and that it doesn't deal with decisions that affect us in our everyday

1

lives. Most of us find politics to be distasteful and government officials to be untrustworthy. Most of us show our disdain for government through our refusal to participate at even the most minimal level of citizenship. The majority of us do not vote, do not attend a single public meeting a year, and do not exercise our First Amendment rights and responsibilities. When compared with other industrialized nations, the United States ranks at or near the bottom on indicators of care and support for our citizens—including health benefits, public spaces, maternity leave, family vacation time, minimum wage, guaranteed retirement plans, child care, and equity of resources for education. Indeed, two thirds of Americans believe that "things have pretty seriously gotten on the wrong track" in this country.

Many of us seem to have given up on the American promise of decency and respect for all. And our youth follow in their parents' and grandparents' paths, continuing the decline in civic participation begun after World War II.

You, our next president, can do something about this. Deep down, we want to be proud to be Americans and, believe me, we are looking for every possible reason to be proud. We want to talk with pride about how our ancestors rose to the challenges of making a life in America, about how generous Americans are in donating to disaster relief, about how youth volunteerism is on the rise, and about how courageous our young soldiers fighting overseas are. But it is getting harder and harder for us, as a people, to reach across our different religious, political, ethnic, racial, socioeconomic, lifestyle, gender, and occupational lines to discuss how we can work together to improve our larger communities. We want to believe in our country, but we need to find ways to make the ideals of democracy, participation, and education the core of our future.

Yet, perhaps if we rejuvenate the core mission of our schools—to educate free-thinking individuals—our schools could help to create an educated citizenry willing to share the burden of a working democracy. Thomas Jefferson, who first proposed that public schools are essential to a democracy, wrote, "Every government degenerates when trusted to the rulers of the people alone. The people themselves, therefore, are its only safe depositories. And to render them safe their minds must be improved." Maybe, just maybe, if we could realize the true promise of public education, we could close the achievement gap and foster an America whose citizens are proud to use their minds to participate in civic life.

How did we fall into the current educational quagmire? The federal Elementary and Secondary Education Act (ESEA), now known as No Child Left Behind (NCLB), was quickly planned and passed shortly after September 11, 2001, at the height of America's concern with terrorism. Educators, civic leaders, students, parents, and researchers knew that—despite the laudable goals of the bill to reduce the glaring achievement gaps amongst various ethnic, racial, special needs, and socioeconomic groups of students—the enactment of the bill would aggravate inequities. They knew it would leave teachers and students with a mess of rules and procedures and would create an education agenda different from what parents, students, and citizens expect from a quality education.

In the first edition of this book, our letter writers predicted that, unless the bill was drastically changed, we would see a further narrowing of curricula, students would be subjected to more and more test-taking preparation for poorly conceived examinations, and that states and school districts would lower their passing levels and manipulate test score data and drop-out rates in an effort to scam the system. They foresaw that student engagement and interactive learning would be pushed aside and replaced by more didactic, "drill-and-kill" teaching. The letter writers also predicted that the mandated formulas the federal government would use for doling out rewards and sanctions to schools would be unworkable.

And it has come to pass. Teachers have been left with a mess. They struggle with whether they should sacrifice science labs, music and art, history and social studies, field trips, and high-interest curriculum to the altar of test preparation. Seventy percent of districts report that this narrowing of learning has, indeed, occurred. Parents know this well, and in survey after survey they complain that their children are over-tested, that curricula are passive and uninspiring, and that there is a lack of balance between the teaching of basic skills and the fulfillment of the democratic and civic purpose of education.

And we should not be surprised that teachers, school officials, and parents—not to mention students—are upset. Elizabeth Debray-Pelot, in the only new letter in this book, explains how legislators and congressional and presidential staff consciously excluded education researchers; assessment specialists; and student, parent, school board, teacher, and school leaders from the planning of NCLB. As a result, NCLB has been criticized, legally challenged, and outright rejected by some states (e.g., Connecticut, Utah, and Nebraska). These states refuse to buckle under to what they see as diminished educational opportunities for their students, the use of bad science to reward or sanction schools, inadequate funding, and an unconstitutional intervention by the federal government into varied and already-proven state accountability systems. Instead of an open, considerate dialogue characteristic of a democracy, criticism of the federal plan—just like criticism about the ongoing war—has been deflected by federal officials. Those who are critical of NCLB have been attacked for being "whiners," "excusers," and even "bigots"—thus ignoring and denying any possible merit to their dissent.

Also correctly predicted in the first edition of this book was that the federal government later would claim success for the enactment of the bill. Unfortunately, the government's evidence of "proven" achievement has been selective at best and—according to a number of independent research studies—simply untrue.

Any government—regardless of party affiliation—that believes its side is right, no matter what, becomes far less a democracy and more a gang of believers who need only to report their version of truth to the exclusion of all else. Absence of open discussion in favor of control of the "truth" is more akin to the authoritarian world of George Orwell's *1984*. In order to flourish, a democracy must always be open to inquiry, study, and human reasoning.

It is time—way past time—to enter a new phase and look at what actually has been accomplished and devise ways to improve education from this point on. The matter at hand, no less than the future of our youth and the future of our American democracy, is too important to ignore. With a new president and administration coming into office in 2008, it is past time to open the discussion about how best to educate students and hold schools accountable. It is time for more citizens to connect to their schools and assist in fulfilling the promise of better education for all.

Let me finish as I did in the introduction to the first edition. These letters are meant to open more thoughts, discussions, and plans about what should be an American education for all the citizens of our democracy. These letters are about the core of America: What do we want future students to be able to know and do, who should control such decisions, and how might we help schools respond to the wishes of parents, students, and communities?

Readers who wish to be part of the strengthening of our public schools can find specific suggestions on how to become involved in the letters and in the new resource section, which includes descriptions of several policy and activist organizations for educators, parents, and citizens and a joint signing statement for changing and improving current legislation.

Ms. or Mr. President, all of us—the writers and readers of this book—would like to open a dialogue with you to discuss what we can do together. Please, during your time on the campaign trail and your time in office, listen to your public speak to the issues ahead. There are many lessons to be learned about ourselves as a nation and as a democracy.

From one citizen to another in respect and in optimism,

Carl Glickman

Sources and Suggested Reading

Bryant, A. L. (2006). Executive director's report: Civic engagement is key mission of public schools. *School Board News.*

Carnegie Corporation of New York & the Center for Information and Research on Civic Learning and Engagement. (2003). *The civic mission of schools.* New York: Carnegie Corporation of New York.

Center on Education Policy. (2006, March). *From the capitol to the classroom: Year 4 of the No Child Left Behind Act; Summary and recommendations.* Accessed March 23, 2007, at http://www.cep-dc.org/nclb/Year4/Press

Croddy, M. (2006, July 2). Have we forgotten civic education? *Los Angeles Times.* Accessed March 23, 2007, at http://www.latimes.com/news/printedition/suncommentary/la-oe-croddy2jul02,1,3428993,print.story?coll=la-headlines-suncomment&ctrack=1&cset=true

Klein, A. (2006). Public dissatisfied over key NCLB provisions, report says. *Education Week, 25*(34), p. 8.

Lee, J., & Orfield, G. (2006). *Tracking achievement gaps and assessing the impact of NCLB on the gaps: An in-depth look into national and state reading and math outcome trends.* Cambridge, MA: The Civil Rights Project at Harvard University.

Leonhardt, D. (2006, September 3) Adding it up: Pockets half empty, pockets half full. *New York Times,* Section Four, pp. 1, 12.

Levine, P., & Youniss, J. (2006). *Options for federal policy in civic education and development.* Paper found online at www.civicmissionofschools.org

Mishel, L., Bernstein, J., & Alegretto, S. (2006). *The state of working America, 2006–2007.* Washington, DC: Education Policy Institute.

O'Connor, S. D., & Romer, R. (2006, March 25). Not by math alone. *Washington Post,* p. A19.

Skocpol, T. (2003). *Diminished democracy: From membership to management in American civic life.* Norman: University of Oklahoma Press.

Wattenberg, M. P. (2002). *Where have all the voters gone?* Cambridge, MA: Harvard University.

PART ONE
SCHOOLS FOR ALL

Journey to a New Life

Dear Future President,

When I think of my childhood home in the Dominican Republic, I remember running past old wooden houses and down narrow streets, holding my twin sister's hand and giggling. As the night approached, our grandmother, Doña Eva, would call us to get back home. We heard her, but we didn't worry. Even though we were only five years old, we knew just where we were in our small town of La Vega, and everyone there knew us by name.

That year, my mother began her journey to a new life in the United States. Until we became teenagers, my grandmother took care of me and my sister, Carmen. In the afternoons, Doña Eva sat with us on the porch and taught us to read and write. Though I would have rather watched the cars and people passing by, she made me read over and over from the newspaper, *El Caribe*. As I struggled to hold the paper against the gusts of wind, she would tell me in her spirited voice to pay attention. "Nothing must disrupt our learning," she said.

We must have the education that she had never had under Trujillo's dictatorship. *Trabajen duro en la escuela para que así puedan ser personas de provecho en el mañana*, she told us—"Work hard in school, so you can become productive people in the future."

The last time I saw Doña Eva, one morning in October 1999, she was standing on the porch as we waved good-bye in the warm Dominican breeze. I could see her big black eyes fill with tears in hopes for our new life in America with my mother.

The next day, I found myself in the streets of the Bronx, in the city of New York—that city we had heard would be the place where our dreams would come true. My sister and I moved into one room with my mother and her husband, in a house shared with many other people. Most were single men in their thirties and, as young teenagers, my sister and I felt afraid much of the time. Neither of us spoke any English, and neither did our mother. Still, Mami found her way to the city's office for education, where an official who spoke Spanish assigned me and Carmen each to a different school.

For better and for worse, his decision had a powerful effect on us both. Carmen would go to a big school with more than a thousand other students. Mixed into classes where nobody knew her name, she would have to learn English with very little support.

Meanwhile, I would enter the ninth grade in a small high school intended just to help students new to the United States. In small and flexible classes that often took us out into the subways and museums and neighborhoods of New York, I would be learning English, and finding my place in this enormous city.

Carmen and I are identical twins, but those very different settings resulted in big differences in our learning. Carmen felt small, scared, and isolated in her overwhelming new school with its overcrowded classes. She ended that year without learning to speak, read, and write in her new language. But in my newcomers' school, each of my teachers gave me the skills and knowledge I needed in order to survive. Starting with the first day, when I learned to say, "I am Rosa, and I am from the Dominican Republic," I was finding my voice in America.

By the tenth grade, I was ready for a small public high school that enrolled about three hundred immigrant students. In a group of seventy-five students, we worked in classes with the same four teachers in each cluster or grade. The classes were longer than at most schools, but they went by quickly because the teachers did not lecture us. We learned to teach each other through discussions, debates, and group activities. If there were five questions to answer, each group would take one question to discuss and come up with an idea or a written paragraph. Everyone had to agree, and then at the end, each group presented their views. We were acquiring essential skills for our lives, for situations in the future where we would have to be talking to people and making agreements.

Of course, in every classroom, people were at different levels. But I didn't see any difference between us. It came naturally being with everybody else, because that's what life is like. In every group project there has to be a leader, but we divided the work. It was all about feeding each other and having something to offer.

I don't think that just because you're a bad student you don't have anything to say. There's something that you react to, something you like, and you have to find it. In order to find it, you need to be exposed to every kind of person. And you have to be given the opportunity to succeed. There's a Spanish saying, *Nadie nace sabiendo*—"No one is born knowing." You learn! Everyone has something to teach and something to learn. Maybe a not-so-skilled student might teach you how to be more patient—a skill that you need for life! This is what you get out of a good, small high school, these little things about knowing yourself.

When I first got to my school I felt lonely—it's normal, like with any other new place. But the difference in a small school is that people notice you. They know that you are feeling just like they felt when they first came. And the teachers know that, too. So they try to approach you, talk to you, let you know that you can ask them anything at any time. Sometimes on our writing, the teachers would ask a question, such as "how are you doing, how are you making the transition to this school?" Even though these are small things—writing a little note on someone's paper—it gives you strength to continue working, because you know that someone knows what you're like.

Small schools are perfect for teenagers, because we need people to be warm and care about us, to be after us—otherwise we might take the wrong road. Mostly we're in school, so school becomes our home. And we want to make sure that we're in a good home.

This is a hard age to be. You're confused, you don't know what you're going to do, you feel alienated. You need adults around you, and friends. And in a small community, it's more likely that you'll find people who know you better—people who can be as understanding and patient as my grandmother, Doña Eva.

Learning in that school day after day made me realize that my voice could be heard. I remembered how Doña Eva had not had her chance to exercise freedom of speech and speak out against injustices. For every time she was unable to speak, I decided, now I would.

As part of the planning team for a new small school in the Bronx, in the past year I have spoken out about the social and educational inequalities that students face. The Bronx is trying to change that by breaking down big high schools into small schools where students can learn better. But at the very same time, the city recently decided to close down the school that helped me through that first awful and scary year, when I was a new immigrant just trying to find my way. I guess they think it is just too expensive to give a hand to the young people who need it so badly. Like my twin sister, Carmen, these students will be left to manage on their own. Like her, at the end of the year they will still not be speaking for themselves.

Even while some people are trying to turn big schools into small ones, even more districts all over the United States keep building huge schools that hold thousands of students. To the young people who attend them, they can feel more like prisons or factories than places of learning. Schools like these do not help develop the citizens your administration is going to need, people who will know how to work out the problems this country faces.

As I go on to college, I hope to become one of those citizens myself, and later I want to study for a degree in law. I have the confidence and the skills to do that because of the setting in which I got my public school education in the past four years. Just as in my small community when I was little, everybody at my school knew my name. And just as my grandmother did, my teachers here taught me to read the paper, to work hard, to think well, and to raise my voice and speak.

When you become the president of the United States, you will have the chance to encourage more schools like mine to start, instead of shutting them down. If you do, you will find that getting to know people like me and my sister, and teaching all of us well, turns out to be a very good investment in the future of this country.

Sincerely yours,

Rosa Fernández

HELPING ME TO
RAISE MY HAND

To the future president

I am nineteen years old, and I have lived in Harlem all my life. This past year, I got my GED, and I now attend Cooper Union in New York City. I work at several jobs to raise the money I need to live on. I can talk like an educated person, and I can talk like the kids on the street. You would probably point to me as a success story, but you wouldn't have much idea of what got me here. Maybe you should.

I didn't have much of a father in my life. He was a teenager when I was born, and he and my mother were not on good terms. Later he moved to another city, where he married and had two children. I saw him once when I was twelve, and then again this year. Maybe because I remind her of him, my mother, who works for the city, didn't give me a lot of support on the emotional side. We lived with her grandmother, who mostly took care of me. My great-grandmother (I call her my grandmother) only had a few years of education, but she would read to me from Mother Goose and from a big book of fairy tales that she had. She didn't read that well, but pretty soon I took the book and figured it out for myself. I was always reading, and I

14

also watched a lot of television. They say that television isn't good for you, but I don't really believe that. I'm a mimic, and I would imitate the way they talked in the programs and commercials.

I was shy and overweight as a kid, and I didn't take well to bullies, so I used to get in fights at school. In my first elementary school they sent me for tests to figure out if I was retarded, and then they transferred me to another school where they thought I would do better. I did, and I graduated from sixth grade as the valedictorian. All the same, I had a lot of troubles. When I was twelve I tried to kill myself.

They sent me to a psychologist, and I started going to this Jewish community center that helps people out. I was written up in the *New York Times* as one of their "neediest cases." A woman saw it and signed up to be my mentor at the center. When I was thirteen, she arranged for me to go to the University of Michigan for a summer academic program. That summer I lost about fifty pounds from walking everywhere I went.

In ninth grade, at a big New York City high school, I felt alone and uncomfortable. Just to avoid being there, I used to cut every day, leave classes early, come in late. It was always about the people, not the academics. Some people like being a face in the crowd, but it made me feel like nothing. I'm smart, and I can do the work. But once, after cutting for three days, I went back and the teacher said, in a sarcastic way, "Why are *you* here? I'm glad you've graced us with your presence." And that was it. I just left and didn't go back. I went to the library. I would read, draw, be depressed. I knew I should be in school—kids *want* to learn—and I felt alone and stupid.

They ended up sending me to Urban Academy, an alternative public school. The school is very small, and the teachers know you really well. They don't assume anything about you based on your neighborhood, race, or class. They aren't afraid to show themselves, and at the same time they maintain a boundary. As kids, we expect adults to give us directions, but it's a balance. To a certain extent, teachers have to have a personality that students respond to. But that doesn't mean they have to be our best friend; if they were, our education would suffer.

Respect and authority are part of a teacher's job. They earn that from kids when their love for teaching comes out, when they get to talk about something they know. The mark of a good teacher is that no matter how weird or boring you might think their subject is, their passion for it pushes you to learn. It could be rat feces or some nasty thing, but the fact that their eyes are glowing when they talk about it makes you want to know something about it. Kids can tell when teachers know and believe in what they are doing, and then we don't have to get into some authority struggle. We can be independent and speak our minds. I like sparring with my teachers to see what they think, and my teachers like to exchange ideas, to turn our viewpoints on their heads.

A lot of teachers feel pressure to teach us what is going to be on the city and state tests, not what will really connect with us and help us learn. In my old school, my history teacher had been in the army and traveled all over the world. He could have tied our history classes to his experiences. But instead, he had to close that off, and get back to the subject we would be tested on.

High school students also feel a lot of pressure to get things right. Sometimes, you don't hand something in at all because you think it's stupid. It's good when a teacher allows you to fail, and accepts something even if it's not right because you're on the road to something right. When I would get confused at Urban, one of my teachers would look over my shoulder and lead me on the way: "Take it easy, you have it right there," or "You only have to do this." Sometimes you only feel comfortable asking a question if you know enough about the thing already. So when we make that effort to raise our hand—and it takes a lot of effort to stand out—we need the teacher to see it, and to support us if we have trouble getting it out. Every student wants to feel special and smart and talented, but at the same time we want to blend in.

One way teachers can keep hooks in kids for longer is by connecting them to someone else who is a good person. One of my teachers arranged an acting internship for me at a small theater in New York, where people come in with plays and one-act pieces. Once I saw what the others were doing, I realized I had something to contribute. You see other people who are older or smarter do something, and you think, "I can do this, too." I wrote a short musical, with text to hold it together. After I got positive feedback, it was easier to take criticism. They said what they liked, and told me how I could make it better.

The internship was good for me because I had problems with authority. I started to listen and take instructions better. I wasn't on my own; I had responsibilities, and people depended on me for things like answering the phone. You do grunt work, like cleaning the toilet, to work your way up the ladder and get skills. Your reward is getting to do what you love. There was a goal; at the end I would be in a performance and work on my play. It gave me a better attitude toward school and homework—and toward life. It's more concrete now in my head.

Even though I had really good teachers at Urban, I didn't graduate from there. The school has a system of portfolios that you have to complete, to show that you are competent in all the required areas, and I couldn't get my math and science portfolios together without staying another year. Once I turned eighteen, my family didn't want me in high school any more, so I took the GED and started working. But I went back to Urban a lot, and my adviser there helped me apply to college.

Why should someone at your level—the president of the United States—care about how I got through my first nineteen years? Maybe because my life shows the difference it makes when kids get support from adults who are not their parents. A lot of times when things got really hard for me, I had someone who knew what was going on with me, who respected me. That fills a void that might not be addressed at home. People are always saying that schools can't do everything. They blame kids' families for all the problems that we have. But my experience makes me think that the family can't bear all the responsibility for keeping kids safe and helping them learn. As president, you could make it a priority to build up every kind of support system that involves adults with kids. I'm talking about the people that care for children, those who counsel kids and connect us up with opportunities, those who teach us the confidence to ask questions, and those who show us that we matter in the world. If you do that, maybe we'll start seeing more adults who think people like me—kids who might otherwise disappear from the screen—are worth their time and trouble after all.

Sincerely,

DEBORAH MEIER

CREATING SCHOOLS
WE CAN TRUST

Dear President,

Every time you think, "What can I do for educa-tion?," I hope you keep the following thought in mind: There is no way we can raise kids well in the company of adults we don't trust. At the heart of good schooling are relationships: relationships between trusted teachers and children, and between trusted teachers and families. No form of curriculum or teaching method can succeed where these do not hold up. No good ends can be bought at their expense. Where trust has never existed, we have never had good schools. Where it has eroded, we have lost ground. Where it endures is where the best education occurs.

We cannot pass laws requiring relationships to be trustful, but we can develop policy that increases the odds in favor of it. Although much of the current wave of state and federal legislation claims to make schools accountable and to restore trust, these laws actually bear little resemblance to the laws we *need*. Rooted in distrust, the laws we have now can only help that distrust grow.

This is really the litmus test for you, as president. Each and every time a policy decision comes before you, you must ask yourself: What impact will this particular policy have on the development of trustful relationships in every local community? Every single law or regulation that comes out of Washington helps or hurts such relationships; none is neutral.

What is needed is simple; getting it is less so. What we need to improve education are adults who are knowledgeable in the fields that they teach, who have the same standards for care that their constituents do, and who are in a position to exercise their best judgment in their classrooms. When I go to a doctor, I want someone who knows me well enough to distinguish a serious symptom from an ordinary bad day. I want a doctor who has been tracking my health, my moods, and my reactions to climate, drugs, and events over time. Furthermore, I want a chance to change my doctor when I have lost confidence in him or her. We must expect no less for our children's schooling.

When pollsters report that the majority of the public does trust their children's schools, they are met with an onslaught of attacks by editors, politicians, and think-tank gurus—all of whom insist that this is proof that the public must be saved from its ignorance. Every piece of good news about America's schools is met with skepticism, and every piece of bad news with headlines. The fact that we are ranked near the top in literacy worldwide is swept under the rug; but the fact that we are ranked in the middle in math and science is headlined as a measure of failure.

This must not be your path. This inflated badmouthing of our schools takes the focus away from where it is needed. There are schools that *are* in crisis, schools that serve the families who are underserved in myriads of ways, as well as schools that must overcome our unfinished struggle against racism. We will not have the resources to deal with them successfully if we persist in treating the whole of public education as a doomed enterprise.

Whenever we look for quick fixes, global solutions, and institutional magic—like those found in the No Child Left Behind Act—we

take attention and resources away from where the emergency correc-
tion is needed most, and we distort the reforms that are necessary in
the vast majority of our schools. Mammoth mandates with draconian
consequences undermine good practice. They lead to a lot of decep-
tive smoke-and-mirror tactics and fail to tackle the details that matter.
They lead to the kind of headline found in the *New York Times* in July
of 2003: "To Cut Failure Rates, Schools Shed Students." If our model
is one of businesslike efficiency, then dropping a losing sector makes
sense.

After thirty-five years as a teacher, parent, principal, and school
board member, I know most of the tricks that schools have used for
raising attendance data, improving reported test scores, and tweaking
anything else that comes with high stakes. But, under your leadership,
focusing on *doing* good, and not simply *looking* good, must become a
priority and not a luxury that only the rich are able to afford.

Here are eight things that are eminently do-able:

1. Get the Size Right: Small Is Better!

We need schools to be small enough that teachers, parents, administrators, and students can get to know each other well over time.
Small schools make trust easier (though not inevitable). Smallness
makes it harder to hide and keep secrets. Ask the kids. In fact, many
students complain about small schools for just this reason—"They're
always in your face," say some adolescents, half-complainingly and
half-gratefully.

There are trade-offs, of course. But we've got the balance wrong.
We may need more generalists and fewer specialists when we reduce
size. There are benefits that come with generalists, such as bedside
manners, that are good for our health and our education. What we
need to change is the habit of neglecting the importance of long-term
and in-depth relationships.

It follows, then, that districts need to be small, too. Probably,
no school board can serve well more than half a dozen schools and a
few thousand students. Unfortunately, at a moment in history when
the evidence for the benefits of smallness is strongest, we are, in fact,

rapidly increasing the average size of both our schools and districts. Only fifty years ago there were two-hundred thousand school boards in America, compared to fewer than fifteen thousand today, and most of my peers went to schools of a few hundred students—not a few thousand. Every federal act that rewards large-scale over small undermines good schooling. Every federal act that supercedes local decisions undermines smallness. The need for smallness is precisely greater now, as our world grows less personal, less stable, and more complex.

2. Encourage Local Decision Making

We need a president who vetoes policies that replace local professional and parental judgment—about matters of teaching and curriculum, a child's competence or incompetence, good behavior or bad behavior—with the judgment of faceless strangers, however well-intentioned. Small schools and small districts are of little value, and soon disappear, if they have no authority to make important decisions. There is little value in knowing our kids and each other well if the only decisions we can make are trivial ones. Such untrusting policies do not attract the best professionals or the best leadership. Small schools, or networks of such schools, must be in a position to have control over a sufficient number of the factors that count (e.g., staffing, curriculum, assessment, scheduling, budget) if they are, in turn, to accept responsibility for outcomes.

You should assume that every parent wants to be able to look the person in the eye who is responsible for decisions about his or her child. There are good reasons for state and federal bodies to gather data that informs policy—for example, to monitor for health, safety, and civil rights violations. However, we don't need a president to tell us if our children are ready or are not ready to move on to the next grade level, or whether they need another year before graduation. Nor do we want a president who tells our children's teachers what reading program to use, what textbook meets his or her approval, what stories should be read aloud, or what disciplinary program to adopt. These are matters that must remain in the hands of those closest to our children and our communities. No matter how much we trust you as president, these

are matters in which parents and teachers may sometimes disagree due
to differing local cultures and values, and neither Washington nor the
state house can resolve that disagreement for us. Hands off.

3. Get Good Information

Democratic decision making rests on the quality and accessibility of
good information. The public that pays for our schools, as well as the
families of the kids who attend them, needs a range of ways to judge
quality. Since no one claims that test data fairly represent the sum
total of what it means to be a well-educated person, we need the kind
of data that can help us see the whole picture. Policymakers, teachers,
parents, and kids all need such information, but they do not all need
the *same* information, on the same scale, or in the same detail. Local
folks and families need more detail about the stuff they see as priorities: whether kids are happy in school, get along well with their peers,
and respect their teachers. We can either create mammoth databases
that obfuscate truth, as we do now, or we can create more ways to get
at the real, hard facts. Until we get the scale right again, parents, teachers, and kids will too often operate without the kind of information
they need and will be forced to rely on what they suspect are highly
manipulatable statistics. In focusing our school work on acquiring
reams of quantitative data, we have distorted the data needed for good
public policy and the data needed to educate each child well.

Schools and districts need to be as open and transparent as possible so that citizens and professionals can arrive at decisions based
on firsthand knowledge as well as statistical reports by experts. As a
parent and citizen, I want to see the evidence the school collects to
tell about how well it is doing. I do not want just numbers and scores,
behind which may lie very different stories about what is represented. I
want evidence that is as direct as possible—for example, biannual tape
recordings of my child reading aloud, or samples of my child's written
work over time. I want high-quality public reviews of a school's work
to be available to all. Sometimes citizens and policymakers need large-
scale, comparative data. But to use *one* system of testing or *one* type of
test to make all decisions about individual children and their teach-

ers *as well as* to provide broad, comparative data for state and federal policy purposes guarantees that we do both poorly. Current policies are leading us to make our schools test-prep centers that serve neither to educate our children nor inform our public.

4. Provide Choice

One size does not fit all—even if all are equally part of the mainstream of American values. Even this nation's top universities interpret our intellectual heritage in different ways and set different priorities about where to focus their resources. Since schools cannot and should not all be interchangeable, we need options if a school's priorities differ from ours (e.g., in its emphasis upon arts or sports, good manners or creativity, and so on).

We don't have to privatize education to get choice; we can offer it in each and every community as part of the public system. We can, as we must in many policy areas, control such choices to increase the odds that children keep company across lines of race, class, and ethnicity. However, controlled choice makes serious reform possible only if we do not mistake compliance and uniformity for meaningful change. The fact that small public schools of choice are harder to regulate and standardize should be seen as a plus, not, as at present, as a disadvantage.

5. Provide Resources for Improving Facilities and Supporting Professionalism

Of course, I would expect that the professionals I trust have the equipment and training that they need to perform their jobs to the best of their abilities. When I go to the hospital, I expect that the operating room is considered safe and up-to-date, that the doctor has access to an MRI, and that he or she knows how to use a stethoscope or a blood-pressure cuff. Likewise, I want schools where teachers have access to good specialists, and the time and resources to consult with them in order to learn about new techniques and ideas. I'd like the school building, itself, to be safe, sound, and attractive. I don't want to be told that only the rich can afford carpeted rooms, air conditioners for hot summers, good acoustics, clean bathrooms, and nice landscaping. These are areas where the federal government can step in without undermining the local control of schools.

Yes, it means achieving greater equity with regard to resources for rich and poor alike. We need a president who promotes policies and tax structures that enable poor communities to pay their teachers well so that they can hire the best, not the least-experienced and least-competent, teachers. We need a president who provides support to colleges that prepare students young and old to become teachers—including funding for the kind of subsidized internships that good teaching requires.

6. Provide Time

The Greeks were right: Being a good citizen is time-consuming. Being small and transparent only helps if we have the time to meet together. We need policies that make it easier for parents to take time off from work or work part-time so that they can be part of their children's lives and support the institutions that serve them. Federal policy could mandate that for all federal employees (and for all citizens) tomorrow. We need a president who reminds the public that teaching is not a part-time occupation. Teachers are at work before children arrive at school and long after the last student goes home, and they often work into the so-called "summer vacation." This needs to be paid work, not voluntary time dependent on teachers' goodwill. The time crunch kills good teaching and good relationship building between teachers and between teachers and families. Look at every measure that crosses your desk and ask: Will this provide more or less time for parents, citizens, and teachers to gather together to talk thoughtfully about an individual child or the larger community of children?

7. Use a Language of Respect

Since kids cannot learn from teachers or schools that they neither trust nor respect, the way we publicly talk about teachers and schools matters. Disrespect comes in many forms, but it starts with our leadership. Our children learn by example: It's hard to be taught by people whom powerful people look down upon. Keep this in mind when you think about how little teachers are paid and what that pay differential says to kids. I have seen too many parents act out the disrespect they read in their local newspapers and hear from their local and national politicians and then act surprised when their kids act up. Please, be careful how you speak of schools and teachers when you address the nation in press conferences and public speeches.

The same is true of the way we talk about our kids and their families. Let's develop a different and less reductive way of talking about our kids. Despite our glamorization of youth culture, we don't seem to like kids much in our public discourse. This begrudging attitude is hurtful to our children and is unwarranted. Most of their faults are simply efforts to imitate what we glamorize for them. They do not own the movie industry or the radio channels, and they do not design the ubiquitous videogames—adults do. We need to spend time recognizing how often they are courageous, caring, and courteous. We also need to think together about how the public can provide better "educators" for them than those that dominate their nonschool hours today. We are also not very mindful about how we talk about parents, above all beleaguered mothers, especially those who are poor. At best, the public discourse about parenting is patronizing.

The same is true about teaching: Politicians and editorial writers suggest that teachers are too dumb to have created organizations that actually represent their viewpoints—and thus dismiss the collective voice of teachers' unions. Parents, kids, and teachers need to be respected, not put down, for their "special" expertise and interests.

Lastly, make sure that you promote a positive image of public enterprises. It's in our public lives that we are first and foremost equal citizens, and it is here that we must restore a sense of publicness as an aesthetic, moral, and social virtue. The virtues of business and the virtues of schooling both have their place, but they are not always interchangeable. While schools can certainly learn from private business, private institutions have much to learn from public institutions—especially in areas such as quality, openness, equity, and accountability.

8. Close the Gaps

Pretending that tough policies and cries of "no excuses" will succeed in wiping out the power gap between the advantaged and the disadvantaged is a cruel hoax that creates cynicism and distrust. Cheap talk about closing the gap between the rich and the poor in school must be matched by expensive talk about closing the gaps outside of school. We pass on to our kids whatever advantages we have, and your concern for children, Mr. President, will speak loudest if you respond to the growing gap between the advantages of some Americans and the disadvantages of others.

ABOVE ALL ELSE, be the kind of person we brag about in school. As president, demonstrate the habits that you want us to value and engender in a good student. Our nation has had a long history of putting down "school smarts." We either need to change schools and what defines "school smarts" so that they match what we honor elsewhere, or we need to be sure the leaders of our nation are in fact models of the kind of smarts we honor in schools. When you are elected, be sure the people making decisions about education on your behalf in Washington have recently spent time in schools and that their own children attend the schools about which they are making policy. Look for people you'd trust to take care of your own kids.

Sincerely

Deborah W. Meier

ASA G. HILLIARD III

IF WE HAD THE WILL TO
SEE IT HAPPEN

Dear President

Urban schools serving low-income and minority ethnic students are best known for chronic patterns of low academic achievement, for being drug-ridden, and for violence. Perhaps the worst thing that can be said about urban schools is that few people, including educators, expect excellence from these schools or the children they teach. In the face of all this negativity, however, students in some urban public schools, including ethnic minority and low-income students, are already achieving at the highest levels, and are doing so without the use of exotic new methods or materials. So far, we have not chosen to guarantee that this happens for all children. Sadly, many who currently lead "education reform" efforts do not know these things.

There are well-documented "savage inequalities" in school leadership and teaching between the services provided to children of privilege and those provided to children who live in the most challenging circumstances. Many of these inequalities are not readily apparent. There is no chance that urban schools will become sites of high achievement if educators and supporters have a false sense of school power or if these savage inequalities persist.

In spite of the "no child left behind" rhetoric and the "every child can succeed" slogans, few teachers or education supporters actually act as if they believe that we can teach *all* children. There is a very simple reason for this apparent lack of faith, often expressed quite explicitly by educators. Few of them have participated in or know that excellent teaching and learning environments exist for urban children. Few of them know about the following:

- In one of the most stunning studies in the history of educational research, Professors Sanders and Rivers showed that even if two groups of students in Tennessee were very much alike, if one group had three good teachers in a row in third-, fourth-, and fifth-grade mathematics, while the other group had three weak teachers in a row, the first group achieved fifty percentile ranks above the second at the end of three years. That is nearly half of the whole achievement distribution! The quality of teaching did it.

- More than thirty years ago, Project SEED began teaching college-level algebra in low-income public elementary schools with large ethnic minority populations. It now teaches calculus to sixth-grade students in urban low-income minority ethnic communities! The mathematics curriculum for these sixth-grade urban students includes topics such as addition and multiplication of integers, calculation of powers and roots, manipulation and multiplication of polynomial equations, graphing linear equations, finding and interpreting slopes and y intercepts, adding and multiplying matrices, finding identity matrices for addition and multiplication, using matrices to solve linear equations, and posing mathematical hypotheses and proving them to be theorems. This is hardly the typical curriculum for urban public education. Yet the students thrive on it. They love it.

- In Kansas City, Missouri, the Chick Elementary School, led by Principal Audrey Bullard, scored in the top ten percent on state tests.
- Led by Principal Freyer Rivers, Sankofa Shule in Lansing, Michigan, showed similar achievement.
- Led by teacher Tommy Lindsey, Logan High School in San Francisco was featured on a national television program because its urban students took first place in the state forensics competition and won national awards as well. Logan's forensic team won the coveted School of Excellence Award at the national competition and produced a first-place individual honor.
- Led by Doris Brevard, for nearly twenty years, the Robert L. Vann Elementary School was among the highest-achieving schools in Pittsburgh. Recently, it has been replaced by the Madison School, led by Mrs. Brevard's intern, Vivian Williams.

There are literally hundreds of other examples that document excellent achievement in urban public schools. Results like those that I have mentioned could be typical, *if we had the will to see it happen*. However, the current expectation seems to be that urban schools can only be saved by large-scale standardized commercial programs, which offer low achievement levels at best.

None of the currently popular minimum-competency school reform programs and high-stakes-test-driven interventions comes close to producing such high levels of student achievement. Focusing on these commercial programs has led education leaders and reformers to abandon necessary reforms that focus on improving the preparation of regular teachers.

Currently, urban districts are moving toward eliminating professional education programs for teachers in favor of lateral transfers from other professions. Likewise, the people who are in charge of these schools are not experienced educators but rather professionals who have been brought in from outside of the education field—for example, ex-governors, bankers, corporate CEOs, accountants, federal prosecutors, generals from the military, and even judges and officials of state departments of education. The rule seems to be that anyone can lead except those who are professionally prepared. Yet these changes have not brought substantial positive changes in student achievement.

Furthermore, for-profit "educational maintenance organizations" (EMOs) have become more popular, and districts are buying their *non-beneficial management* and *non-beneficial instructional* services on a massive scale. In fact, "education reform" has come mainly to mean purchasing school leadership and instructional services from a cafeteria of "programs." As a result, the leadership role of public school officials has been diminished significantly. These new "teacher-proof," standardized, and scripted instructional services are touted proudly as being "research-based." It all sounds so scientific. Yet student achievement in the urban schools that use these programs remains at low levels, with few independent evaluations of reform programs.

Every day we hear of failed and abandoned educational reform programs that have moved their failures to new districts. Most of these reform programs claim victory when they reach narrow minimum-competency achievement goals. High-level academic goals that go beyond standardized tests and socialization goals are rarely evaluated at all. Offerings in areas such as performing arts and physical education are being dropped from the curriculum as the panic sets in over meeting the minimum-competency high-stakes standardized test goals. What's worse, these current school reform *experiments* use urban children as guinea pigs.

The unique use of reform programs in urban schools is a new form of segregation. Virtually all of these "school reform" programs are almost exclusively sold to schools and districts that serve ethnic minority and poor students. Even within the same public school district, schools that serve wealthier children rarely, if ever, use the commercial "reform packages." I cannot even imagine that the currently popular reform program would be offered to the headmasters of elite private schools. There is a vast gap between the intent and the quality of school services provided to urban schools that serve poor and minority ethnic children and those that serve the wealthy.

What is the real reason for coercing schools that serve poor and ethnic minority children to use these weak and even harmful programs? Why are historically Black colleges and universities given grants to teach their education faculty a particular scripted, cookie-cutter, minimum-competency reform program called Success for All? Why not teach these wonderful skills to teacher educators in prestigious mainstream colleges and universities?

To make matters worse, although a large part of my professional work is devoted to the location and dissemination of information about powerful teaching and learning, I know of *no* widely used educational maintenance organization with a standardized, cookie-cutter-based, commercial "reform" package that has produced excellence for the ethnic minority and poor children in the districts that they serve. None! Yet it seems that the more these "programs" do not work to produce excellence, the more they are adopted, or even mandated!

If we continue on the present path, I predict that we will continue to see wholesale academic and social failures worse than any failures that have been blamed on traditional public education and its leadership. Further, I fear that abused, unappreciated, poorly supported, and increasingly demoralized urban professional educators may drift into fatalistic acceptance of the status quo of low achievement.

Those who deny that urban schools can be successful in teaching all children show a profound lack of commitment to having urban students reach high standards of achievement. Ron Edmonds asked, "How many successful schools would you have to see to be convinced of the educability of all children?" He then answered his own question: "If your answer is more than one, then I submit that you have reasons of your own for believing that children's success is due to family background, rather than to the school's response to family background."

If we truly love our children, and if we truly intend to create positive, supportive learning environments for them, then we cannot ignore the obvious fact that educators who know how to get students to achieve at high levels succeed largely because of hard work and simple, straightforward teaching and leadership, not magic. Most of them do not use "research-based" or standardized and scripted minimum-competency programs. Their success is not due to the adoption of these "reform" programs.

Teachers and school leaders who produce excellence in education share the following simple things:

- clarity of purpose
- a sense of mission
- a shared vision among teachers, leaders, and communities
- high or rigorous goals and standards
- time on task
- deep academic backgrounds for teachers
- basic effective teaching methods for teachers
- strong school and district leadership
- elimination of "savage inequalities" in school services

Yet many urban schools and school systems continue to be led by ineffective and inexperienced leaders who have no track record of success with urban schools and whose school reform efforts do not address the important factors listed above. This is especially true as the school leadership job description has begun to shift from *leading* instruction and reform to *purchasing* instructional services from private vendors, such as Success for All, Project Grad, The Edison Project, and others.

Reform efforts should be directed at building the capacity of teacher education institutions and related staff development in schools. *Unless educational leaders and policymakers know about how existing powerful staff development is making great teachers and school leaders, they should not have any part in designing solutions to the problems in urban education.*

I HAVE NEVER BEEN MORE WORRIED about those who care for our children than I am now. Public-school and public-school-teacher bashing is a national sport. Teachers and school leaders struggle under the burden of impossible and invalid demands, with virtually no respect paid to them as human beings or as professionals. Turning urban teachers into robots executing scripted programs has not solved the schools' problems. Disrespecting teachers and school leaders as professionals and giving more influence and control to leaders brought in from other noneducation professions and the monitors of scripted programs has not solved our problems. Worse, by reducing our urban teachers to "robots" and "zombies," we take away one of their greatest teaching tools: the human bond they develop with their students.

Some of the best urban teachers who I know—master teachers who have excellent track records of encouraging high student achievement—find this new academic terrorism intolerable. They must *comply* and be *monitored* to see if they follow ridiculously inane required routines. They must endure "teacher training" programs that treat them more like children than like the professionals that we require, and that teach them lessons of little value in the process. Many teacher educators know how to do excellent staff development work. Yet increasingly we see the work of teacher education turned over to those who do not know how to teach urban ethnic minority and poor children and who have never produced excellence with these children. What value do these teacher educators have to aspiring teachers?

Recently, Carrie Secret, one of the most successful teachers in this nation, called me to talk about her work in a low-income urban area. Carrie said, "This last group of children has presented real challenges for me because of their high energy and headstrong behavior, and especially because of their unconquerable spirits and unconquerable intellects. I have to be ready for them every day!" Do most urban school teachers see their students in this way?

All children in the United States can be learning to their fullest potential in schools that offer rigorous and joyful curricula. If they wish, they should have the opportunity to take advanced classes in literature, higher mathematics such as algebra and calculus, foreign languages, science, the performing arts, health education, and recreational studies. Urban public schools exist already where this is done. It is time to pay attention to and learn from those educators who know how to achieve excellence.

Asa G. Hilliard III-Baffour Amankwatia II

Suggested Readings

Berliner, David C., & Biddle, Bruce J. (1996). *The manufactured crisis: Myths, fraud and the attack on the public schools.* New York: Perseus Books.

Cookson, Peter W., & Persell, Caroline Hodges. (1985). *Preparing for power: American elite boarding schools.* New York: Basic Books.

Darling-Hammond, Linda. (2000). Defining highly qualified teachers: What does "scientifically-based research" actually tell us? *Educational Researcher, 31* (9), 13–25.

Delpit, Lisa. (1995). *Other people's children: Cultural conflict in the classroom.* New York: The New Press.

Education Trust. (2000). *Dispelling the myth: High poverty schools exceed expectations.* Washington, DC: Author.

Haycock, Kati. (2002). Toward a fair distribution of teacher talent. *Educational Leadership, 60* (4), 11–15.

Kozol, Jonathan. (1991). S*avage inequalities: Children in America's schools.* New York: Crown Publishers, Inc.

Perry, Theresa, Steele, Claude, and Hilliard, Asa G. III. (2003). *Young gifted and black.* Boston: Beacon Press.

Peshkin, Alan. (2001). *Permissible advantage: The moral consequences of elite schooling.* Mahwah, NJ: Lawrence Erlbaum Associates Publishers.

Sanders, William L., & Rivers, June C. (1999). *Cumulative and residual effects of teachers on future student achievement.* Knoxville, TN: University of Tennessee.

Schmoker, Michael. (1999). R*esults: The keys to continuous school improvement.* Arlington, VA: Association for Supervision and Curriculum Development.

Suzuki, Sinichi. (1984). *Nurtured by love: The classic approach to talent education.* Smithtown, NY: Exposition Press.

Getting Our
Responsibilities Right

Dear President:

Our public elementary and secondary schools have for too long failed to educate too many of our children, especially those children most lacking in social and financial resources. The seeming intractability of the problem has led some people to give up on public education altogether and to turn instead to measures such as vouchers and privatization. Others advocate bypassing school districts and supporting charter schools. While these ideas may have some merit, it is my firm belief, based on almost twenty years at the Panasonic Foundation, that the best hope for improving our schools and bringing that improvement to scale lies in the systemic revitalization of school districts.

Some critics of pubic education will say that it is an exercise in futility, that districts are neither interested in nor capable of improving. Our experience at Panasonic Foundation has been otherwise. In eighteen years of working in partnership with districts across the country to help bring about fundamental and system-wide reform for improving teaching and learning for *all* students, we have never been at a loss for districts wanting to partner with us. To the contrary, we have had to turn away many more districts than we could accommodate—this, despite the fact that Panasonic Foundation provides no money to districts, but rather sends in consultants to work directly with them in ways that are often intrusive and demand real commitment and demonstrable change. Overwhelmingly, we have found intelligent, caring, and hard-working people at all levels and in all parts of school systems who truly want to do much better than they are currently doing.

The magnitude of the changes that must occur is huge. That many individuals in schools and school districts currently lack much of the knowledge and skills for bringing about that change and educating all children well should not surprise us. Teaching, leading schools, and running districts are immensely difficult and complex undertakings, even in the best of circumstances—those of Garrison Keillor's Lake Wobegone, for example, "where all children are above average," come from comfortable homes, and begin first grade already reading proficiently. Most educators do not work under these circumstances, and many schools and districts—the ones receiving the greatest amount of public criticism—serve student populations of which the majority must surmount the most severe social and economic disadvantages.

We should also recognize the enormity of what schools and school districts are being asked to do. In asking them to "close the achievement gap" and "educate all children to high levels," we are in effect asking schools to do what our nation as a whole has been unwilling and unable to do—namely, to overcome the pervasive and persistent inequities of opportunity that exist in this country. Rather than putting in place resources to ensure that—at minimum—all children are well-fed, well-clothed, and well-housed, we are in effect asking schools to fix society. Yet we are *shocked* that schools fall short. We call educators lazy and incompetent, and we demean them by offering measly amounts of money as incentive to do better—as if they were holding back their best effort in a haggling match. It's a wonder that anyone in this country is willing to go into public education and that, indeed, millions of individuals stand ready to serve.

Still, schooling for our students does need to improve, and improve significantly. The question is how? Providing students with vouchers to attend any school of their choice—whether public, private, or parochial—is an idea with many flaws, the least controversial of which is the assumption that there are enough schools of quality worth choosing. There are not. Chartering every school and letting each do its own thing does keep public schools in the public domain, but there is often little real fiscal or educational accountability, and, to date, the performance of charter schools in the aggregate has been mixed and not markedly better than that of regular schools. Focusing on individual schools and fixing one school at a time in the hope that the good ones will naturally embarrass, infect, or force the bad ones into shape has never worked in the past, and, in any case, with more than ninety thousand schools in the country, how many decades will it take to reach the tipping point, or a critical mass?

Our best hope, as I said earlier, is to improve *school districts*—that is, to take the *district* as the unit of change. In part, this is a question of practicality. The vast majority of children attend schools in districts; it is where the children are, and destroying or bypassing districts will take even more time and effort. But districts also *matter*. For one thing, schools need them. Schools should be about teaching and learning and *only* teaching and learning—not labor relations, fundraising, performing personnel checks, making sure the buses run on schedule, contracting for food or janitorial services, and filing the myriad reports that state and federal agencies require. These are services that a district central office can and should provide.

Districts also matter because schools, especially public schools, should not be concerned only about the particular children attending them or simply reflecting the values of those children's families. Schools are part of a larger community, and it is a school district's responsibility to embody the values and aspirations of the community as a whole. It can and must ensure that every child within the district is served well and equitably, and it can and must allocate the district's human, financial, and material resources so that each school and each student receives the support needed to succeed.

Then there is the scale-up issue. Schools do need to improve one at a time. However, like people, they learn best when they learn from and with others. Yet, most of our schools, and even most classrooms, operate in splendid isolation, with virtually no knowledge of what is going on down the hall or across the street, much less what "best practices" are being developed outside the district. The result is complacency (we're doing just fine), frustration (we're trying our hardest, but it's still not working), or despair (we may as well give up). Effective district central offices can break down the isolation of schools by creating opportunities for them to learn from each other, by bringing in local and national experts to conduct professional development, as well as by working with schools to analyze their strengths and weaknesses and plan and implement improvement strategies. In so doing, districts not only help individual schools to improve, but bring that improvement to scale—to *all* their schools for *all* their children.

What, then, must a district do to become the kind of institution we would all want? First, the district administration, the teachers' union, the principals' association, and the school board must all work together for the improvement of the system as a whole. For too long, these key stakeholder groups have treated each other as adversaries, not as allies with a common mission: to improve children's learning. They have let adult differences overshadow children's needs, forgetting that each group cannot accomplish this mission without the active cooperation of every other group. From our work with districts, we have learned that, even as an outside organization, excluding any of these groups is a surefire route to failure. Conversely, we have learned that working with all of them as equal partners in a system is eminently possible. The union, principals, and school boards, no less than the superintendent, want their schools to succeed. Working as a team and letting go of past biases may require new skills as well as initial mediation, but we have been tremendously gratified by their eagerness to do so and by what they have been able to achieve collaboratively.

At the same time, while having buy-in among the stakeholders is a necessary precondition for reform, it is not in itself sufficient. School systems also need to align every part of the system to focus on their instructional mission. How? Panasonic Foundation has developed a framework called "Essential School System Purpose and Responsibilities," which can serve as a diagnostic tool and guide for a district's reform efforts, and which our partner districts have found very useful.

According to the framework, school districts must first embrace as their essential purpose—their reason for existence—the provision of high-quality education for all their students, regardless of socioeconomic background. This purpose must "drive" everything they do. This may seem self-evident, but, traditionally, the main function of districts has been to ensure school compliance with local, state, and federal rules and regulations. These rules and regulations address both trivial and important issues: Do the clocks run on time? How many minutes are spent on a particular subject? Are teachers using a particular set of textbooks? Are schools following civil rights guidelines? Ensuring instructional quality, including how well teachers taught and students learned, and helping schools to become better places of learning, were not part of the job description. They are now, especially with the No Child Left Behind Act that was signed into federal law in January 2002 and that holds districts "accountable" for the performance of their schools. This is a seismic shift in how we think about districts that calls for a correspondingly seismic shift in how districts must operate.

Based on the essential purpose of educating all children well, the Panasonic framework goes on to enumerate the eight "essential responsibilities" of districts:

1. The system must uphold the core value and belief that all students can and will learn at high levels. This value must be communicated clearly throughout the system, instilled in every employee, and reflected in every action. In the past, it was acceptable to believe or act as if not all students could learn.

2. Having established its core value, the district must promote a culture and climate of trust, respect, honesty, and openness throughout the system. Individuals should be encouraged to seek new solutions, take risks, admit mistakes, and learn from both mistakes and success. In the past, the rule of thumb was "playing it safe," not risk-taking.

3. School systems must establish high learning standards that define what all students should know and be able to do at each level of schooling, and guide the work of students and adults alike. Holding different students to different standards on the basis of their race, ethnicity, and class race can no longer be tolerated.

4. The system must establish adult performance expectations for all personnel that are explicitly tied to helping all students achieve the learning standards. All personnel, from maintenance workers to the superintendent, play an important role and must understand not only *what* they must do but also *how well.*

5. Having established adult performance expectations, the system must ensure that its human capacity is up to the task. This means having recruitment and induction processes for placing the right people in the right positions and providing relevant, ongoing, and differentiated learning for all personnel so that they continuously learn and improve. "Any warm body" and one-size-fits-all training will no longer do.

6. The system must allocate the fiscal and material resources needed to support its purpose and core value. This may entail providing some schools with more of one kind of resource and others with less, depending on the needs of individual schools and their students. Equality, or sameness, was the guide in the past, not equity.

7. The district must establish an accountability system that holds everyone—including the district itself—accountable for meeting performance expectations. This can only happen after the district has provided the human and fiscal resources to enable students, schools, and central office personnel to do their work well. Accountability in the past focused on following rules, laws, and regulations; not on how well students learned.

8. The system must mobilize support and engage in advocacy at the local, state, and national levels for the policies, practices, and resources needed to achieve the system's essential purpose. Districts in the past have felt powerless and behaved as victims. They must now become activists.

While there is a sequential logic to the responsibilities listed above, the work of school systems is not linear, and system leaders must address several fronts simultaneously. And getting the responsibilities "right" requires deep knowledge about instruction, finance, organization development, systems thinking, human dynamics, learning theory, data management and analysis, and a host of other areas. Since these are not the kinds of knowledge usually provided by schools of education, everyone in the system must learn on the job.

This learning, in turn, requires money, which is in short supply, especially in these times of deep and widespread budget cuts. It requires time—an even rarer commodity for teachers and administrators, who already routinely work overtime: time—during the school day, after school, on weekends, and in summers—to participate in extensive and intensive professional development; time to absorb new knowledge and to practice and hone new skills; time to disassemble old systems—including old technologies—that no longer work, and to be deliberate in developing and implementing new ones. And, because the kind of district revitalization that is needed will not occur overnight or even in a year or two, especially since students cannot be sent home while the system transforms itself, it requires patience on the part of both the larger community and those within school systems. Fundamental school reform has been likened to rebuilding an airplane while it is in flight. I believe school reform is probably much harder.

GIVEN THE CHALLENGES OUR SCHOOLS AND SCHOOL DISTRICTS FACE, what can you, as president, do to help? In the policy arena, you can direct national resources toward improving the lives of our neediest children, so that they have a fighting chance at succeeding in school. You can direct resources toward reforming public schools, rather than toward strategies such as privatization or vouchers that risk increasing the inequities that already exist. You can work to ensure adequate funding for districts serving the most disadvantaged students so that they may successfully compete for qualified teachers and have facilities that are as clean, safe, and well-equipped as affluent districts. You can roll back the high-stakes testing frenzy that has been exacerbated by the No Child Left Behind Act so that teachers can focus again on helping students use their minds well rather than simply knowing which boxes to check on the answer sheet.

As president, you can also use your bully pulpit to help the public understand the new kinds of responsibilities that school districts must carry out, so that they will support and not deny educators the time and resources needed to acquire new knowledge and skills. You can advocate for higher and more equitable salaries for teachers and administrators, so that public education—even in "difficult" schools and districts—will be a viable and attractive career choice. Finally, you can galvanize support for high-quality public education of *all* our young people as a genuine, national responsibility—not only because they will be paying for our pensions, not only because they *are* our future, but because it's the right thing to do.

Sincerely,
Sophie Sa

Note: I would like to thank Andrew Gelber, Scott Thompson, and Paul Liao—respectively senior consultant, assistant director, and board member of the Panasonic Foundation—for their suggestions and input. However, the views expressed in this letter are mine, as are any shortcomings.

IT'S PAST TIME TO FUND
WHAT WE MANDATE

Dear President,

In the nineteenth century, Horace Mann, who is often credited with developing the American public school system, said that every human being who comes into the world has the right to an education. Two centuries later, we, as a nation, seem to still be baffled as to how we can provide a quality education to all who seek it.

I don't believe the solution to this dilemma is that complicated. *The federal government must increase its role in funding public education.* In the late 1940s, with the creation of the GI Bill, the percentage of the total federal budget dedicated to education was 10.7 percent. Some sixty-plus years later, that amount—which covers funding for elementary, secondary, and higher education—has dwindled to slightly less than three percent. The federal government must reach back into history and return to dedicating ten percent of the total federal budget to education.

In 2004, the federal government provided fifty billion dollars in discretionary funding for education. This compares to four hundred billion dollars for defense programs. Providing sufficient funding for defense is very important. However, it is just as important to provide the necessary funding and leadership for us to have one of the world's greatest education systems. Some may ask, "Where can we find the money for education?" We can find the money when we all finally understand that it will be a severe detriment to the survival of this nation if we do not.

Since this nation was founded in the late 1770s, we have struggled with the roles the various parts of our government should play in our public education system. In 1867, President Andrew Johnson signed into law a bill creating a Department of Education. However, the first commissioner of the department was not popular, and the department became a mere bureau. Over the next century, the Bureau or Office of Education, as it became known, was primarily responsible for collecting data—not developing or implementing policy. With the ascent of the civil rights movement in the 1950s and 1960s, education became a focal point in national politics.

The first significant financial influence by the federal government into elementary and secondary education occurred in 1965. In that year, under the leadership of President Lyndon Johnson, the Elementary and Secondary Education Act (ESEA) came into existence. The original purpose of the ESEA was to distribute money to needy schools in order to compensate for inequality of educational opportunity and to stimulate plans for school integration. Throughout the last forty-two years, that purpose has continued to be the foundation of the Elementary and Secondary Education Act. However, sufficient funding has never been provided and the purpose has yet to be fulfilled. Since its inception in 1965, Title I—the heart of the ESEA law, which provides funding to school systems across the country to improve education for children at risk of school failure who live in low-income communities—has served less than fifty percent of the children who should be served under the program.

When I first arrived in Congress in 1975, one of the first bills I worked on was the Individuals with Disabilities Education Act (IDEA). The purpose of this legislation is to ensure that children with disabilities receive the special education and related services that they need to learn. Because children with disabilities often require specialized services, educating them can be twice as costly as educating children without disabilities. In order to ensure that schools can afford to provide a satisfactory education to students with disabilities, IDEA authorizes the federal government to pay up to forty percent of each state's excess cost of educating children with disabilities. Unfortunately, our government has failed to actually provide the states with that forty percent. We are currently only providing slightly over seventeen percent of the forty percent we promised thirty-two years ago.

Our education system is also stressed at the post-secondary level. We have a higher education system that is the envy of the world. However, many in this country are not able to pursue post-secondary education opportunities because of the astronomical financial burden. One third of all seniors graduating from higher education institutions do so with at least twenty thousand dollars in debt.

The financial strain of post-secondary education is having a direct impact on our job market. A good example of this is seen in the current shortage of qualified teachers in almost every community in our country. How many graduates leaving college with at least twenty thousand dollars in debt can afford to sign up for a teaching job that pays, on average, a beginning salary between twenty-five thousand and thirty-five thousand dollars? The cost of higher education is also a particular problem for the high-tech and health-care industries. A number of jobs in these two areas require postgraduate study. Yet financial hardship prevents many of our college students from going on to graduate programs. This has been a factor in the dramatic increase over the last decade in the number of H-1-B visas (which allow companies to recruit skilled workers from overseas) that have been issued.

Our country is lacking the skilled workforce necessary to address many of our needs. One initiative designed to address our job training needs is the Workforce Investment Act, which provides job training activities for adults and youth. Unfortunately, federal funding for job training programs has dropped $1.63 billion since 1985.

As I HAVE OUTLINED, there are a number of federal programs that have improved and could further improve our public education system if sufficiently funded. By vastly increasing the federal government's monetary responsibility for public education, we would go a long way to provide the resources needed to:

- serve every student who needs Title I assistance;
- sufficiently meet the requirements of many of the mandates included in the No Child Left Behind Act;
- provide quality early childhood education;
- provide additional funding for Pell grants and other student financial aid programs to improve access to post-secondary education;
- provide quality professional development for all school personnel, with a special emphasis on math and science; and
- provide the full federal share for the Individuals with Disabilities Education Act (IDEA).

Both the president and the Congress should work together to see that the federal funding commitment to education is at least ten percent of the total federal budget. For the sake of our children, this is the least we can do. For the sake of our country's future, we must make it happen.

WILLIAM J. MATHIS

FINANCING AMERICA'S FUTURE— HOW MONEY COUNTS

Dear President —

Two hundred years ago, our nation's founders ratified a Constitution to build a government based on the will of the people. Today, we hardly grasp just how much of a staggering task it is to build a government on such an untested notion. When the Constitution was signed, it was barely conceivable that a people could govern themselves free of a king and an aristocracy. Likewise, it was unprecedented that citizens could express opinions, move about freely, choose their own religion, and actively participate in government. These were breathtaking risks.

Thinking such a doubtful venture was doomed to fail, many of our founders said that the illiterate, uneducated common people were not capable of governing. The rabble would make a mess of things, and that would lead to bloodshed and anarchy. They believed that government should be run by the landowners, the educated, and those who were privileged by education, refinement, and family background.

Yet statesmen such as Noah Webster and Benjamin Rush argued that if we are to have a democracy, all the people must be prepared

47

to govern themselves wisely. They must be educated. "I know of no safer depository of the ultimate powers of the society but the people themselves; and if we think them not enlightened enough to exercise their control with a wholesome discretion, the remedy is not to take it from them, but to inform their discretion by education," said Thomas Jefferson. As time passed, we established a system of universal education. The system is far from perfect, but it was the engine that established the United States as the world's leading democracy and preeminent power.

Our founders had an intense interest in education. In the magnificent 1787 Northwest Ordinance, Thomas Jefferson and Nathan Dane proposed that education was an essential factor for building new self-governing states in the wilderness. In the darkest hours of our Civil War, Abraham Lincoln worked with Vermonter Justin Morrill to establish land grant colleges across the nation. In 1890, the second Morrill Act opened higher education to freed slaves and Native Americans. In 1944, in the late hours of a world war against dictatorships, Franklin Roosevelt signed the GI Bill, which gave the nation the skills and knowledge it needed to escape a depression and emerge as the globe's predominant economic force.

These noble and historic acts expanded our vision of democracy. They enhanced the opportunities of the citizens. They were founded on the realization that the education of all citizens was essential if we were to preserve and enhance democracy and freedom. Our forbears believed that the government and the people could do great things. With the provision of scholarships, aid, and land grants, they provided the commitments to match their promises.

Today, mired in a dark, bleak, and fearful vision of education, we ignore our greatest educational accomplishments and deny our greatest failings. In the never-ending criticism of our schools, we give ourselves no credit that national assessment test scores are at historic high and steady levels in reading, math, and science. In fact, mathematics and early reading scores have dramatically increased since 1973. Drop-out rates have steadily declined since 1972 and are today at a historic low. More students than ever are going on to college and other institutes of higher education. Almost across the board, minorities have seen the fastest improvements.

These are not signs of a failed education system. They are signs of a magnificent success! We should celebrate all we have accomplished! But we must also look at our true problems. Our much maligned "average" international test scores do not mean that our schools are bad. They mean we have schools that score exceptionally high and schools that score terribly low. UNICEF ranks the equality of U.S. education an abysmal twenty-first out of twenty-four industrialized countries. Also, while our international test scores are in the middle of the pack, our investment of our nation's immense wealth in education is mediocre. For elementary schools, we are merely average—thirteenth out of twenty-three countries. For high schools, we are fifteenth of twenty-four nations in our commitment of our per capita gross domestic product to education. Twenty-five of our nation's state supreme courts have said our educational funding systems are inequitable or inadequate. Education spending has gone up, but not for all children.

It is a sorry reflection on our nation that one of the richest countries in the history of the world ranks twenty-first out of twenty-two developed countries in the percentage of children in poverty. Only Russia has higher child poverty, says the United Nations.

If we want to maintain our democratic heritage, then all our children must be educated. We have the knowledge and the power to make it so. Yet, study after study tells us that schools are able to buy only one sixth of the teachers, technology, and tools needed to help our children in greatest need. Despite talk of "historic" federal investments, total federal monies spent on education represent only about seven percent of all education spending, and the amount targeted to help children in need is a mere four percent.

Instead, we are told that some dark alchemy of endless testing and financial pressure from state and federal bureaucrats upon a community and its school will magically restore broken buildings, provide new textbooks, and place a highly qualified teacher in every classroom.

Testing will not make any student's toothache go away, nurture his spirit, or teach him to read. Newspaper reports labeling his school as "failing" will not make him believe that he, too, can have a chance—just a chance—of getting his slice of the American pie. The constant threat of loss of funding will not ensure that every child can read, write, and do basic arithmetic, particularly when the schools close early because they can't meet the payroll.

This is not a failure of our teachers, our principals, or our schools. It is a failure on the part of our government to provide that bedrock entitlement of an equal and adequate opportunity to all children. Ultimately, it is a failure of will, a failure of caring, and a failure to match our commitments to our promises.

Some rationalize these failings by saying schools have "more than enough money." Still others say that money doesn't matter or that, when it is given, it is being frittered away. Federal bureaucrats brag about their "massive increases" in funding for education, but we must remember that a massive multiple of a very small thing is still small.

During the early 1990s, there was a fierce fight about whether money mattered. Those who stood for equal and adequate education for *all* children presented an impressive array of well-designed studies showing that money, quality, and equality all matter. Those fighting for low state support for schools and against broad-based and progressive taxes countered with their own lineup of experts and think-tank reports.

Although echoes still resound on talk radio and among some econometric number crunchers, by 1996 the battle was basically over. The weight of the evidence consistently shows that even moderate increases in spending on education provide significant increases in achievement. Parents who want the best opportunities for their children know that safe and adequate facilities, good and caring teachers, and computers and quality textbooks are essential to a good education. They don't need a research study to confirm the obvious.

Common sense began to prevail in the courts as judges went into decrepit buildings, examined forty-year-old textbooks, and sat on broken furniture in overcrowded classrooms. Court decisions across the nation declared that the basic human right of an adequate education is not available to all our children. Money *does* matter. It particularly matters to our promises of democracy and freedom whether we keep our commitments to provide a decent education for every child.

As standards-based reforms took hold across the nation, the question became: Where can our resources be best used to make sure that all children learn? Fortunately, research began to emerge finding consistent and positive results for good preschool programs, full-day kindergarten classes, small schools, small class sizes (particularly in elementary schools), extra help and family support for struggling students, adequate and safe facilities, up-to-date textbooks and learning materials, access to technology, and qualified teachers. Providing these essential resources to all students then became the base for estimating what it would truly cost to give every child access to a good education.

A number of studies in different states using different methods and different researchers began to calculate the costs of providing these resources to all children. In independent studies, they found that fundamental new investments of between twenty percent and thirty-five percent of our national total education expenditure would be needed if we are really to leave no child behind. Unfortunately, the federal government has fallen woefully short of making that investment. Title I remedial monies *may* rise to $12.5 billion, but the research says the amount needed is between eighty-five and one hundred and fifty billion dollars. States, wallowing in an estimated eighty billion dollars in deficits, do not have the capacity to make up the difference. Stressed local schools, predominantly tied to tapped-out property taxes, also do not have the resources to close this gap.

The inevitable consequences are already unfolding. If a school has low scores, the state must help it improve. Yet, with near uniformity, most states admit that they cannot provide meaningful help. Legislatures in Maine, Nebraska, New Hampshire, Nebraska, Utah, and Vermont have made public statements that they have no such ability. Success is virtually impossible for schools without the promised help and without the money to hire teachers, repair buildings, and buy textbooks.

Furthermore, if these same low-scoring and resource-starved schools do not make big enough test score gains, they will be publicly labeled as "in need of improvement." In newspaper listings they will become the "failing" schools—regardless of the fact that the teachers taught the best they knew how, worked hard, and cared about their students. They never got the resources and the support their wealthier neighbors take for granted. Yet our government lets them be called "failures."

Not since Puritan times have we locked people in stocks on the town square. Yet this public shaming is glorified as the answer to the unfairness of our own system. The only real shame, however, is that a nation of enormous and unprecedented wealth chooses to ignore the needs of its children.

In time, if test scores do not go up fast enough, the school or district may be forced to offer vouchers or adopt some form of alternate or privatized governance. Despite thirty years of research, there is no body of evidence that shows that vouchers, charter schools, or privatized government will solve the problems of society or of schools. To dangle the "choice" carrot before parents who can only choose among schools in the same resource-poor district, whose voucher amounts to only a fraction of the tuition cost, or who cannot get transportation to another school, is not a choice. It is merely a masquerade of our denial of opportunities to children.

The delivery of a public good by a private corporation, whose central value is profit and competition, has no inherent incentive to ensure a more just and equitable society. Eliminating the democratic governance of schools does not teach children the values of democracy, nor does it empower or encourage them to participate in government.

While some use words of caring, our care should not be measured by either some sweet sound-bite in the rose garden, or by a politician's photo-op while he reads to a child of color perched upon his knee. Public postures of piety do not show that we care. Our caring is manifested in our deeds. Our caring is measured by how our society chooses to allocate its resources.

What a government considers important, there it places its wealth. The federal compensatory education fund was funded at only two thirds of what was authorized. Even if funded at the full eighteen-billion-dollar level, we know that keeping the promises of this fund will cost at least eighty-four billion dollars.

While we have not kept our promises to our children, we have enough wealth to provide three hundred and fifty billion dollars in tax cuts where the major beneficiaries have been the wealthiest people in society. We also spend uncounted billions on the war in Iraq and the restoration of the oil fields. We may not have found weapons of mass destruction in the desert, but we are at great peril if we ignore that we are making them in the wastelands of our cities and communities.

This neglect is cloaked in the proclaimed "failure" of our nation's greatest success, our education system. We forget that leadership must be based on the *best* vision of what schools can be rather than on a dark obsession with what they are not. In 1983, *A Nation at Risk* said that America's economic well-being was at risk if we did not better educate our children. Today, we have a superb record of educational improvement and we are the only economic superpower. This is a testament to education's success over these twenty years, not a sign of its failure.

Our failure is a failure of faith in our democratic ideals. It is a failure to recognize that an educated citizenry is the most essential prerequisite to our freedom.

We do not measure the effectiveness of our schools in glaring headlines about test scores but in the gifts that educated citizens provide to the richness and well-being of our society. We do not measure children by their suitability as "products" for the workforce. Instead, we must measure ourselves by how we open up the opportunities we give to children. We do not measure education by policies that separate our children by family wealth or religious affiliation but by the fairness in how we share this most precious resource of hope and promise with all children.

GREAT IMPROVEMENTS IN OUR NATION ARE DRIVEN BY DREAMS. Throughout history, our greatest leaders have shown us how to achieve these dreams by lifting the hearts of those who must carry us there and by opening and expanding the fields of opportunities. This dream is an essential part of a greater vision of a more perfect society, where children are taught the knowledge needed for the twenty-first century along with the civic ideals that all are free and able contributors to the advancement of that society. And it is founded on a government where our commitments match our promises.

Sincerely,

Will J. Matt

JOHN I. GOODLAD
_____

WHY WE NEED
PUBLIC EDUCATION

Dear Mr. President,

For several years, there has been a widening
disconnect between parents and schooling
in our nation. Many people hear from pre-
sumably dependable sources that America's
system of public schooling is a near-disaster, something an enemy
country might have imposed on us. However, for most people, it has
not yet grown to include their local school—the one their children
attend.

The local school provides the cheapest, safest day care and an
educational oasis available to most families. In the sample selected
each year in the annual Gallup Poll of the public's view of our schools,
local schools get high marks, but public schooling, in general, gets a
D or F. Our political leaders and the media have done a fine job of
telling us that we have a malfunctioning school system. Many people
think that there are a lot of bad schools out there because they are
constantly bombarded with these negative messages, but they aren't
familiar with any of these "bad schools;" they know only the good
ones in their neighborhoods.

The trouble is that when the larger school district needs more money—as most chronically do—many people do not vote in favor of providing the funds the district needs to improve its schools because they assume it will be wasted on unknown "bad" schools. And so, Mr. President, the gloomy message that has been coming out from our federal and state political leaders for the past three decades or so has been increasingly withering the public support that our schools must have.

We now have a bundle of research on what citizens expect from their schools. High on the list is that their children be safe, that the teachers make an effort to get to know their children, and that their children receive equal educational opportunities in the classroom. Parents want to be kept informed about what is going on and listened to when they express their views. Contrary to much conventional wisdom, few parents want to be heavily involved in matters of curriculum and instruction. Most do not have the time. They would like to believe that the educators at the school are well-prepared, competent, caring professionals who are capable of taking care of these matters.

It is abundantly clear that the federal government, with its roughly seven percent annual expenditure on education, is a minor player in the financial support of public education. But this seven percent is what makes it possible for many districts to keep their schools open and functioning for one hundred and eighty days a year. Many of the requirements for getting these additional dollars restrict local ability to use their own dollars for district priorities. In other words, with its seven percent expenditure, the federal government holds districts hostage regarding how they spend the other ninety-three percent.

There is often a devastating ripple effect from one-size-fits-all federal laws and mandates. Never before has this been more apparent than with the current No Child Left Behind Act. Not only must states and local districts spend part of their seven percent on the administration of mandated testing, but the accountability requirements built into the system virtually force them to abandon many of the hard-won changes they have made in order to better meet parental expectations. Consequently, even though the local school has managed to sustain considerable public affection while public schooling has fallen from grace, politically driven school reform appears to be well on the way to trashing what Robert Maynard Hutchins (former president of the University of Chicago) described in 1972 as "the bright and shining beacon . . . the source of our enlightenment," the public school.

For some years in this great country, we have been moving steadily toward the public view that democracy is something that takes care of us. We speak much of our freedoms; much less of our responsibilities. High school and college commencement addresses speak less to the relationship of education to democracy, and more to its link to economic success. Leaders in philanthropic foundations have noticed this, and several are supporting programs of civic engagement for the young. But some are noting that, although such programs are important, they fall short of the apprenticeship in democracy that only education can provide.

Major studies and surveys reveal that a large majority of the people—and particularly parents—expect schools to teach the young more than academics, which they see as dominating practice. Since there recently has been a weakening in the bonds between home, school, and local religious institutions, parents expect schools to pay parentlike attention to their children's personal and social attributes. Indeed, many parents see as much need for this type of instruction as they do for vocational and academic instruction.

The continued high ratings of the local school, except in areas where the nation's congenital malaise of prejudice and educational inequities have not yet shamed us into corrective action, suggest that people close to schools still believe these expectations are being met. How else might we account for the high satisfaction index? Lately, I have had a rash of school principals tell me that they are frustrated in trying to address the increased parenting role being thrust upon their teachers. They feel caught between parental expectations that the school will take care of their children and district expectations that the school will raise test scores, even if they are already high.

Only a few parents turn to the local school board for answers to their questions and concerns. The principal and teachers of the local school are much easier to reach. Day after day they must answer parents' questions: Why has recess been eliminated and the lunch break shortened? What happened to that wonderful music program we had?

Why is physical education being reduced when we know that obesity is a serious problem in this country? Why is it getting harder and harder to find out how *my* children are doing? They aren't coming home excited about what's going on in school. What *is* going on, anyway?

Two principals who visited with me for a couple of hours last week poured out *their* concerns. They feel guilty in trying to defend the policies and practices they are called upon to support. They empathize with these parents and would like to meet with groups of them to openly discuss their common concerns. They are torn between coming out into public discourse regarding their concerns on these difficult questions and supporting the district's need to comply with federal law. The dilemma keeps them awake at night.

Is it better for a principal or administrator to appear stupid, or should one be honest in trying to answer likely questions? For example, if you succeed in raising those test scores, will this mean that our children are likely to be more responsible citizens and parents? Will they be better prepared to deal with the circumstances of daily life in this fast-changing world? Are the high scorers more likely to be better problem solvers, more creative thinkers, and perhaps happier than the low scorers? I can hear the conversation now:

> "Well, not exactly, Mrs. Brown. A considerable body of research shows that there is very little relationship between academic achievement test scores and the desirable human traits you mention and many others."
> "Yes, Mr. Thompson, but I thought the central purpose of our schools was to prepare honest, decent, problem-solving, responsible citizens."
> "Of course, Mrs. Brown, but don't you see . . . ?"
> "See what, Mr. Thompson?"

Wow! It's no wonder principals are so hesitant to get into conversations where questions like these are likely to come up.

Once upon a time, schools and their practices were exceeded in the conversations of parents only by the weather. Indeed, visitors to our country cited the conduct of school affairs as the essence of the American democracy. When a little book, *Why Johnny Can't Read,* entered the ongoing educational debate in the 1950s, local newspapers featured conflicting reviews, coffee klatches sprang up nationwide to discuss it, and local school boards joined "the reading wars" over whether to teach reading through phonics or through whole-word and whole-language approaches.

Today, I hear that the educational debate has gone to Washington. When one goes to Washington in search of this debate, one doesn't find much. What one gets at most meetings of the Department of Education is more information about the requirements of the No Child Left Behind Act—some of which dismayed even members of Congress after they had voted for it.

And so, Mr. President, the most important educational initiative I'm asking you to support during your watch is to restore the central school mission that served us so well in the past: the development of democratic character in the young. It embraces the social, personal, vocational, and academic purposes that parents expect of our schools. The first step toward this end is to restore the educational debate in local communities nationwide. You will have no trouble finding able and willing individuals and agencies to help you do this. It cannot be done by federal mandate.

Four school reform proposals have received considerable recent attention. One is to make schools of choice open to all parents. A second is to hold back all children who fail to reach grade-level performance on academic achievement tests. A third is to put a qualified, caring, competent teacher in every classroom. An exceedingly dominant fourth is to institute a standards-based testing and accountability system in every state. When respondents are asked to choose just one of these as being most likely to ensure school improvement if we were to concentrate on it over a period of years, the third is the nearly unanimous choice. Strangely, in commission report after commission report on school improvement from the 1950s into the 1990s, the education of the nation's teachers was rarely mentioned. That good teachers are central to good schools and to affecting any effort to make them better would seem obvious.

Over this same period of time, all the major professions have seen that a broad and deep general education, grounded in the concepts and principles upon which the profession has historically been tied to, and a range of internships to ensure the abilities necessary to competent practice are necessary to the quality of their practitioners. As a consequence, there are professional schools on major university campuses—architecture and urban planning, business, dentistry, engineering, law, medicine, nursing, and more—that, in many cases, have become the universities' primary educational business. Increasingly, these schools are reaching out to practitioners for purposes of learning how they can be more effective in preparing new professionals and providing services to the experienced.

Ironically, the most neglected of these professions has been education—the one held accountable for preparing teachers for the nation's schools. For more than a decade, there has been a surge of agreement on the need for a partnership between arts and sciences departments in universities, schools of education, and local elementary and secondary schools in the education of teachers. Yet, just as this surge is gaining attention and action, a countermovement is shortening preparation, leaving many beginning teachers to learn good teaching practices on their own.

As I have written above, parents assume that their children's teachers know a good deal about what and how to teach, even though they also assume variation in competence. At first, ill-prepared teachers will show up in our most neglected schools, which will continue to be disadvantaged. Later on, however, when they are hired for the more advantaged schools, local schools will begin *their* downward slide in the public's affection.

I'm requesting, Mr. President, that you do two things about this growing problem early on. First, get the federal government out of providing financial support for routes into teaching that bypass the type of professional preparation that every other major profession has made mandatory. Second, assemble a commission of a dozen independent education leaders to prepare a proclamation of what every parent should expect to be the credentials of each teacher appointed to the risk-laden responsibility of teaching in his or her child's school.

You must make clear to all, especially your policymaking colleagues, that one may leave the local school but not his or her responsibility, as a citizen in our political and social democracy, for the maintenance of a robust system of public schooling.

I pay taxes for the maintenance of nearby Interstate Highway 5, whether or not I use it. Having paid these taxes for many years, surely I should own a few hundred yards of it where I'm allowed to post the lower speed limit I would prefer. Our children graduated from a public high school many years ago. However, we now pay taxes for the schools of a different state, even though we don't personally need public schools any longer. Or do we?

Having observed our fledgling democracy carefully, Alexis de Tocqueville observed that "there is nothing more arduous than the apprenticeship of liberty." Thomas Jefferson concluded that education must provide this apprenticeship. During the intervening years, we have maintained a system of public schooling primarily to serve this end. We have charged no other agency with this responsibility. To take care of the local schools that make up this system is, in large measure, to take care of our democracy. Whether or not we use them for our own private purposes, we dare not walk away from them.

Most of us sense that we live together in a moral ecology of multiple communities, rhetorically committed to and ever striving toward liberty and justice for all. Entry into the twenty-first century has brought to many of us the realization that this ecology is fragile, that what we have been taking for granted can readily erode.

We look to you, then, to take the lead in restoring the educational debate that once thrived in these communities. There is readiness now to address and provide the necessary resources for an agenda in local schools designed to educate *all* children and youths in the rights and responsibilities of citizens in a social and political democracy and the behavior necessary to living wisely and well in it.

In hope and with respect,

John I. Goodlad

PART TWO
LEARNING FOR ALL

DERRICK ATTAKAI, EVALENA JOEY,
BRITTA MITCHELL, MELODY RIGGS, &
MANUEL THOMPSON WITH MARK SORENSEN

BROKEN ROADS AND THE GREAT MOTHER EARTH

Mark Sorensen with teacher Evelyn McCabe and students Melody Riggs, Manuel Thompson, and Derrick Attakai

Little Singer Community School is located in the high desert of the Navajo Nation in northeastern Arizona. It is surrounded by sand dunes with sparse vegetation and sheep and goats grazing, features that are common to many of the more remote communities in the Navajo Nation.

The school is unique in that it was not built by the federal government to accomplish federal goals for Indian education. In fact, initially it was not built by the state government or by the tribal government. It was built by volunteers from families in the Navajo community of Birdsprings and by college volunteers in order to honor the vision of respected medicine man Hatathlii Yazhi, or Little Singer, who had told the people of the community before he passed away that they needed to bring the community's children back from the boarding schools to which they had been sent. Hatathlii Yazhi told the people that with the children gone there was an unnatural silence in the community. They could not hear the laughter of the children. "We must bring the children home," he said.

Since those days in the mid-1970s, Little Singer Community School has sought to honor that wish. However, it has become obvious that the children not only need to attend school near their homes, but that they also need to see the relevance of the school to the concerns of their community. With an unemployment rate of thirty-five percent, with thirty percent of parents not having received a high school diploma, and with the school only reachable by a seven-mile-long dirt road that is at times impassable, one might think that our students would not have a sense of hope or a clear vision of what they need to improve their education. The letters from these students of ours make it clear that they are very capable of seeing the problems before them and identifying what is needed.

It is our hope that these letters will be a sobering view of the state of education in some areas of this country as well as a statement of hope about the strength and promise of our children.

Mark Sorensen—Director, Little Singer School

Dear Mr. President,

MY NAME IS BRITTA MITCHELL. I have completed the eighth grade here at Little Singer. I think this is a great school. I have learned a lot from this school. The junior high has graduated many students, who are now either still in high school or who have graduated from high school. Some students are in college. I have a little brother who is going to school here, and I want him to have a good education.

I want to let you know that our school is in need of many educational supplies and well-educated teachers that are really, really interested in teaching Native American students. I want my little brother and all of the other kids that are going here to have a good elementary education here at Little Singer School. In order for these kids to learn all they can, they are going to need new textbooks in the classrooms.

Our school has old and not-so-old computers. It's awful when you don't have a computer and you are trying to do a research paper.

Pretty soon you just give it up and get an incomplete assignment. I don't want my little brother and other students to go through that. They have the right to have a good education. I know with the right supplies, we will all improve in our grades. It will be more fun to go to school. I think this is true of all American students.

Another thing that is important is that most people and children all over the United States and in other countries look up to people who care for and respect them. Here at Little Singer Community School, we have many people who care about our education. They teach us many things and that's why I like to be here at school. Next school year, I will be going into high school. I hope I meet some people that care—people who will be more than willing to help me. You see, I am handicapped.

When I was little, I was in a car accident with my parents. I almost lost my right arm. I was born right-handed. I had to learn to use my left arm and hand. I don't use my right arm very much, but that is not going to stop me from getting an education. My teacher, Ms. McCabe, told me never to say, "I can't." She's a good teacher. I'm going to miss her a lot.

All across Mother Earth, schools and education should be number one. Every school should have all the updated equipment, reading, and other supplies right there for the teachers and students to use. Mr. President, I have shared my ideas with you. Now, can you help my fellow Native students as well as other students across our great Mother Earth to have a better education?

Sincerely,
Britta Mitchell

Dear Mr. President,

MY NAME IS DERRICK ATTAKAI. I am a fourteen-year-old Navajo boy from Birdsprings, Arizona. I have completed the seventh grade this past spring. I will go into eighth grade in the fall. Right now I am taking summer courses here at Little Singer. Little Singer is in a very remote area in the southwest Navajo reservation. Our school goes from pre-school to eighth grade.

I am writing this letter to you because of my concerns for my education. I have been attending Little Singer for two years now and I have seen where things are badly needed. Our junior high school is in need of new computers in the classrooms. When we are assigned to do research, we have to stay in line and wait until two or three people get done with their research before we can start our own research. We could also do our homework on the computer if we had more computers. Most of the students who attend this school live in a remote area of the reservation, where we don't have electricity or phone lines to get a computer hooked up. So, we depend on the school computers to complete our assignments.

Our school is also in need of new books. Our library only has old, outdated books that are torn-up and falling apart. They are not fun to read. In our classrooms, we do not have textbooks. We have a lot of books that were given to us from other schools. They, also, are old and not interesting to read. I would like to read a brand-new book for a change. Next school year will be my last year here at this school, and I would like to see some new, updated literature books and textbooks.

I would like to study science, but there are no supplies to do science projects. Because materials like microscopes and other tools that are needed are not available for teachers and students to use, our teachers cannot help us sometimes.

When I was in fifth grade, I got my first tribal clothing. I thought it was a very nice thing for our tribe to do. The next year, I did not get anything. I have not received any tribal clothing since fifth grade. I know some kids do not have any clothes to wear to school so they just stay home. I know tribal clothing will help some of us a lot. School is fun to go to when you have nice clothes to wear. I also feel that children of all nationalities who are of school age and who are in need of clothes should be eligible to get these clothes, whether they have census numbers or not. All students should be treated equally.

Our teachers are very smart. They can come up with great ideas without having a lot of supplies and materials. In junior high, we do service-learning. We go out into the communities that surround our school and we help our elders with whatever they need help with.

So, Mr. President, I have mentioned some problems about my school. What can you do to help my people get a better education?

Sincerely,
Derrick Attakai

Dear Mr. President,

HELLO. MY NAME IS EVALENA JOEY, "Evie" for short. I am fourteen years old and soon to be a freshman in high school. I live on the southwestern part of the Navajo reservation in a small community called Birdsprings. We have a small community school where I have just completed eighth grade. I really don't know what to expect in high school. I know it will be hard, but I want to complete my education and, one day, find a good job.

Our school is very culturally traditional. The staff knows that we need help with our native languages and that we need to know about our culture. We have some Navajo teachers, but they do not teach the Native language; they teach regular classroom lessons. I think it would be nice to have a Navajo teacher who would only teach the Native language and the Native culture. I want to know more about my ancestors and where we originated.

Sir, I think that you should improve on your own personal feelings about students and their education. It is like we are your children. You need to look at our schools. We need better places to learn. Some of us travel many miles to get to school and by the time we get there we are tired and hungry. The cafeteria food is another story, but at least we have food. We need elementary, middle, and high schools close to our home.

Well, sir, thank you for listening to me.

Sincerely,
Evalena Joey

Dear Mr. President,

HI. MY NAME IS MANUEL THOMPSON. I am thirteen years old. I went to Winslow Junior High School last year. I am attending summer school here at Little Singer Community School. I have been here for two weeks and I can see what they need to make it a better school for the students.

The school really needs sports equipment so that students can play basketball, soccer, and volleyball. They really need a new track field so the kids can run on it instead of running around the rough campus road. When they run around the school campus, they could slip on rocks and hurt themselves or they might step on a rattlesnake and get bitten. The school also needs new playground equipment.

The buildings here are old. The school needs money for repairs. The greenhouse is a great idea, and with repairs it will be as good as new. The kitchen and cafeteria building is where they really need new supplies and a new building. What I like about the cafeteria is that they keep it clean and the food is better than it was at my school in Winslow.

Even though they need many new things for the school, they are learning all the time. Within two weeks, we did a lot of neat things. The school allows the kids to learn about their cultural clans and other things about the Navajo. We don't have that at our school in Winslow. Please help my people here at Little Singer Community School.

Thank you,
Manuel Thompson

Dear Mr. President,

MY NAME IS MELODY RIGGS. I was in the seventh grade. I am passing into the eighth-grade class. I am attending Little Singer Community School here in Birdsprings, Arizona.

I am a student with many concerns about our school. Our school is in need of many things. We need supplies such as computers and books for our teachers and students so that they can accomplish their lessons.

We need a school nurse at our school because the staff members can't give us medicine. They always try to find someone to give medicine or treat some student who is hurt. They take us to Indian Health Services in Winslow, which is a long way from our school. If we had a school nurse, then we can get treated here at school.

We also need new buses. Our buses break down all the time out in the middle of nowhere and we have to transfer to another bus before we get to school or before we get home.

We need better roads to our school, too. Because of the bad roads, our buses always break down, and the staff's cars get flat tires and then they are late to work. The dirt roads cause a lot of problems for all of us. Sometimes, after it rains or after the snow melts, we have lots of mud. We all get stuck. Believe me, it's not fun. We would appreciate it if you could do something about this for us.

Our school is very special to us and we enjoy going to this school every day, and every year we go into a different grade. Our teachers are very nice and very good at teaching us. Thank you for understanding.

Sincerely,
Melody Riggs

LISA DELPIT

IN STRUGGLE AND HOPE

Dear Madam or Mr. President,

Recently, a new teacher told me that she did not know what to do when an eighth-grade African American student came up to her and said in a shy voice, "So, Ms. Jones, they made us the slaves because we're dumb, right?" Because children become what they believe, and because, when left unexamined, schools reinforce societal stereotypes, this story says much to me about why we have been so unsuccessful in teaching *all* of our children. Based on the results of most standardized tests, we have particularly failed American children of African descent. Most of our schools are not organized to ensure that these children get a quality education. The majority of our teachers are not educated in how to create classrooms that provide the instruction that these African American children, particularly those from low-income families, need in order to achieve. I believe that if we can design schools and educate teachers to provide excellence for this most vulnerable population, then we can create schools to educate all children.

There are teachers and schools that *do* know how to ensure that low-income African American children excel. Good examples are Harmony-Leland in Cobb County, Georgia; Sankofa Shule in Lansing, Michigan; the Prescott School in Oakland, California; and the Chick School in Kansas City, Missouri. Also, there are teachers who can turn any classroom into a class of achievers. Among many others, there are Carrie Secret in Oakland, California; Stephanie Terry in Baltimore, Maryland; and Paula White-Bradley in Atlanta, Georgia. The question for me has always been: Why don't we have more of these good teachers and schools? What do teachers need to know and do to deliver a quality education to all children wherever they live, whatever the color of their skin, and whatever their family income? Answering that last question and getting the answers implemented in schools is my life's work.

There are three factors I'd like to discuss that I have found essential to creating the educational excellence that we, as a nation, seek. First, we must have schools and teachers that, despite widespread societal stereotypes, understand and teach to the brilliance of African American children. Second, we must have schools and teachers that seek to learn about and respect the culture, the communities, and the intellectual and historical legacies of their students. Finally, we must have schools and teachers that can translate knowledge about their students into appropriate and rigorous instruction. Let me speak to these three factors before I try to suggest some policy implications.

In our country, African Americans have been historically *stereotyped* as being inferior to other citizens. From the days of slavery to the present, our society has consistently held and disseminated demeaning views of the intellectual capacity of people of African descent. Without attempting a detailed account, suffice it to say that many of our founding fathers, many of our revered "scientists," and even recent "scholarly works" (for example, *The Bell Curve*), have argued against the intellectual equality of the races. These views have become embedded in literature, the arts, and the media. As a result, they are typically buried somewhere in the subconscious, if not conscious, mind of everyone who grows up in this country. It is no wonder that the young man quoted above has internalized feelings of inferiority. Since no child can learn if he does not believe he can, we must have teachers and schools that can help students fight the negative stereotypes leveled against their communities.

What could the teacher above, Ms. Jones, have done to help her student? First, she must herself believe in the brilliance of her charges. She must know enough about their intellectual heritage—for example, the universities in Africa that existed thousands of years before those in the rest of the world; and the scientists, writers, philosophers, mathematicians, physicians, and so forth, who practiced their respective crafts long before African enslavement and who continued to do so even during the harshest years of that enslavement. She must understand that when African American children do not succeed in school, it is actually a *break* in historic precedence and not "the way things are supposed to be." Then, she must ensure that her students are also made aware of this information about their own heritage, that they understand the brilliance that is their birthright.

In order to ensure that such brilliance is actualized, schools and teachers must not "teach down" to low-income children of color. These children may come to school with a different knowledge base than their middle-class European American peers, but they are no less capable of tackling complex information. It is important, however difficult it is, to avoid classes and packaged instructional programs that teach them the so-called "basic skills" (which are only considered "basic" because they are what middle-class children learn at home) and teach them so slowly that advancement is all but impossible. These kinds of scripted, rote programs "dumb down" the curriculum that poor children receive. If we are to ensure success beyond the earliest grades, these children must be exposed to *more* information, at a *faster* pace, than their middle-class, mainstream peers. If teachers are forced to use these scripted programs, which resort to constant repetition of small steps and which primarily require rote memorization of answers and little or no critical thinking, then these children will never excel. They may show apparent gains in early grades on "basic skills," but these are soon washed out when critical thinking is required in later, more demanding subjects. If teachers are not educated to understand

and believe in the intellectual competence of *all* their students, then they will not provide the deep, rigorous instruction necessary to ensure that low-income African American children will close the so-called "achievement gap."

The second factor in developing teachers and schools that successfully educate low-income children of color is to make certain that educators learn who their students are. I always ask my graduate students to imagine that they just received a letter indicating that they are to begin teaching next week in a distant country with which they have absolutely no familiarity. I ask them to tell me what they will need to know to be able to teach successfully. They list many elements: the language, the foods people eat, organization of the families, expectations of parents, the music and culture, community taboos, the history of the community, the religious beliefs of the students and their families, the kind of work available for school graduates, previous educational successes and failures as seen by the community, the beliefs the community might hold about Americans, male and female roles, what children do outside of school, what roles the children have in the family, what chores they are responsible for, what their houses are like, and so forth. I then ask them how they would find out this information. They suggest becoming friends with people in the community, reading local newspapers and books on the area, attending dinner at a community member's house, visiting the community's places of worship, visiting shopping places, and participating as much in community life as possible.

I then ask how many of them teach students who are from different cultures from their own and how many live more than three miles from their students' communities. Many of them fit into both categories. The next question is, since we know what we need to know to teach well and we know how to learn about it, why do we continue to assume that we know enough to teach children from cultures different from our own? Why don't we do what we know we need to do in order to be successful in teaching these students? Most times, the answer is that the teachers' schools are not organized to help them do it. Schools exist as islands, not as integral parts of the communities they serve. Can they become the institutions we need to teach children who are not from mainstream cultures? Not unless that is made an explicit goal and structures are set into place to allow teachers to learn about the students they teach.

The third factor involves tying the information teachers acquire about their diverse students to classroom instruction. In order to motivate students to connect to complex subject matter, it is critical to have the ability to get their attention. Teachers who are successful at getting students' attention create metaphors for advanced subject matter in mathematics, science, and literature based on students' experiences. They excite students about the history of the students' communities and connect that history to the history found in books. They utilize aspects of the students' lived culture (such as familiar interaction styles) to present and review academic material. Furthermore, they connect student learning and problem solving to issues found in the students' communities.

A few examples might serve to clarify the above points. My own mother, a math teacher whose career spanned both segregation and desegregation in Louisiana schools, always connected her teaching to her students and their communities. When one of her students got married and became pregnant during the school year, she taught plane geometry by having her class make a baby quilt for the baby. All of the theorems were taught in the context of cutting the shapes and piecing them together to form the quilt. Thus, she not only connected math to the biggest issue in the eleventh-grade class, she also connected it to a specific value which the community embraced—building a strong network to care for a new life.

In her book, *The Dreamkeepers*, Gloria Ladson-Billings writes of a teacher who taught the Constitution of the United States by having her African American students collect the bylaws and articles of incorporation from their churches. The teacher compared the minister to the president, the deacons to the legislators, and the church board to the senators. As the students learned about the Constitution through comparing it to the church documents and personnel, they also learned that people who looked like them could create and maintain important institutions.

The Algebra Project, instituted by Dr. Bob Moses, is another prime example. Moses, a former freedom worker in the civil rights movement in Mississippi, says that mathematics is "the new civil rights." He points out that, unbeknownst to many poor parents, mathematics is the key to being admitted into college. If students do not take certain math courses in high school, they will not be on a college track and, therefore, cannot be admitted to most colleges. Moses has been successful teaching high-level mathematics to low-income children of color all over the country because he finds the metaphors and strategies that make the math meaningful to the students. For example, in Cambridge, Massachusetts, Moses took the students on subway trips. Later, the students talked about the trips and, with their teacher, connected the trip to understanding negative and positive numbers. They set different subway stops as "0" and then added positive and negative integers to those stops to determine which subway stop would be the new destination.

Moses also talks to students about the civil rights movement. His style of organizing the classroom is strongly connected to the kinds of strategies he used in voter registration campaigns in the Deep South. The Young People's Project, an offshoot of the Algebra Project run by young adults who participated in the Algebra Project when they were in middle and high school, motivates current middle and high school students to delve deeply into math and other subjects that students consider to be "hard." The program engages students in discussions about the civil rights movement and about the responsibility they have to do well in order to help their community.

If we can create teachers and schools that can implement the three factors indicated above, then we can begin to create the instructional settings necessary to ensure that African American and other low-income children of color can achieve at high levels. How can we create policy to allow this to happen? I make no claims of expertise in the policy arena, but I do know that the federal government has had tremendous influence on what happens to education in the states. In the Higher Education Act of 1965, Congress approved a National Teacher Corps designed to educate cadres of teachers specifically to teach in urban, disadvantaged areas. Working through schools of education that received special funding, teachers-in-training received small stipends as they lived in the communities in which they planned to teach; learned from community leaders; studied the history, arts, music, and culture of the communities; and learned about the children from their parents. This kind of program comes closest to what I believe we need to educate those children whom we have failed.

In general, schools of education can be influenced to try new strategies if there are funds available to fund new strategies. Were we to have government-sponsored programs that allow schools of education or school systems to apply for funds to help teachers learn about their students and their communities, develop curricula based on what they learn, and create rigorous and engaging instruction based on students' academic, political, and cultural heritage, then we would be able to provide better-educated teachers for our students and greatly improve the quality of education provided in our schools.

We also need to allow teachers who are trying to make a difference in the education of previously underserved children to have more control over their teaching lives. Teachers in Japan work collaboratively to study their students, to study their teaching methods, and to collectively develop curriculum. In our individualistic society, we do not provide time for the same kind of collaboration to allow teachers to ameliorate problems and plan for success. Again, funding allocated for schools, school systems, or colleges of education to develop programs of teacher collaboration to address the factors indicated above would help encourage the widespread sharing and promotion of knowledge and better methods of teaching among our teachers.

Civil rights leader Victoria Adams-Gray once said that we educators should be "the seed people of the world"—those who prepare the ground and plant the seeds of the future. We have somehow abdicated our seedlings. In order to provide the kind of nourishment they need, we must enrich the soil where our students grow with the belief that they are brilliant, we must weed out the stereotypes that make them question their intellect, and we must fertilize new buds with rigorous, relevant, engaging instruction. Then, we will actually grow the democracy our country has only hoped for.

In hope and struggle,

Lisa Delpit

NINE MILLION VOICES

Dear President

You may be surprised to learn that more people live in rural America now than did in 1950. In the 1990s, the population of rural America increased by more than ten percent due to a combination of natural growth, migration from urban centers, and an influx of immigrants. Even more surprising is that forty percent of the nation's public schools are in rural communities or towns with populations of under twenty-five thousand and that twenty-eight percent of the nation's children attend these schools. Even by the most stringent definition of *rural*—that is, communities of two thousand five hundred or fewer—almost one third of the country's schools are in rural areas and twenty-one percent of public school students (one in five) attend rural schools. In twenty states (mostly in the South, Appalachia, northern New England, and the Great Plains), more than thirty percent of students go to school in these small rural communities. There are more than nine million students attending schools in America's rural places, and their voices need to be heard.

You may also be surprised to learn that rural America is far poorer than our country's metropolitan areas and nearly as poor as our poorest inner cities. Mr. President, if child poverty matters, then rural Mississippi matters, as well as rural West Virginia, rural South Dakota, and rural New Mexico, among many others. Moreover, while many people cling to the notion that rural America is homogeneously White, it is, in fact, as diverse as the rest of the nation. Most Americans would be astonished to learn that if you are African American or Hispanic, your chance of living in poverty is greater if you live in rural America than it is if you live in a central city.

In this next year, approximately one hundred small rural schools and eighty rural districts across the country will close. This great loss to rural children, their families, and their communities comes at a time when urban school reformers trumpet the growth and success of newly created small schools and the breakup of another two dozen dysfunctional mega-schools. Although the news for urban schools is good, the elimination of small schools in rural communities is a tragedy.

What is especially irrational about this trend is that there is overwhelming evidence that smaller schools are beneficial for kids. In recent years, research results from multiple studies in dozens of states; in urban, suburban, and rural places; and in schools with high numbers of poor children, immigrant children, or children of color have found advantages to learning in small schools. Research concludes that, when compared to large schools, smaller schools tend to have

- better attendance rates,
- stronger academic achievement,
- lower drop-out rates,
- higher grades,
- fewer failed courses,
- greater participation in extracurricular activities,
- less vandalism and violence,
- fewer behavioral incidents, and
- especially strong academic results for low-income children and children of color.

In response to this research, and because parents and communities have demanded it, both state policy and private investment have begun to focus on breaking up huge schools into smaller units, or creating schools within schools. Likewise, the charter school movement has led to more small schools at all grade levels. The consensus is that small schools work. Yet, in many rural regions, despite the fact that long bus rides have finally reached outer limits of decency and expense (one and a half to two hours each way), saving small rural schools and making them better has not yet become popular. It should.

Small schools more often have elements associated with higher academic achievement than large schools. For instance, small schools tend to have smaller class sizes, and smaller class size is, in turn, associated with achievement gains, lower drop-out rates, and fewer grade retentions. Small schools, often out of necessity, encourage mixed ability grouping and classes that cross grade levels—two elements that promote increased learning and positive student attitudes. Small schools intrinsically foster close relationships that not only help children feel connected to the school community and reduce alienation, especially among older students, but also lead to increased student learning. The close relationships inherent in small schools also have a positive impact on educators. For example, teachers in small schools tend to be more satisfied with their jobs, have less absenteeism, and take more responsibility for ensuring that their students are successful in school. Furthermore, teachers and school leaders are more likely to implement innovative instructional methods that have been shown to increase student learning—the numbers just make it much easier to manage.

The great detractors of small schools have often quoted the high cost of creating such schools. However, because their drop-out rates are so low, small schools—in addition to being more academically effective—prove to be more cost-effective than large schools when measured on a cost-per-graduate basis.

Schools in rural communities perform an essential community development function. They are often the central meeting places for communities, the location for most recreation and cultural events, and the repository of articulate leaders for community organizations. They are frequently the rural town's art museum, symphony hall, sports arena, fitness center, polling place, and a venue for public meetings. Young people can provide energy and leadership for community betterment through the school's service-learning projects and through membership in school programs and groups. Indeed, when a school closes in a rural community, the community's population declines faster and community organizations lose their energy.

A 2004 study by sociologist Tom Lyson at Cornell University compared small rural communities in New York that had schools with those that did not have schools and found stark differences between the two. While all the communities had roughly the same percentage of households with school-age children, communities with schools had higher housing values, better infrastructure, less poverty, fewer welfare recipients, and more jobs. Communities with schools also tended to gain population.

The purchasing power of schools and their employees is also significant. In a study of six Minnesota communities, school district expenditures made up between one and three percent of the county's retail sales and the take-home pay of employees ranged from five to ten percent of retail sales. In Lund, Nevada, retail sales dropped eight percent when the community's school closed. In two North Dakota towns, the local grocery stores closed after schools consolidated, largely because of lost revenue from the schools and their employees.

For rural children of all races, education has often been assumed to be the pathway out of poverty. The paradox of this is that the education that provides a pathway to greater individual opportunity more often than not has led young people out of rural communities, leaving those communities more impoverished and depriving them of the very talent that offers the most hope for the future. This is starkly apparent on Indian reservations, where schools are often seen by Native people as partners in cultural genocide. But this problem is not limited to Native Americans. The same complaint is heard from Appalachia to the Mississippi Delta to the Northern Plains. Too many schools just teach kids how to count and read so that they can be commercially useful in a world that does not respect who they are. Schools should teach kids how to live well anywhere, how to build good communities, and how to commit themselves to making any place they live the best place it can be.

Instead, the division between schools and communities is tragic and widening. It is fueled by the national obsession with standardized testing and the implicit drift toward a rigid and narrow curriculum of particulars as well as a system of discipline and accountability that reduces teachers to test coaches and converts our most challenging young people to little more than skilled test-takers, at best, or dropouts, at worst. In some cases, this division between school and community is a reflection of longstanding poverty, racism, and social injustice. Sometimes, the division is a product of professional educators (many well-intentioned, some merely cynical) who do not trust parents or communities to take responsibility for the education of their children. In other cases, the division is the result of communities that do not trust or value education. In the worst cases, the divide is a product of all of the above. Of course, these are all mutually reinforcing factors.

This division is unnecessary. Schools need the wisdom and support of the communities they serve if they are to educate their children well, and communities need schools that produce educated citizens who are committed to making good communities no matter where they choose to live. Children raised in such communities and taught in such schools may choose to live their lives elsewhere—though many will not, especially if there is a meaningful opportunity to stay home. There *should* be vibrant, thriving, sustainable rural communities with high-quality schools, and we, as a nation, should work every day to help rural schools and communities improve together. You cannot leave democracy behind when you enter the schoolhouse door, and you cannot isolate learning from doing good in the world. Schools need to be engaged in the communities they serve, and communities need to be the centerpiece of school governance.

Every child deserves a good school that is close to home. Mr. President, you have a unique opportunity as a leader to assure that geography does not dictate which children receive an excellent education and which do not. You can make a difference for more than nine million rural children. In the sections that follow, I will outline some of the things you can do to support rural schools.

Use the bully pulpit. Be an advocate for small rural schools. Research supports small schools for student learning. Rural communities need them to partner in development. The mantra that bigger is better has been recited so often that people have forgotten to look at the evidence. And the evidence is mounting that there are significant costs to children and families, to learning, and to communities from creating larger schools and transporting kids long distances to attend them. At the same time, there is abundant evidence that there are significant benefits to small, community-based schools, especially for children from poor communities.

Change the adequate yearly progress requirements in No Child Left Behind. When small numbers of students are tested at each grade level, as they often are in small rural schools, the year-to-year changes in the student population can cause wild fluctuations in school-level scores. This random variation based on small cohorts means small schools will often not be able to sustain progress from year to year as NCLB requires, no matter how well teachers perform. This misuse of statistics to judge school performance is hitting hardest the schools that serve the most vulnerable students in the politically weakest regions of our nation. Ultimately, this practice is less likely to lead to school improvement and is more likely to lead to school closure.

When a small school is needlessly labeled as low-performing, children suffer. States are now required to publish annual report cards on the performance of school districts. Likewise, districts are required to submit similar reports to the public with school-level data. For rural schools, this could mean publishing results for very small classes in very small communities. When newspaper readers find out, for example, that five out of eighteen fourth graders scored below proficiency in reading, there will likely be open speculation about who the five kids are. Putting pressure on adults to perform better as teachers and school administrators is one thing. Publicly humiliating children is another.

Increase federal resources for teachers in schools that are hard to staff. For hard-to-staff rural schools—many of them in communities with significant minority populations and high poverty rates—the requirements of No Child Left Behind will make it even harder to attract and retain well-qualified teachers. These are schools that already face serious teacher shortages and serious gaps in teacher pay when compared with urban and suburban schools. The average rural teacher makes only seventy-seven cents for every dollar earned by his or her suburban counterparts and eighty cents for every dollar earned by peers in urban areas.

A 2006 College Board report made a series of policy recommendations for improving America's education system. The report acknowledged that schools with the highest challenges must be staffed with the most experienced teachers and that teacher pay must increase by at least twenty percent across the board, and even more so for hard-to-staff schools and subjects. Additional significant financial incentives are needed to recruit and retain teachers in these schools. Raising the average rural teacher's salary up to the average for non-rural teachers would involve an investment of $1.6 billion—or $201 per rural student. A strategy of additional federal investment in hard-to-staff schools is needed in both urban and rural schools. There are federal programs for getting doctors into underserved areas, so why not have programs for getting educators into underserved schools?

Continue support for the E-Rate and make greater investment in appropriate technology and its use. Since 1998, the federal E-Rate program has provided discounts of between twenty and ninety percent to schools and libraries for telecommunications services, Internet access, and internal connections. The program has provided rural schools with affordable access to the Internet and new information technologies. It must be continued and improved.

In addition, many rural schools are creating regional consortia to share their best teaching resources by interactive TV or blended interactive technologies. Investment in careful research and demonstration is needed to assure quality as new distance learning technologies emerge. Large national for-profit vendors are unlikely either to provide the instruction suited to rural regions or to build upon the strengths of local schools and communities.

Support a demonstration program for community learning centers. In the poorest rural regions, where levels of adult education are very low and the economy must be reinvented, collaborations between

Community Development Corporations, K–12 schools, and community colleges to focus on community and economic development should be encouraged. Schools are significant community assets, and they could provide much more than a traditional K–12 education if we expand schools into community institutions. These "reinvented" schools could provide early education such as Head Start and programs for mothers and infants. They also could provide seamless access to community college courses, adult education, workforce training, and perhaps even micro-business startups. In successful examples of this type of collaboration, the school is the center for community health and fitness, hosts community events using the auditorium for theater and the cafeteria for dinners, and provides services such as child care and fire and rescue. Students and teachers at these schools contribute to community development through curricula and connections with the community.

Multiple funding streams and divergent bureaucratic cultures make this work difficult to start, but a federal program combining waivers for existing funds and modest new resources could lead the way to new opportunities in the most distressed regions.

IN SUMMARY, MR. PRESIDENT, you have a real opportunity to make a difference to the nine million children who go to school in rural America, to their families, and to the continued vitality of their communities. I hope you will use your leadership to set an education agenda for all of America's children—no matter where they live.

GEORGE WOOD

HOW OUR HIGH SCHOOL
MAKES A DIFFERENCE

Dear Future President,

Think of this as a letter from the front lines. For the past dozen years I have watched politicians and citizens debate about public education and educational policy from my desk as a high school principal. I am writing this to you at the end of another school year, when the question of what difference we make as a school weighs heavily on my mind. When I contemplate the future of our graduates—young people who live in Appalachia, one of the poorest regions in our county—I wonder about how my staff and I may have changed their lives.

There is no doubt in my mind about the quality of our school. After a decade of fierce commitment to making whatever positive change we can in the name of doing what is right by our students, we have come a long way. Our daily schedule is built around long class periods, with teachers having fewer than eighty students a day, providing the time and connections necessary for students to learn. Our teachers push themselves continually to find more ways to reach our students through multiple forms of instruction. Our curriculum reflects a sense of place and a deep respect for our local community and traditions—often requiring teachers to write their own texts as they use the local surroundings to teach content.

We have developed an advisory system that ensures every student is closely followed throughout high school by an adult who knows him or her well. There is an internship program that places students in real-world situations where they put to use what they have learned. Each student develops and carries out a senior project, contributing to our school or community. And graduates all prepare and present a portfolio of their work, which they defend in order to justify earning a diploma.

All of this has led to improved achievement at our school. State-required test scores have climbed, discipline referrals have dwindled, attendance is up, and more students are now going on to college. We have received Ohio's Best Award for our internship program, have been recognized nationally as a First Amendment School for our work in promoting democratic citizenship, and have received a wide number of grants and awards. Our history would seem to tell you that we are a successful high school.

As I write to you now, however, I am specifically thinking about the 100 or so kids my staff and I are graduating this year. I am wondering about the impact that we have had on the lives of the kids we have spent so much time with over the past four years. Of course, I know that we are only a small part of their lives over this period of time. Yet, if you figure it out, we have their attention for about twenty-one percent of their waking hours during the four years that they attend our high school. That means that they most likely spend more time with us in school than they spend doing anything else throughout these four years. Does it matter?

I am also thinking of our annual portfolio day, the day when all of our seniors carry out their final task on the way to graduation—the presentation of their graduation portfolios. The portfolio is an account of the students' four years with us. It is a chance for the students to tell us how they feel they have met the school's mission for its students to be lifelong learners, active democratic citizens, and flexible in their career choices.

For a full day, each and every hour, every senior presents his or her portfolio—each student's personal statement of readiness for life after high school—to a panel of faculty and community members. The presentations are as varied as our students. Some take the form of trips down memory lane, with the students wandering through the school to a series of stops on their academic development; some students put together meals that represent their development; some take us to athletic fields to show us their "field of dreams;" some run interactive computer simulations; some dress as knights, doctors, firefighters, and lawyers; and some even put on mini-concerts. Each presentation is built around a theme, each pinpoints the students' strengths and weaknesses, and each tells us about who these kids are.

Not only do I judge some of the portfolios as a member of the faculty, but I also try to observe as many of the others as I can. Nothing impresses me more than the fact that every student, regardless of social class, handicapping condition, or any other factor, is expected to meet this challenge—and they do.

This year I must have been listening a little more closely than usual, however, because a theme emerged that I had not heard before. That theme was change. There it was in the student who decided in her sophomore year that she should quit being so self-centered and take on more of a life of service. Another young woman recounted how she decided to give up cheerleading so she could concentrate on raising her achievement in math and science. One young man decided halfway through his junior year to give up "fighting my teachers and to try liking them to see what I could learn." Yet another, in his senior year, gave up feeling sorry for himself and set out to "take on a bigger challenge to work with people who had less than I and to make something of myself that I can give back to my community." Again and again, there were stories of change, either dramatic ones like these or simpler ones like giving up a job to devote more time to family and school.

As I was hearing these stories, it came to me that the ability to change and to devote oneself to helping others was not only the biggest difference we were making in these kids lives, it was also the most important. Our mission as a school is to prepare young people for the roles they face in life after school. First and foremost among these is the role of citizen in our democracy. An active citizen is always dealing with change, and the most powerful citizens direct or work to control such change while the weak or apathetic simply acquiesce. Clearly, our kids, having been able to work through and direct their own changes, were on their way to taking the mantle of involved citizenship.

As I watched the portfolio presentations I wanted to know how teenagers—who are so concerned with peer pressure, so bombarded with media images of who they should be, so overwhelmed, at times, with issues of love and romance—find the courage and ability to make these life-altering, even self-sacrificing, changes in their lives. After hearing similar stories numerous times I decided to ask the students, and the answer was the same every time: I changed, every student said, because change is expected, encouraged, supported, and even celebrated at our high school.

That is the difference that we make, and that every high school could and should make. We make it possible for young adults, at a crucial time in their lives, to rethink themselves and who they want to be. Somehow we take away the fear of change and make it possible for our kids to become something more than they thought they could be. They have to be the ones to make the change, but we seem to be able to create the impetus and sense of security that such change requires.

How do we do it? My best guess, based on what the kids and staff say, is that we have created several sets of complementary structures that make this possible.

First, we do not just say kids are equals, we treat them that way. Our core courses are not ability grouped, which means that students of many different backgrounds and with many different talents and abilities rub shoulders with each other every day. We insist that *all* students have access to *all* leadership and internship positions, and sometimes push them to take these spots. We also structure the school day to provide "slack time" for all students (through a long lunch with access to the entire campus) so that all the students in the school can freely mingle.

Second, we give our students a real say in how their school operates. Students engage in a yearly review of school policies and procedures, in which they create the first draft of the annual rewrite of the school handbook. They have an equal say in the hiring of new teachers through a student committee (appointed by the student government from volunteers) that assists in screening applications and conducts interviews of candidates. They serve on many different committees, including our site-based governance committee, curriculum committees, school change panels, and departmental meetings. They manage all student affairs, such as fundraisers, social events, clubs, and any request for student involvement in community affairs. Citizenship here is not a class kids take; it is a way of life.

Finally, and perhaps most importantly, we work hard to put our kids in close proximity to our staff. Long class periods, an advisory system, the development of the portfolio, an extended lunch period, and other tools give students and staff the time to get to know one another. We do this because students are more willing to take risks in front of adults whom they know well, and change certainly involves risk. They are also more likely to model productive adult behavior when they have the chance to be near productive adults. Time and time again in the portfolio presentations I hear our students talk about the one particular teacher who, through his or her actions, gave them a model of action to which they aspired. In the very last presentation I heard this year, a young woman said, in response to a question about why she had taken on a commitment to community service: "Well, I am around [a certain guidance counselor] a lot and she is always talking about community service. I finally got that it was what I should be doing."

Most of our students become different people because of the four years they spend at our high school. This does not mean they receive the highest scores on the ACTs or that they will all go to college. It does mean that, more importantly, we have provided them with the tools and confidence to choose their own paths and to live reflective lives. Our school has done this not through a particular course or by simply telling students about these skills, but rather through encouraging the direct experience of exercising these skills. What they face after school may make some of these choices impossible—the economy, the prejudices they face because of their skin color or heritage, and family crises can all conspire against who they can become. However, at least once in their life they will know that they had a choice, and most of them, to their benefit, exercise it.

I believe that every school could make this type of a difference in the lives of the children they serve. What more could we ask for? This is the highest aspiration for a system of public education: to equip our nation's young citizens with the tools to self-govern, to make choices, and to contribute to the public and private good. Yet so little is said or done to help schools be places where we nurture the habits of heart and mind that make democratic citizenship possible.

Instead, over the past two decades, we have lived through a federal policy environment (mirrored in most state policy) that is not about making a difference in the lives our children lead—at least not a positive one. Focused primarily upon raising standardized test scores, educational policy has prescribed curriculum and teaching methods, narrowed what counts as learning, and has punished schools when externally imposed standards are not met. It is not my experience, as the principal of a public high school for more than a dozen years, that these strategies work. Nor is there any evidence available that our schools have improved after over two decades of the implementation of such policies. In fact, I think I could argue that the quality of our public schools has worsened as unique, locally designed programs are eliminated to make room for test-preparation programs. What is taught is more often than not limited to what is tested, and, as a result, some of our most creative and insightful teachers leave in response to having their professional hands tied by external standards.

Let me now direct your attention to what I think you could do, back there in Washington, to help those of us like the teachers with whom I work make a difference in our students' lives. What could you do that would allow us to build the personal relationships that learning requires and that would allow for schools to be places where, through experience, the tools of citizenship are learned and the habits of good community members are nurtured? At the risk of being simplistic, here is my suggestion in a sentence: Treat public schools the same way you treat any industry or business that you are trying to grow or improve.

Allow me to elaborate on this point. For years I have been, I must admit, somewhat jealous of the treatment my friends in the business world have received from the federal government. When a business sector goes to Washington for help, it is often treated to fewer regulations, assistance in finding markets, and increased funding for research. Often the president is a visible inspiration—giving pep talks, meeting with workers, and convincing citizens that such public support of business is in our collective best interest. Decisions about how to restructure are left to owners or managers of the business, there are incentives for highly skilled workers to join the effort, and entrepreneurs are made to feel as if they are central to fulfilling the American dream. In short, when Washington wants a business or industry to advance, your office does the following:

- The president leads by providing a vision of our goals and the methods we will use to achieve them.
- Funds are made available for innovations and multiple approaches are welcome.
- Decision-making authority is localized and decentralized.
- Regulations are limited or waived.
- Outcomes are broad, with multiple measures of success embraced.

What would it look like if you were to take this approach in education? How could you use these tools to make it easier for people like me to make a difference in the lives of the kids who walk through the doors of our nation's schools every day?

First, you could help us, as a country, clearly define what it means to be well educated and what role our public schools play in achieving this level of education. Do we really want to limit our vision of education to producing good test-takers? This seems to be the only notion of success that Washington currently accepts. I think you could raise the conversation about schools to a higher plane by calling for an educational system that lives up to our highest vision of ourselves—that of the engaged democratic citizen. This is the one role we all share in our republic, and it is the reason public schools were begun. The goal of our public education system has always been to equip every one of us—regardless of race, social status, class, or creed—to be good citizens above all else. You should challenge us to live up to this heritage and history.

Second, you could authorize increased funding and support for ongoing and new efforts to educate for citizenship. This should not be about a specific program, but rather about completely restructuring schools so that the core of their work is citizenship. Part of this would involve the promotion of the structures that we know make a difference in building the relationships that citizenship education requires: smaller schools; a curriculum that makes sense to students and is also challenging and engaging; a school structure that allows students to be involved in genuine decision making regarding school policy, staffing, and curriculum; incentives for service-learning; and greater availability of internships to allow our students to explore many different possible career paths.

There is one caveat to all of this: There is no one model that best meets this vision of education for students and schools everywhere. Communities and their children differ, and so should their schools. Our diversity is something we Americans proudly point to when we talk about what makes our country great, and we should encourage our schools to exemplify this greatness through diversity.

This brings me to my third point: Put decision-making authority at the local school level. So much of what schools do is dictated at the state or federal level that innovation is next to impossible. School administrators' days are filled with paperwork, the school day is built around external mandates, and teachers' lessons come from prescribed texts. When we look for leadership in this country in restructuring an industry or business, we often turn to the people doing the work. Again, local control is something that Americans are fiercely proud and protective of—and often for good reason, as many of the decisions forced on them by bureaucrats and "experts" do not fit their local reality. At the federal level, you should work to leave every decision about life in schools to the most local body of decision makers possible, and you should provide financial incentives for states that do the same.

Of course, local decision making only works in an environment with limited regulations. My fourth suggestion, therefore, is that you undertake a sweeping revision of all federal regulations regarding public schools. For years, federal limitations on local action have piled up like barnacles on a ship, never cleaned off but frequently added to. Some regulations will need to be kept; federal intervention is warranted, for instance, when it comes to protecting minority rights and ensuring the health and welfare of children. Spend money on these historic, constitutional priorities and leave everything else—issues of curriculum and methods of assessment, for example—to the schools and local communities. Create a climate where federal policy asks how to *help*, rather than how to *prevent*.

Finally, speak to us in the broadest possible ways about how the success of our schools will be measured. Honestly, few people care about two-percent increases in standardized test scores by disaggregated racial groups (as specified in the recent No Child Left Behind legislation). What most of us *do* care about is whether more of our fellow citizens vote, volunteer for community activities, find productive work, and are good neighbors. Use these as measures of our schools and you will be surprised at the real changes that occur.

Rather than worry about outcomes such as test scores, we should focus on the quality of the daily life inside the school and *the school experience as an end in itself.* Does the daily life in every school engage every student in the practice of the skills and the acquisition of the knowledge that it takes to assume the ability to take on the highest office in the land—that of citizen? I am convinced after working with literally thousands of young people, their parents, and members of our communities, that Americans want schools with this focus—schools like mine, where students' lives change through strong connections with what is taught and, more importantly, who is teaching it. I am also convinced that you, as president, could help create and nurture such schools, if you choose to.

Sincerely,

George Wood

REYNOLD LEVY

PUTTING THE ARTS
BACK IN AMERICA'S ABC'S

DEAR MR. PRESIDENT:

As the leader of the most powerful nation on Earth—what some have called "the indispensable country"—your agenda of major challenges is simply daunting. I write this note of appeal appreciative of the pressures and priorities that you must balance and of the thousands of supplicants pursuing their interests and advancing their agendas with the office of the president.

However, my request, animated by public interest, not by private gain, does not seek major resources so much as your attention and an honored, modest place on your cluttered agenda. If you are persuaded by my entreaty, little you could do in your presidency would have a greater impact on our nation while requiring less of your time and of the country's treasure.

Perhaps the best way to present my request, and what I hope you can accomplish in the next four years, is to begin with a personal story.

As is the case for millions of Americans of my generation, attending public elementary and secondary school was compulsory, not a matter of choice. Private school education was then, as it remains today, prohibitively expensive for the vast majority of Americans. In my first eight grades of education at PS 100 in Brooklyn, the arts were an integral part of the curriculum. All students were offered the opportunity to play an instrument. All students were invited to participate in the orchestra, the marching band, and the chorus.

In the seventh grade, the students of PS 100 were told that there was to be a visit by important authorities from Abraham Lincoln High School—the high school that we would all attend upon graduation from eighth grade. At first, we thought our honored guests must be the coaches of the football, basketball, and track teams. We were wrong. Our visitors were the directors of Abraham Lincoln High School's orchestra, chorus, band, and theater programs, and they were eager to find enthusiastic, talented students and to recruit them two years in advance of enrollment!

Those visits sent a strong signal to us as students that the arts mattered and that they were important for everyone, whether you were to become a performer on stage or an appreciative member of the audience. And the experiences that followed offered us a sense of poise and self-confidence as well as a glimpse into the demands and joys of the creative process.

Many municipalities, including New York City, experienced a major fiscal crisis in the middle of the 1970s, and one of the first expense-saving acts was to virtually eliminate all fine and visual arts programming from the public school system. Almost thirty years later, public elementary and secondary schools are still recovering from that major blow.

As a result of this vacuum in arts education for youngsters all around America, orchestras, theaters, dance companies, festivals, and performing arts centers are experiencing difficulty attracting a new generation of audiences.

Today, there is growing recognition of the positive impact of arts education on student learning across the curriculum. There is growing appreciation of a renewed emphasis on the arts as being complementary to, rather than competitive with, the back-to-basics movement that stresses language and math literacy. There is a growing engagement across the country between nonprofit performing arts institutions and schools acting in partnership to restore and renew arts offerings. These partnerships in their best form can provide more than simple exposure to the arts, they can provide a continuing engagement with works of art that has benefits across the curriculum.

Lincoln Center Institute is proud to play a leadership role in this movement. The institute reaches approximately 188,800 elementary and secondary school students across the New York metropolitan area and around the nation. It works with 2,500 teachers and 332 schools in seventy-five school districts throughout the country, and serves as a model for twenty-nine similar institutes in the United States and around the world. For more than twenty-five years, it has developed and refined its own distinctive approach to the arts and education, one that challenges all students to learn about—and through—the arts. Working in partnership with educators and education programs, the institute develops experiential studies focusing on works of art, including dance, music, theater, visual arts, and architecture. The institute holds that works of art provide an inexhaustible resource for exploration, research, reflection, and discussion. Every individual—child as well as adult—has the capacity to explore and respond to any given work of art in ways that challenge preconceived notions and promote fresh insights. By stimulating the perceptual abilities and critical thinking skills of young learners, Lincoln Center Institute supports learning across the curriculum. This process-based approach demonstrates the role that the arts can and should play as an integral component of educational renewal.

It also stimulates understanding of the cultural context in which a work of art was created, which brings me to the other driving force behind the need to increase emphasis on the performing and visual arts as vehicles for communication and learning: globalization. The need for Americans to appreciate the language and the culture of the many countries with which we conduct security, diplomatic, and commercial business has never been greater. By exposing our children to art and culture from many different areas of the globe, we can help them to learn about and appreciate the beliefs and values of different types of people.

There are many ways to better accomplish this objective: more emphasis on studying abroad, more priority given to language training, more encouragement for foreign students in America to return home, an enlarged Peace Corps, the continued lowering of American trade barriers that now pose obstacles to poorer countries endeavoring to develop business relationships with us, and promoting American tourism. But only a small portion of Americans can be directly engaged in such initiatives compared with the order of magnitude that can be transformed by more film, dance, opera, theater, music, and visual arts coming into the United States and going from America to countries around the world. Through an understanding of the arts, the unfamiliar can become knowable, both to us as we look at the rest of the world and to the world as it looks at us.

There is no argument that counters the need to understand one another better. This has been thrown into sharp relief by America's engagement in areas of the world that were so entirely unknown to us just a decade ago, such as the Balkans, Afghanistan, Rwanda, and Liberia.

How can you, in your role as president, lend momentum and legitimacy to both a renaissance of the arts in our public schools and a significant increase in cultural exchange between our country and others? My agenda for the future, submitted humbly for your consideration, includes the following items:

First, what the president values occupies his or her time. At home in the White House and on your travels, attend performing arts events and visit schools where the arts are being featured. Honor artists. Invite them to the White House. Host symposia that bring dancers, musicians, painters, singers, and actors into government quarters and to the airwaves. Send a signal that the quality of American culture matters.

Second, revive government programs that subsidize artistic tours abroad. At a time when apprehensions in the world about American motives and intentions are high, who better to neutralize them and represent our country well than the men and women of opera, theater, ballet, modern dance, the orchestra, and the museum?

Similarly, consistent with new national security needs post-9/11, accelerate the process by which visas are granted to those artists from abroad whom institutions such as Lincoln Center have engaged to perform. Today, delays and uncertainties about pending approval of artists to travel play havoc with the ability to plan a schedule with any measure of confidence.

Third, adjust federal funding formulas for aid to poverty-impacted public schools to at least allow for—and, more emphatically, encourage—the use of existing or expanded funds for arts purposes, especially for curricula that offer sustained and meaningful study of works of art.

Fourth, increase funding for the National Endowment for the Arts and Humanities. If direct government support for the arts is a measure of how they are valued, then most European and many Asian governments place a higher priority on artistic endeavors of all kinds than does America. They not only recognize the intrinsic benefit of the arts to children and adults, but they appreciate the impact a thriving arts community can have on neighborhood and community development, on job creation, on tourism, and on the economy overall.

Finally, the gap between what the federal government appropriates to its arts institutions located in Washington, D.C., measured in the billions of dollars, and what it expends directly on the arts in the rest of the country is egregious and growing. Billions of dollars go to the Beltway of the Smithsonian, the National Gallery, the Holocaust Museum, and the Kennedy Center for the Performing Arts—to name a few—and a couple of hundred million dollars or so goes to arts institutions in the rest of the nation. The nation's arts appropriations water must rise to the handsomely funded arts bridge of our nation's capital.

MR. PRESIDENT, the nation enjoys a vibrant, vital, and heterogeneous arts landscape. It is supported by state and local governments, corporations, foundations, and individuals. With a little more encouragement from the federal government—in the form of your own involvement and commitment, steady increases in federal appropriations to arts institutions and public schools, streamlining of visa processes for arts visitors, and attention to tax law changes that would encourage gifts of art and cash to artistic institutions—a renaissance in the American arts education is possible.

The forces in our culture that would "dumb down" discourse and that would promote mediocrity—on film, television, the Internet, and in print—are very strong. The federal government should strengthen the elements of the American artistic community and provide our teachers with the knowledge and skills they need to actively participate in arts education. As a nation, we should raise our sights and elevate our thinking and demand far more of our native creative and intellectual capacities.

Mr. President, put the arts back in America's ABC's, for the sake of the next generation of artists, schoolchildren, and audiences.

Yours sincerely,

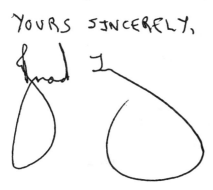

Lilian Katz

When Does $1.00
Equal $7.00?

Dear President:

Nowadays, just about everyone agrees that any provision for young children that is not of good quality—whether in the children's homes or outside of them—represents a missed opportunity to make a substantial contribution to the rest of their lives.

However, there's still plenty of disagreement about what "good quality" is. Indeed, the arguments are often bitter. Some people argue about what constitutes a good-quality preschool curriculum, some argue about who should be responsible for monitoring and ensuring the quality of programs for our youngest, and many argue about who should pay for these programs, since—as you well know—those children who have the most to gain from good-quality early childhood programs are from families who can least afford to pay what they really cost. But today, everyone with serious interest in the future of our children agrees with the basic idea that the experiences of the first half-dozen years of life have a powerful influence on the rest of it.

I'm sure you've been told many times about the substantial long-term savings generated by good preschool education. Past research indicates that, when compared to their peers who did not have good-quality preschool experiences, low-income children who had good-quality preschool experiences at ages three or four were more successful in completing education and in staying employed well into adulthood. In fact, in the 1960s and 1970s, economists estimated that for every dollar invested in high-quality preschool programs, the long-term savings of public funds are anywhere from four dollars to seven dollars. These savings were due to reduced need for special education, lower school drop-out rates, and fewer employment difficulties.

These estimated savings of public funds were the result of pre-school programs that were based on what we thought was good quality in the 1960s—the early days of what we used to call "compensatory education." We have learned a lot about children's early development since then. If we offered preschool education to all of our children based on what we know today about early child development, who knows how much greater our savings might be? Of course, in every profession there's always a gap between the latest knowledge and current practices. It's inevitable because professions are always developing new knowledge, and it takes a while for practice to catch up with it. Yet, the gap between what we now know about child development and our current practices in early childhood programs is much too large.

Since the National Education Goals Panel was launched in the 1990s, helping children to get ready for school has become a major goal of preschool education. Please notice that I deliberately avoided using the phrase "all children enter school ready to learn." In my view, that phrase is misleading. I think it would have been more accurate to state the goal as "all children enter school ready to learn *what the school wants them to learn*."

To say that all children should enter school "ready to learn" implies that they haven't been learning all those years before entering the school doors. But one of the truly impressive facts about young children is that, not only are they all born ready to learn, but they are all very busy doing so from day one! Granted, some learn faster and more easily than others. Still, the point remains: Our *schools* should be ready for *young children* who have been busy learning throughout the years before school.

So, what kinds of programs and methods of teaching best help children continue to develop their capacity to learn?

By now you are probably weary of hearing about what's referred to as "brain research." Popular discussions in the media about brain development hammer away at the importance of brain development in the early years without being clear about what kinds of experiences should and shouldn't be provided for young children.

One important insight from recent neurological research is that helping children get ready for school isn't simply a matter of providing stimulation—as was often claimed in the 1960s. After all, watching television and movies can be stimulating—especially if there is lots of dramatic and vivid action such as explosions, disasters, and scary monsters! In fact, many of our youngsters growing up in poor neighborhoods have *too much* stimulation. What they often need help with is how to make sense of it all. So, stimulation, by itself, will not provide the high-quality preschool education our children need.

Our brains are designed for pattern *seeking* rather than just for pattern *receiving*. This means that helping children make fuller and better sense of the patterns of events around them is a major responsibility of adults both at home and in the preschool. For many of our neediest children, the adults in their lives have their own heavy burdens and stresses that keep them from helping their young children make good sense of their experiences. In the face of chaotic environments that, by definition, cannot be made sense of, the most adaptive response is to give up trying. This suggests, again, that a major criterion of quality in preschool programs is the ability of the staff to help the children make sense of their environments and experiences.

The case has been made that early and frequent interchanges between the very young and those who care for and educate them actually lead to the growth of the neurological connections between the midbrain, the part where basic emotions and motives come from, and the forward part of the brain, where decisions and plans for action originate. The earliest examples of these interchanges are often the typical kinds of behaviors we've all seen when an adult interacts with a little baby. The adult makes funny faces and noises to engage the baby's attention. When the baby is engaged, everything slows down except information processing. Breathing rate, pulse rate, heart rate, and limb movements all slow down as the baby "makes sense" of what's going on. What's really interesting, however, is that if the adult persists in making precisely the same funny faces or sounds, the baby will turn away out of boredom and seek other input. When the adult responds to this turning away by making new funny faces or sounds, the baby will return to the interaction! This "causing" of the adult's behavior is a very early form of what later becomes task orientation and planfulness!

As I suggested above, such interactions stimulate the development of the neural pathways inside the baby's brain. This means that throughout the first half-dozen or so years of life, children need to experience these kinds of continuous interactions often so that these essential neurological connections can be developed. The importance of these connections between the emotional and the decision-making parts of the brain cannot be overestimated; they make possible the initiative, effort, and task-oriented actions that must be in place for successful adaptation to life in school classrooms and, ultimately, to life in general. Indeed, these are the very capabilities that kindergarten teachers most prize in their students—not their ability to recite the alphabet, but their ability to undertake and follow through on the many different kinds of tasks appropriate for them in the first year of schooling.

One of the implications of this recent "brain research" is that very young children must have frequent, meaningful, engaging *inter*action throughout their infant, toddler, and preschool years rather than heavy doses of stimulation to which they are simply required to *re*act. For every age group and every subject, good teaching is essentially interactive in nature. Yes, teachers tell and explain things, give directions, guide, and make demands. But to do those things well also requires interaction, sometimes of a subtle variety. We might say that, in principle, the younger the children are, the more interactive the teacher has to be.

Another important insight suggested by recent research is that what appears to work well for children's preschool education in the short term may not turn out to be what is best for them in the long term. It's difficult to conduct long-term follow-up studies for both technical and financial reasons. But the data we do have indicate that children of low-income families who had a formal, teacher-directed preschool curriculum appeared to do better on tests at the end of preschool than children who attended programs with more child-sensitive approaches.

This apparent benefit of formal instruction in the short term is hardly surprising when we take into account that the closer the curriculum content is to what is on the test, the more likely those who experience it test well. What really should give us pause for thought is that such early academically focused and test-preparation types of preschool curricula do not have the expected long-term benefits. On the contrary, children who had more opportunities for *inter*action versus *re*action, and more opportunities to be initiators and investigators versus having to be passive, reactive receivers, were notably better off in school later on. So there are differences in the short- and long-term effects of different curriculum approaches—just because effects appear positive in the short term does not guarantee benefits in the long term.

It should be noted here that a more child-responsive and informal preschool program is unlikely to provide a long-term advantage unless it is a really good one. Just because children are not having formal, teacher-directed lessons does not ensure that what they are doing will give them the long-term benefits we hope for. The early childhood curriculum must offer frequent meaningful interaction—not just cutting and pasting, coloring, trike riding, and other pleasant but insufficiently challenging and mind-engaging experiences. Young children's minds should be fully and consistently engaged as they investigate their environments and explore their experiences in the company of thoughtful adults who know well how to interact with them in ways that will support their motivation to apply early literacy and mathematical skills in the service of their intellectual work.

What would it take to provide good-quality preschool provisions? The kinds of preschool educational experiences that would be most likely to yield long-term benefits, especially to children of low-income families, require well-trained and well-paid staffing. There is no way around it. The current level of training and income of those who take care of our young is a national disgrace. Average wages for preschool and child care are about sixteen thousand dollars per year. Such low pay leads to very high staff turnover rates, so that even the benefits of good in-service training are frequently lost as highly qualified child-care workers leave preschool education for more lucrative jobs—to say nothing of the often devastating effects on children of the frequent loss of adults to whom they had become attached. Most people who work in these programs do not get the kinds of benefits K–12 teachers expect and receive. Let's face it, Mr. President, would you really advise a capable, high-achieving, and thoughtful youngster in your family to make a career in the field of preschool education? Unless we resolve to meet the costs of highly capable early childhood personnel, especially for those families least able to pay for them, we cannot hope to realize the full potential of their value to children and of the savings to society to be had by ensuring good-quality early childhood programs.

ON MOST MONDAYS when I hear about how much was spent over the weekend on a given new movie, I wonder what kind of people we are. Huge amounts of money are spent on these films—for example, the last *Terminator* movie made $72.5 million in its opening week-end—yet we haggle about spending more money on the education of our children! Surely we could find the necessary funds to ensure that the adults who are responsible for the future well-being of millions of our young children are well compensated for their work. Better curriculum and better-trained and much better-compensated staff: These are the elements of good-quality early childhood programs. We need your leadership to get us going in that direction.

Let me know if there is any way I can help.

Julian S. ....

LOUIS B. CASAGRANDE

WHAT THEY DO WITH THE OTHER 73 PERCENT OF THEIR TIME

Dear Next President

What makes America the land of opportunity for people from all over the world is not only our public school system but also the rich array of learning and educational opportunities throughout our society. I am sure that you have heard from many different people on how we can improve our public schools and the educational futures of our children. My concerns, however, go beyond having a good school in every neighborhood. I believe that all our children also need and deserve equally imaginative and inspiring prospects for learning *outside* of school. Therefore, to enrich the minds and spirits of *all* our children, I am asking you to consider establishing a national voucher program for out-of-school learning. Here are the reasons why.

I am sure you are well aware that our children only spend about twenty-seven percent of their waking hours each year in school. The other seventy-three percent of their time, they are engaged in all kinds of other learning, for better or for worse.

As you know, new studies suggest that kids who get absorbed in educational activities outside of school do better inside school. This is not possible for all kids. Put simply, it appears that the damaging effects of unequal access to good schools are compounded by the similarly damaging effects of unequal access to a much larger learning landscape beyond the traditional schoolyard.

In your travels around the country, I am sure you have heard parents and local community leaders plead for more high-quality after-school programs. In response to the growing desire for such programs, Congress, state, and local governments, as well as numerous foundations, have significantly increased the funding for such youth programs. Moreover, I am pleased to report that my colleagues in the nonprofit world are also doing their part. Nearly every local museum, library, zoo, YMCA, computer club, music or art school, youth organization, and neighborhood community center has signed on as an educational resource in support of our public schools by providing after-school, vacation, and summer programs for their communities.

Yet, despite all of this new funding and universal concern, we are only making a dent in meeting the need for enriching extracurricular opportunities for learning. The great majority of communities, including most of America's most beleaguered cities, enroll less than fifteen percent of their eligible youth in any structured, out-of-school learning activities. Not only is new program funding insufficient, but there are also the barriers of providing transportation, finding safe spaces to meet, and training qualified community educators. Also, there is the basic challenge of how to promote the value of such learning opportunities to families whose immediate problems are food, clothing, and shelter.

I am not advocating that all of our nation's youth should be required to enroll in formal after-school or summer programs. Nor am I trying to suggest that kids cannot learn important things about themselves and life by just being kids and "bumping into" new knowledge as they cruise the Internet or the mall. Rather, I believe that, as a matter of national educational policy, we need to place much more importance on how our children use their out-of-school learning time. In particular, we need a national policy that offers incentives and says explicitly and clearly to parents, "Be your child's learning partner," not just in choosing your child's school, but also in choosing how, where, and what your child learns outside of school.

This is where the idea of vouchers comes into play. To be clear, I am not endorsing vouchers for choosing among public or private schools. (I am against that idea—but that's another letter). Instead, I propose that we create a national voucher program that helps pay for informal out-of-school learning that directly supports the teaching and learning in our local public schools. These vouchers would allow parents and children to choose from a vast array of unique learning opportunities that local school districts could "certify" as being related to local learning standards and school curricula. Lessons at every grade level and in every discipline could be coordinated to reinforce extracurricular programs at area cultural institutions, providing a variety of innovative ways children and parents can explore a particular topic. Although I do not have all the details worked out, I envision a program that would have tremendous positive benefits for our children and the whole American educational system.

First and foremost, such vouchers would help level the playing field for poor kids. We already have several national programs that identify kids and families in need—for example, food stamps and school lunch programs. To poor families, vouchers of roughly five hundred dollars per child per year would make a huge difference in the number and quality of enrichment programs they could afford—from art classes at museums to technology classes in church basements. Yet this would not be a program exclusively for the poor. All American families would receive vouchers for their children, the amount of which would be determined by need.

Second, these vouchers would motivate parents to get involved in their children's overall education. There would be a quantum leap in the number of parents checking out the education programs at the local children's museum or science center. There would be "get acquainted nights" for parents at the local library or community center. At their workplaces, in grocery stores, and at beauty parlors or barbershops, parents would share with each other their opinions on the "best" educational enrichment programs for their kids. Children and youth, too, would become increasingly motivated to take advantage of such enrichment activities because of their club-like appeal as well as for the chance to earn extra credit; gain recognition from peers, community members, and teachers; and build confidence.

Third, a voucher program of this sort would stimulate creativity and entrepreneurship among the providers. Since parents would receive and choose where to spend the vouchers, nonprofit educational organizations would be encouraged to respond to this new "market" by creating even more engaging, relevant, and fun learning experiences for a greater diversity of children. As the president of a children's museum, I personally know how hungry America's arts and cultural institutions are to attract new audiences. Here would be their chance to expose an entire generation of children to the wonders they hold.

Last, but not least, such a voucher program would strengthen the connections between teachers and all the other venues on America's learning landscape. I think teachers should be in charge of "certifying" these enrichment programs, or at least should become the key liaisons between these formal and informal learning opportunities. Teachers could become summer curators or learning consultants to technology training organizations, or they could help work with program providers to relate sports to science or boating to marine biology, for example. One of the reasons why many of our public schools are in trouble is that they have become isolated places where teachers feel both divorced from, and more often than not, misunderstood and disrespected by the larger society. Good teachers cannot survive in such lonely places. This voucher program would help break down that isolation if teachers had the chance to become mentors and advisors to out-of-school program providers, and if staff from cultural or youth organizations were encouraged to spend more time inside our schools.

Of course, there are obvious barriers to such a voucher program for out-of-school learning: cost, bureaucracy, and maybe even a negative reaction from the NEA or AFT, since this idea could be seen as taking funds away from needy schools. Yet such programs would actually relieve schools and teachers of some of the pressure to provide a greater variety of diverse learning opportunities. Moreover, a broader, full-day commitment to our children's learning would only serve to enhance our collective political will to improve our schools.

Please consider such a national voucher program. I believe it is in the best interest of American democracy that each and every child learn to navigate and access all of the diverse opportunities available to them in this great American learning landscape and that all children have the chance to find their true passion for learning whether inside or outside of school.

Most sincerely,

Lou Casagrande

PART THREE
TEACHING FOR ALL

KAREN HALE HANKINS

MY STUDENTS, MY SCHOOL

photo by Loralle Swindell

Karen Hale Hankins and former student Laura Davis

Dear Candidates,

My life is marked by the scent of crayons, the sound of Velcro shoe closings, and the taste of animal crackers washed down with lukewarm coffee. Small arms try unsuccessfully to hug my middle and end up patting me *wherever* their hands happen to land. (You haven't *really* been hugged until you've been hugged with the express intent on the part of the hugger of wiping his or her nose on your stomach.) My closet is full of dresses that hang from the shoulder (nonbinding) and adult shoes that still allow me to shimmy to the top of the monkey bars in a "rescue emergency." You know me. I teach some of our youngest children, first graders. Trembling fingers compose this letter, trembling from pure adrenaline at the hope that your eyes will take in a first-grade teacher's vision of education.

The country thinks it can recite my job description: "Teach the children to read, write, and do math; treat them well and all the same." Yet I have children who come to me still confusing the letters of the alphabet and children who are reading as proficiently as a third or fourth grader—all are different and all are longing to learn

113

something new, *now*. I have learned to cherish the mix and have found methods of bringing the curriculum together in ways that do help them *all* learn something new. It took a master's degree and a PhD to figure it out . . . not to mention a lot of my own money. My curriculum is not magic. It cannot be boxed up, sent out, and made into a national curriculum. However, it meets the needs of the population that *I* teach. It changes year to year because my children change every year. Good teachers—many of them more proficient and gifted than I—everywhere at all levels do the same.

One of the most difficult parts of my job is to use the proliferation of mandates and lists of benchmarks passed down from the state and federal governments to enhance rather than hamper the progress of my students. A one-size-fits-all reading program is a misnomer. Children are not always well served by even the best of blue-ribbon committee designs. Such programs leave little room for difference, and there is rarely any way of validating progress made outside of that one program. Real learning is much bigger than anything that can be packaged and prescribed.

The hardest thing for me to bear is that the most beautiful aspect of my classroom—the different colors, religious backgrounds, financial pictures, narrative styles, and languages—becomes its curse in the eyes of the public every time a set of misinterpreted data crosses the lips of a news anchor. The public is beginning to fear me and my classroom of beautiful children.

A deepening cycle of fear is grabbing hold of Americans at the mere mention of schools. I tell you as honestly and sincerely as I would speak a vow: I do not fear school problems at all. I do, however, carry an alarming level of anxiety over the destruction the public's growing fear is sure to unleash. Sure, I face discipline problems, time constraints, culture and language barriers, lack of funds, lack of public respect, and huge gaps in ability and performance with certain angst. Those "problems" lace the reasons I teach. Yet, the fears of the public are unfounded and keep teachers from advancing the work we are called to do.

Many years ago John Dewey advanced the idea that education could serve the masses as well as the elite. The heated counterargument was that the masses had no need for subjects like Latin and probably did not have sufficiently developed brains to learn abstract concepts, anyway! From that crossroad of debate rose the concept of a public school system. The next one hundred years have been spent changing, shaping, and studying public education. It has been hotly debated, grossly neglected, highly funded, publicly glorified, and just as publicly maligned. I have often said that, now that the Cold War is over, public education has replaced communism as America's greatest angst. Unless you, as president, help redirect this fear, the education legacy of this century could be the demise of the public schools.

Recent metaphors have not worked. There is the business metaphor, which turns all principals into managers, calls all teachers the labor, and labels the students as the product. Children are not products to be standardized, homogenized, dehumanized, and devalued. The business metaphor glorifies the ability of the standardized test to act as a quality control for sorting children and schools into the categories of "consumer-safe" or "consumer-beware." Yet the fundamental purpose of public education is the exact opposite of this. We keep all of our "products."

Then there is the military metaphor, which describes schools as battlefields, the students as besieged prisoners, and the teachers as commanders of curriculum. Parents are encouraged to "join the war" and to "counterattack" the "battle" schools are supposedly waging against excellence. One has only to turn on the news to realize the fear exacted by a vocabulary of war. This fear, though subliminal, hits its mark. People who are afraid either lash out or fold up. Yet neither of those stances will sustain the efforts of educators and students to attain excellence.

It is easy to see how the public has come to think of *crisis* and *education* in the same breath. However, you, as our president, have the public ear. You can change the way people perceive us by speaking about education and teachers in a way that is positive. Let's face it: All of life rides on language, and education is no different. Today, the words used to take a position on education borrow from a negative vocabulary, even when the people who are using those words are in support of schools. The talk is always about the "crisis."

I am not here to tell you that there is no need for vigilance and standards, but I would like for us to dismantle the idea of there being a "crisis." I would like us to diffuse its power to hold us hostage to an ill-projected fate. I would rather we allow ourselves to think of ourselves as being in "a quandary." Let's embrace that metaphor of inquiry to shed light on our struggles, support questioning, and aid the search for new ways and for new insight. It's such a small nuance of vocabulary, but look at how it unlocks the mind and how it places hope at the end of a question.

You and I have lives that are so different from one another. Perhaps the most important difference is that my role as teacher is my defining contribution to America. For you, that essence of my life is reduced to a place in your platform. Believe me, I'm glad it is an important focus for you. Still, it is why I read faces and you read numbers. I see individual needs and school needs while you must look at nationwide needs. People bring a set of statistics to you for inclusion in a speech and you have little human confirmation or denial of those numbers.

Data can both yield facts and obscure the truth. Recently, a sentence ran across the bottom of the nightly news stating, "Fourth-grade test scores higher while high school scores dropped on the SAT nationwide this year." One could possibly conclude that elementary schools are improving instruction but that high schools are not. What was left unsaid, however, was that the SAT score included non-college-bound students for the first time—even though the explicit purpose of the test is to predict the success of a high school student in college. This is just one pointed example where "crisis" reads "catastrophe" unless *someone in a quandary* asks, "What else could that mean?"

I see my students up close—magnified humanity through a narrow-angled lens. It would be impossible to hold twenty-five individuals so personally for a year without that specificity of focus. Through them I see the world brand new and know so often the joy, and pain, of innocence. The six-year-olds I teach are just beginning to internalize thoughts instead of having *every* thought come straight from brain to mouth. It is not hard to reconnect to your own questions when they speak them aloud *all day long*! I'm often moved and amazed at the range of emotion, sophistication, and candor their questions, stated dreams, and hopes reveal:

> "Why can't they just share? . . . I mean who started this war anyway?"
>
> "Did Mrs-Dr-President Laura Bush write a letter to Afghanistan like she did to us on the computer?"
>
> "Hey, hey, hey! . . . Does she wish that helicopter didn't get on her grass?"
>
> "Why do some kids get divorced mommies and daddies?"
>
> "Why do the red crayons get too short so fast?"
>
> "Mrs-Dr-Hankins, does Osama Bin Laden have a mother?"

All of those questions, asked nearly one on top of the other and some at exactly the same time, were caught on tape at the writing center in my class. I transcribe them in their idiomatic speech to give you the joy of "hearing" them and to put forth the plea that we never lose sight of the fact that schools are places to ask questions. As long as we hold to that chief idea, we will be able to recapture the lodestone of truth that sent us toward the idea of schooling *all* children in a system that is free to each and every child in America. It is our questions that bring the new century into being. A quandary makes for deep thinking, and deep thoughts beg to find ways of being expressed. That, I believe, is the epitome of education.

Schools hold multiple voices and share the goal of bringing all children in to comfortably ask, seek, discover, and explore . . . together. Our public education system is the only system in place where so many who are so different can live and learn together productively. I do fear the power of short-sighted and ill-advised reforms such as vouchers to undo that system and to polarize us.

The thing I fear most, however, is that we will become a nation of nonthinkers. Nonthinkers don't vote. Nonthinkers assume their thoughts make no difference and that democracy does not involve them. Schools that reduce curriculum to facts that can be measured on a statewide multiple-choice test also reduce the time that students have to participate in conversations that allow them to attain the skills of democracy: debate, conjecture, synthesis, and construction. I teach toward a vision of a world where we would live with eyes, arms, and ears boldly open to each other. I teach to see what children can generate, demonstrate, question, and compare rather than to find out what they can parrot back.

The high-stakes testing frenzy that has taken root in our nation in the name of progress is sadly the opposite of learning. It reduces the curriculum to teaching the way to take a test. For most elementary students, real teaching ceases during the testing preparation because the taking of the test does not reflect the way, nor the *what*, that children have learned. We cannot afford to allow fact-driven curricula that are tested out of context to replace learning. Focusing on *facts* rather than *meaning* further undercuts participation in a democratic way of life.

The cry of "reclaiming our schools" rises from the very steps of the inaugural platform. Urging today's diversely populated schools to become more standard seems to unveil our long-hidden fear of differences. Just what are we hoping to reclaim? Separate but equal? A time before laws protected the right of children with physical and mental differences to go to school? A time when, in answer to the Industrial Revolution, we put all children in nailed-down desks with individual task sheets all day long? A day when the Jewish child had to memorize the Lord's Prayer because everyone was doing it for a grade? Do we want to reclaim a time when only those who could pay got to eat lunch? A time when only White children got to ride a school bus?

Even successful leaders often forget that childhood memories are interpreted by the present. Those golden memories where everyone (who *came* to school) could read and behave nicely is just a fairy tale. Wishing for everyone to talk, act, and look the same will not make it so. You can kiss that frog all day long but it will yield no prince!

Therein is the *true* crisis, not in the messiness of the present but in the myth of the golden past. History records the many times we have renewed and rethought schools. We will always have things to rethink and renew as long as there are people who are able to think and are free to make choices. The radical truth here is that democracy begets the need for change over and over again. We can lament that by-product of democracy or we can celebrate the strength that comes from freedom of expression and the possibility of discovery that comes with the freedom to make choices.

Schools can engage minds for six hours a day, but we cannot give a graduate a job. Teachers can feed, clothe, love, and teach our youngest, but we cannot wipe away the pain that keeps them unfocused and often angry. We can entertain the questions of the most gifted orators of the future, and hone the investigative skills of future journalists, but we cannot give them the issues they will address before they live them. Schools are but one cog in a series of gears both being turned and turning the other interlocked parts of America.

Our classrooms will give birth to the best and to the worst as they always have. Yet presidents and painters, critics and crusaders, mechanics and missionaries, gardeners and generals all harbor in our classrooms, anchored but already floating in the waters of the mysterious unknown journey they will make.

I LONG TO WALK INTO MY CLASSROOM knowing that my president views me as a professional and my children as learners, thinkers, and strugglers together on a journey built on curiosity instead of competition. I yearn to hear that journey spoken of with respect. Our itinerary encompasses literature, math, science, and history in all the ways that it wraps around the human condition and the life of our planet. Schools are a promise to the future, a hope in the present, and an amalgamation of gifts and legacy from the past. So where is the real crisis in education?

Perhaps the crisis is in the gift of a question and in the courage to envision possibilities. The solutions reside both in those who must see schools at a distance in order to see the whole picture—like you—*and* in those who, of necessity, must see schools as close up as too-short-red-crayons and snaggle-toothed-grins—like me. I believe that double-sighted view, when taken together as a whole, will feed our quandary well enough to birth a new vision of education.

Will you come with me?

Karen Hale Hankins

JACQUELINE JORDAN IRVINE

TEACHING DARIUS TO DREAM

photo by William Mercer (© 2001)

Dear Future President,

I would like to share a true story with you about a brief conversation that I had with a nine-year-old African American male. This story motivates me daily to work as hard as I can to make sure caring and competent teachers reach all kinds of students, particularly poor and urban students of color. I hope you are similarly inspired.

Several years ago, I was sitting on the steps of my church, located in a poor Atlanta neighborhood, waiting for the locksmith to open my car, when an inquisitive little boy spotted me and jumped on his bike to get a closer look. After he was persuaded that he did not have to break into my car to retrieve my keys, I asked my newly made friend, Darius, to sit down to talk. I asked him the usual boring questions that adults ask children: What's your name? How old are you? Where do you go to school? What's your teacher's name? And finally, I asked, "What do you want to be when you grow up?" After responding quickly to the other questions, he stalled on the last, and then said, "I don't wanna be nothing."

120

"Oh, come on," I coaxed. "There are so many wonderful and exciting things to dream about being: a teacher, an astronaut, a businessman, a mechanic, a policeman. Just close your eyes and let me know what you see yourself doing when you get to be all grown up."

Darius hesitantly followed my directions. He closed his eyes, folded his arms over his chest, and lifted his head toward the sky, as if he needed divine inspiration for such a difficult task. After fifteen seconds of what appeared to be a very painful exercise, I interrupted Darius's concentration. "What do you see?" I asked impatiently. "Tell me about your dreams."

The young boy mumbled, "Lady, I don't see nothing and I don't have no dreams." Stunned by his remark, I sat speechless as Darius jumped on his bike and rode away.

Darius, this bright, energetic, handsome young man, is not likely to end up in a college or university. In fact, statistical data predict that Darius has a better chance of ending up in a state prison. If Darius ends up in prison, taxpayers will spend approximately twenty thousand dollars a year for his incarceration. For that amount of money, we could pay his college tuition at most institutions of higher education.

Sometimes we forget that a large number of children, such as Darius, "don't see nothing and don't have no dreams" when we ask them to envision their futures. Often, their nights are filled with nightmares from horror movies or scary books that all children experience. Their days, however, are filled with horrors and "daymares" associated with the harsh realities of poverty, violence, hunger, inferior schools, drug addiction, insensitive policies, and privileged people who sigh in hopelessness and outrage, wondering why Darius's family and community have failed him.

I have spent my entire career researching and writing about the school experiences of African American children like Darius and their schools and teachers. It should come as no surprise to you that most of the research in this area, including my own, is directed at identifying correlations, causations, and interventions aimed at reversing the dismal achievement statistics of many low-income African American students. On most indicators and measures of academic achievement, African American and Latino students' performance lags behind their

White and Asian peers. Although African American students have shown some increased performance on standardized test scores, the gains have been relatively small and inconsistent over time. Reports from the National Assessment of Educational Progress (NAEP) reveal that the gap between White and Black students has widened over the past twelve years. In reading, for example, only ten percent of African American and thirteen percent of Latino fourth-grade students could read at the proficient level. Overall, average scores for seventeen-year-old Black students in reading and math are about the same as the averages for thirteen-year-old White students. In addition to low academic achievement, schools are places in which Black and poor children are disproportionately placed in low-ability-level tracks and special education classes, suspended, and expelled.

Too often we focus on trying to explain *why* certain students do not achieve as well as others instead of *how* teachers can be trained to help alleviate discrepancies. All too often, we neglect to focus on the cultural influences that shape teachers and on what can be done to educate truly great teachers who acknowledge their cultural lens and attempt to make the necessary adjustments based on their student population. Far too many pre- and in-service teachers proclaim a color-blind approach in teaching diverse students, hesitant to see them as cultural beings. Moreover, many practitioners believe that ethnic and cultural factors do not influence the ways in which they relate to diverse students or practice their craft. Although many teachers prefer to apply a color-blind approach to their practice, research data support the claim that an individual's culture and ethnicity do influence attitudes and behavior toward the cultural other.

In addition, many teachers erroneously believe that if they recognize the race of their students or discuss issues of ethnicity in their classroom, they might be labeled as insensitive or, worse, racist. However, when teachers ignore their students' ethnic identities and their unique cultural beliefs, perceptions, values, and worldviews, they fail as culturally responsive educators. Color-blind teachers claim that they treat all students "the same," which usually means that all students are treated as if they are, or should be, both White and middle-class.

Educating teachers for cultural competency is a complex undertaking that requires reflective thought, inquiry, and guidance by experienced mentors. Cursory and superficial understanding of cultural differences does not result in increased student learning or significant changes in teachers' attitudes and instructional behaviors. In fact, inadequate cultural knowledge can lead to *more*, not less, hostility and stereotyping toward ethnically diverse students. I have come to understand these complex issues about culture by contemplating my unique K–12 school experiences. Rather than simply looking at rather obvious differences in ethnicity, social class, and verbal and nonverbal modes of communication, I have concluded that the most important cultural match for school success is a type of seamlessness between home and school that is connected by vision, shared values, and a sense of mission and purpose.

My schooling is an affirmation of these very points. I am a non-Catholic who attended an all-Black elementary and secondary segregated Catholic school in Alabama that was administered by White priests and nuns from the Midwest. This curious mix of conflicting cultures is pertinent and instructive because it illustrates the resilience and adaptability of African American children—in fact, most children—in handling contradictory and contentious worlds.

For example, as a child, I practiced two religions—the faith of the African Methodist Episcopal Church (commonly known as the AME Church) and the faith of White Eurocentric Roman Catholicism. Although I was not Catholic, I attended mass and catechism classes five days a week in school and weekly AME Sunday school classes, church services, and youth group meetings outside of school. I understood the Catholic sacrament of private reconciliation and the AME practice of public testimonials. I admired the White Catholic priest and the Black AME preacher. Latin masses and Stations of the Cross posed no problem for me; nor did gospel singing and revivals. I unabashedly interacted with White nuns in black habits and as well as Black ushers in white uniforms. I am amazed how well I mastered this fine art of cultural switching as a child, and I am reminded that children and adults can retain and celebrate the culture of their ancestors yet be at ease in multicultural settings as well.

I believe that my school experiences did not result in school failure because there was more of a "match" than "mismatch" of cultures than was obvious to me as a child. What the Catholic nuns and priests shared with my parents and the African American community were strong, dogmatic beliefs in the power of education over oppression and discrimination and values such as discipline, achievement, and hard work. They shared a common mission and vision that was clearly articulated and passionately executed. My parents were more insistent upon my school success than the zealous nuns and priests who taught me. Although my family warned me that Catholics were "misguided in their religious perspectives," they were to be respectfully tolerated because they held the key to our educational future. This belief in education served as a common foundation that minimized the potential for cultural misunderstanding, hostility, and alienation between the Protestant African American community and the Catholic school.

I have often used this story in classes with my mostly White preservice teachers to explain how differences in culture, religion, race, ethnicity, poverty, and geographical origins are not excuses for student failure. I emphasize to teachers that the successful outcomes of my segregated schooling have little to do with the fact that the school was administered by a religious order. What seems more relevant is the fact that competent and dedicated teachers worked with parents and community to make a difference in the lives of all children. Caring and competent teachers make schools places where all children become successful learners and productive citizens.

Far too many programs and legislation for educational reform underestimate, ignore, or devalue the influence of teachers who look at the Dariuses of this world and see hope and possibility rather than despair. Contradicting popular portrayals of incompetent and disinterested urban teachers, I have concluded in my work that there are many teachers who make a difference in reversing the cycle of despair and school failure among African American and other nonmainstream students. The teachers with whom I have worked in CULTURES (the Center on Urban Learning/Teaching and Urban Research in Education and Schools, which I founded and directed) represent the best of urban teachers. Focusing on models of best practices is an important step in finding solutions to the seemingly intractable problems in urban education.

CULTURES has enrolled more than 159 teachers from five culturally diverse school districts in the Atlanta metropolitan area. The voices of the teachers, not just researchers, are important to include because these teachers have taught me so much and because, unlike most university-based researchers, teachers have an intimate knowledge of students like Darius and their daymares. The typical CULTURES participant is an African American female teacher from an elementary or middle school in the Atlanta public school system with more than sixteen years of teaching experience. In addition to providing forty hours of classroom instruction to these teachers, I read their journals, projects, lesson plans, and transcripts of their entry and exit interviews and visit the schools and classrooms where they work.

These veteran teachers are competent in their subject areas and they are experienced and masterful at what they do. They are excited about learning new teaching methods and keeping abreast of knowledge in their instructional fields. However, these necessary but insufficient attributes are not the characteristics that distinguished them from their equally competent peers. They believe that students needed a demanding curriculum, yet they seldom are advocates of a particular teaching strategy or program. The teaching method is less important than their belief about the very nature of teaching itself. Teachers in my research not only view teaching as telling, guiding, and facilitating mastery of content standards, but also believe that teaching is defined as "caring," "mothering," "believing," "demanding the best," "a calling," and "disciplining."

What Darius, my own childhood education experiences, and the participants of CULTURES have shown me is that as we continue to work on research models that explain or predict conditions of children who have daymares, we have to convince policymakers and politicians with power and authority to act on behalf of what Lisa Delpit calls "other people's children."

We will not and cannot achieve our vision of providing all children with an education and a future by ignoring children who have none. It is not enough to think of a child such as Darius as a research subject, a service project, or just another child who is doomed to fail. Somehow we should start to think of him and our future as inextricably linked. I am convinced, however, that eager, well-educated, committed teachers can and do make a difference. We already have the knowledge, skills, and technology to transform children's daymares into dreams. What we lack is the collective will to do so.

MR. OR MS. FUTURE PRESIDENT, currently a myriad of government agencies is defining what a "good" teacher is. These agencies are coming up with lists of standards and prescriptions that suggest that there is, in fact, one prototype of a good or effective teacher for all types of students, for all subjects, and for all schools. I urge you to invest energy and resources into defining the complex qualities of caring and competent teachers and providing support for programs that encourage eager and well-educated teachers to cultivate their own cultural understanding as well as a passionate conviction that all children can, and must, succeed.

Sincerely,

Jacqueline Jordan Irvine

JANE ROSS

WHY WE CONTINUE TO STAY

Dear Mr. / Mrs. President,

I write this letter to you with a sad yet hopeful heart. The sadness comes from the awareness that our nation's schools are in need of something more than what currently is given to them; the hope comes from the possibility that you will set a national tone toward education that reflects the belief that teachers have the desire and ability to affect sustainable change that benefits all children. We need you to support teachers rather than punish them. Please do not allow anyone to commit instructional crimes when they make or support policies that harm schools and harm children through institutionalized racism or education bashing. These practices demoralize children and teachers. If you asked our students how you could help them, they would give you raw responses of:

> "Can you explain why so many people leave us every year?"
> "Can you speak Spanish?"
> "Would you look at me as more than a score on a standardized test?"

"Can you believe in me?"

"Can you believe in my teachers?"

"Why does our school's air conditioning keep breaking down?"

"Why do many of my teachers leave without giving me a reason?"

"Can you make my mom stop crying every night?"

"Can you remove all the labels from me?"

"Can you give me back my childhood?"

"Why am I called *at-risk*?"

By setting a national tone that inspires everyone to become a partner with schools, you can make sure that all of these questions, and the deeper implications behind them, are addressed.

How Others *Describe Our Campus*

Our middle school is located in the zip code area that has one of the highest reported crime rates in the city. More than ninety percent of the students live near or below the poverty line, some students have probation officers, and most come from single-parent homes. Ninety-eight percent of our students are Hispanic or African American. Our campus has a high student mobility rate, and approximately forty percent of our students receive either special education or English as a Second Language (ESL) services. Our achievement scores fluctuate, but are far from exemplary. Each and every year, our teacher and staff turnover and transfer rate is one of the highest in the district. We have seventy teachers, and there are only five still at this campus who were here my first year. For many years, we had a crumbling building that required a ten million dollar renovation to make it a safe and adequate place for students.

How We *Describe Our Campus*

Those of us who have stayed experience the honor of working with nine hundred brilliant and capable students who bring beautiful diversity to the school. Despite years of lacking facilities, our students rarely complain about the conditions. In the years before and during our renovation, we often had no gym, no library, no courtyard, and a field covered with work trailers. We had an air conditioning system that usually did not work and often produced hot, uncomfortable classrooms—once during a state test—and still the students rarely complained. They possess a cultivated resistance to these substandard conditions. Our students speak multiple languages and bring an endless flow of creative talents to our campus. Those of us who have stayed do not see deficits in our students; we see deficits in the larger system that repeatedly fails them.

I began my teaching career at this middle school twelve years ago as a math teacher and could likely stay here my entire career. Although I am certified in secondary English, language arts, and math, I realized quickly that math is a high-needs area in terms of teacher availability and student fears of the subject. I often joke with teachers that I was demoted to an assistant principal position because the greatest work takes place in the classroom.

Nationwide, our schools are haunted by a yearly mass exodus of people within and beyond our walls. They originally join our schools eager to climb up the mountain of success for all children, yet become exhausted from constantly getting knocked down by avalanches of systemic dysfunction and distrust. I cannot count the number of times I have taken over a class because a teacher has walked out permanently, often midday, sometimes mid-class. Our students have come to expect their teachers to walk out on them and rarely appear shocked when someone leaves. When teachers stay for more than a year, the students embrace them with unparalleled trust and affection. Until then, they are wary and distrustful of promises made to them. One year, we had five teachers rotate through one language arts class and four teachers rotate through one math class. One day, I was explaining to a class why they were going to have a long-term substitute until we hired a new teacher. Scott, an eighth-grade African American student said, "Miss, don't worry about us. We're used to this. We didn't expect him to stay. It's no big deal." It was actually his resigned indifference that worried me more than the fact that another teacher had quit midstream. I sensed his and the other students' deep-rooted belief that people simply will break their commitments and promises to them. Our yearly high rate of teachers leaving weakens an already fragile system that needs continuity and stability. Ironically, my personal experience has been that when someone from the outside believes that those of us who stay are doing meaningful work on our campus, they rarely encourage us to continue staying. Instead, they often offer us other—usually better-paying—jobs. I become saddened when people hear me explain why I stay at my campus and then respond by encouraging me to contribute to the systemic culture of abandonment. Often, they rationalize their offers by telling me that I'd help more teachers and more children if I were in a higher, more influential position. In my opinion, the trickle-down theory rarely works in education.

Why do we, albeit just a few, stay at a school in which for years we walked around inadequate facilities and unsupportive structures with a resigned indifference that comes only from systemic failure? We stay because we believe teachers should not abandon their students, who already are abandoned by so many in our society. We stay because the heartache in the struggle is minor in comparison to the beauty of the children we serve. We stay because we worry for our students' futures in a world that assumes they will fail. We do not stay to "save the poor kids;" we stay because the students are simply amazing in their resilience and certainly not in need of being saved. We do not stay out of pity; only others' negative attitudes toward them—not the students, themselves—are pitiful. We do not stay because there are only a few career options; there are many other options that we reject to stay at a place that makes us constantly improve as educators. We do not stay because it is an easy job; on the contrary, staying on our campus requires tremendous intellectual, physical, social, and emotional work.

Four years ago, at the end of the day as kids were leaving, tornado weather came through our area. After many hours of the faculty trying to contact as many parents as possible to pick up their children and having to make difficult decisions about when to allow the buses to leave, we were down to approximately ten adults and one hundred children in the building. By seven o'clock at night the weather had reached unparalleled harshness and we were informed that one of the tornados had landed and was heading directly toward our area. We all went to the lowest wing in the school and sat under the lockers. The adults tried to comfort the terrified students. After I said a few reassuring words to Jessica, a Hispanic student, she replied, "Mrs. Ross, I'd rather be here with you than at home. I feel safer with you than anyone because I know you'd never leave us. I'm not worried about the tornado. You'll take care of it." Although I admit that I wasn't sure how one "takes care" of a tornado, I *was* certain that the other educators and I would take care of all the children with us. The other students chimed in with similar statements, basically comforting themselves that, over time, some people in their lives have proven that they will not leave them.

To the students, "taking care" means not abandoning them or giving up on them, whether during a tornado or during their educational journey. We stay because our students feel broken by a system that appears to, and often does, discard them. We try to create worlds for students who rarely leave their neighborhoods. We fear that our students will live down to the low expectations that many people have for them instead of living up to our high expectations. We stay because we have faith that things will get better. We hold on to the belief that one day there will be trust in, and support of, our schools as the basis for a national philosophy about education.

To keep excellent teachers at our most challenging schools across the land, this is what we need from you:

> *Listen to teachers.* Encourage policymakers to listen not only to the voices of the business community, but also to the voices of the educational community. Any policy that silences educators ultimately harms businesses and schools. Encourage educational policymakers at all levels to model the same collaboration that we want from our students. Teachers and students are the greatest think tanks, but often they are regarded as invisible when decisions affecting them are made.
>
> *Create multidimensional assessments.* A single, one-shot, black-and-white assessment will not give you the feedback that you need to make decisions about a field whose success

or failure affects every single person in the United States. Society judges low-income, minority students—often harshly, often unfairly, and often by only looking at a small piece of who they are—and then gives them a permanent label. Do not use this same model to assess schools, teachers, and students. Instead, increase the standards and expectations by assessing us holistically rather than narrowly.

Change the national tone toward public education and remove fear and humiliation from models of judgment. Educators receive painfully mixed messages. Businesses give us donations and the government gives us funding, but then they both turn around and slap us in the face with fear tactics and systems designed to humiliate us rather than support us. Set high standards for educators, but also set equally high standards for government, businesses, and communities to develop reciprocally supportive and collaborative relationships with schools.

Provide incentives to attract and keep excellent teachers at the neediest schools. At the heart of all solutions to make our school successful, we simply need the top educators to make long-term commitments to the neediest schools. Most educators do not run to our school beating down the door looking for jobs, especially when they can work at what many call "easier campuses with fewer challenges." If we were able to offer an increased salary for working at a high-needs campus and stipends for multiple-year commitments, we would have a larger and more qualified group of applicants from which to choose. In an ideal world, the very best educators would come to our campus without needing additional financial incentives. We do not live in an ideal world, and the raw fact is that many people choose to work at other campuses.

PEOPLE OFTEN COME ONTO OUR CAMPUSES with clipboards, promises of assistance, and a smile for our campus. Our students and teachers always smile back because—miraculously—they cling to the belief that maybe this group is more sincere than the last group who walked through our hallways. Then those same people who smile at us later demoralize us, exercise one-dimensional judgment, and leave us with little more than pages of demands. Please have high expectations of teachers, but do not bash and belittle us and then expect us to raise our heads from a pool of blood and create miracles.

Look at teachers through the eyes of the children they teach, who entrust their minds and hearts to us. Look upon us from the viewpoint of the classroom desk rather than the government office. If you did, you would see that teachers work hard to create a place that is a safe harbor for children where deep thinking occurs and self-confidence grows.

If you support us, we will not disappoint you. In most schools, there are pictures of presidents on the walls and in textbooks. Most people associate each president with a national priority, a time period, an event, or a persona. We long for the day when we will look at a president and think, "Thank you," because we feel your unparalleled support of our schools. We long to stand next to our students in successful, creative, enriching, and democratic classrooms across America and pledge allegiance to the flag, to the nation, and to you—a president who upholds and protects the ideals of an education for all.

With faith in your commitment to education in America,

Jane Ross

THE GAP BETWEEN
WHAT WE SAY AND WHAT WE DO

Dear Future President:

I write this letter not only from the perspective of a parent and a teacher, but also from the perspective of a lifelong student whose life has been enriched and transformed by good teachers. Teachers have always been present in my life, not only during my many years of schooling, but also as colleagues, as teachers of my own children, and as students in a well-respected teacher preparation program at a college where I served as dean for a decade.

As a child of Mexican immigrant farmworkers, I am one of the lucky ones who survived schooling. I know that many of my childhood peers didn't have the opportunities of good schools and good teachers, and they were forced out of school early due to the demands of work and family responsibilities. Although I am now a mature adult, I still consider myself a student and a keen observer of good teachers.

Currently, I use my knowledge of what constitutes good teaching and good teachers to prepare new teachers for jobs in the public schools in my community of El Paso, Texas. El Paso is a working-class, urban community of seven hundred thousand on the U.S./Mexican

134

border. Upward of eighty percent of the one-hundred and sixty thousand schoolchildren in our community are Mexican American and poor. Although it is impoverished economically, El Paso is a community that is rich in cultural tradition and that believes deeply in the power of education to transform our community. We continue to have strong faith in the importance of high-quality public schooling, and we know that good teachers are critical to opening up new opportunities for all students.

Addressing the issue of how we can prepare the kind of teachers that every parent and student would want assumes that we know the answers to the following questions: What qualities do parents want in the teachers of their children? What qualities do students want in their teachers?

What Do Parents Want?

Parents in most communities want teachers who are nurturing adults of good character and who care as deeply about the children they teach as they do their own children.

Parents want teachers who are smart and well-prepared, teachers who have a deep knowledge and understanding of the subjects they teach. Equally important, good teachers must know and understand young people—how they develop, how they are best engaged and motivated, how they learn, and what they care about. They should connect their expert knowledge of their subject matter to pedagogy in order to create an environment where learning flourishes and students are both challenged and engaged.

Parents want teachers who understand and are respectful of the neighborhoods where their students live. They want teachers who are culturally responsive to the students and their communities and who know how to use the students' backgrounds and storehouses of knowledge and experience in order to move learning forward. Parents want teachers who treat them as partners in their children's learning, not as problems or obstacles.

Parents want teachers who recognize that they are not only stewards of the young but also stewards of our democratic society's future.

They want teachers who prepare the young to be active participants and informed citizens of a democratic society. They want teachers who model in their classrooms the core values of a democracy: equality, social justice, honesty, fairness, and participation in the process of being a good citizen. Finally, parents want teachers who believe that all children can learn and who acknowledge that it is their responsibility to maximize the potential of every student.

What Do Students Want?

Students want most, if not all, of the above. Depending on whether they are fourth graders or high school seniors they may phrase it differently, but, when pressed, their list of ideal teacher qualities is much the same as their parents'. They want smart teachers who know their subject well and understand how to teach it effectively. Students want teachers who know young people, who care deeply about their development, and who listen and respond to what is important to them. They want teachers who know about teaching and learning and are willing to learn from their students as well as teach them. Students appreciate teachers who make learning both challenging and fun, who remain passionate about their subject matter and curious about the world, and who see learning as a way to improve the world. Young people want teachers who have a deep commitment to fairness and justice. Students often have a strong sense of right and wrong and of ethical and fair behavior, and they expect their teachers to be exemplars of these ideals.

How Do We Prepare the Teachers We Need?

We have very high expectations of teachers and we recognize the importance of their role in society. Indeed, in a 1998 Harris poll taken for Recruiting New Teachers, Inc., teachers were ranked first as the professionals who provide the *most* benefit to society—higher than both lawyers and doctors. Yet, when we consider how we prepare and treat teachers, there is a mismatch between what we say we want and value, and what we actually look for in terms of preparation. Yes, there has been some recent attention given to increasing the requirements for teachers' subject-matter knowledge, and this is a very important development. Although they may possess teaching credentials, too many teachers continue to possess low levels of preparation in the subject matter that they teach or are teaching subjects other than the ones that they are qualified to teach. This is particularly true in our middle schools and high schools and in critical subject areas such as mathematics and science. We need to examine the rigor and depth of subject-matter preparation for all teachers. We should require teachers to hold a bachelor's degree in the subject area that they teach, and we should also do more to ensure that teachers—especially in middle schools and high schools—teach only in those areas where they are qualified.

Yet we want and we need much more in teachers than subject-matter knowledge. To demand far higher levels of subject-matter competence of all teachers is not to diminish the importance of all of the other attributes and areas of expertise that we want in our teachers. Here, too, we fall far short in terms of the connection between what we want in teachers and how we actually prepare them. We want our teachers to demonstrate competence in child and adolescent development, in cognitive development, in theories of learning, in assessment of student work, and in understanding and implementing content and performance standards. Furthermore, we want our teachers to be prepared to teach *all* students in *all* types of communities. Aside from the occasional course in multicultural education, we often do little to prepare new teachers for culturally responsive teaching in urban or rural classrooms. This knowledge is not just something of interest to teachers in "minority" communities. In our increasingly global society, this knowledge is essential to all of us.

When we examine the complex set of attributes, knowledge, and skills listed above, it seems highly unlikely that this set of competencies can be squeezed into an undergraduate teacher education program without decreasing the quality of these programs. We may need to think about requiring a post-BA year for this additional preparation, not unlike the post-BA preparation required in other professions, such as law and medicine. This is not the language that policymakers like to hear—especially in difficult budget times and in the face of teacher shortages—but if we are serious about what we want in our teachers, we need to be serious about how we go about preparing them.

How Will We Know When We Have the Teachers We Want?

As much as some of us think we know good teachers when we see them, it doesn't hurt to check the evidence. The bottom-line evidence is, of course, the academic achievement and well-being of the children in our schools. We want *all* students to graduate from high school having taken a rigorous academic curriculum and to be ready and able to attend college. This means they will have taken a college preparatory curriculum and will have successfully completed it. We want and need this in working-class communities like El Paso, where some students may have to work before attending college or must work while they attend college part-time. A high-quality, rigorous curriculum that prepares students for college is even more important to the future of these working-class students than it is to their upper-class or middle-class peers. Nothing less is acceptable.

This goal—that all students graduate from high school and are prepared for college—demands an even higher level of necessary skills and attributes from teachers. They must actively and consistently pay attention to each and every student in their classrooms, not just the thirty to fifty percent they think may be headed for college immediately after high school. There must be a complex shift in the expectations that teachers hold for students, both in terms of their academic potential and in terms of the skills and the work necessary to ensure their academic success.

In addition to the academic achievement of their students, other formative assessments of teachers are needed. Not all people are well-suited to become teachers, especially good ones. Unfortunately, the old adage that "those who can, do; those who can't, teach," still has some resonance because we have been too lax in our belief that any adult with a college degree can teach. In reality, along with rigorous intellectual preparation and the ability to be clear, concise, and articulate, there are a number of sociocultural and emotional dispositions that are important to good teaching—including patience, empathy, sensitivity, openness to others, endurance for sustained hard work, tolerance for ambiguity, good character, motivational skills, and altruism.

Some of these attributes, dispositions, and abilities can be assessed early on in an undergraduate program. Others may need to be assessed in the natural setting of a classroom. Almost none can be assessed by the simple paper-and-pencil tests now administered as exit tests to students leaving teacher preparation programs and entering their first year of teaching. However, they can, and should, be assessed. These assessments are complex and difficult, and they can't be done inexpensively—despite some of the claims by commercial testing companies. Some of the standards-based performance assessments developed for experienced teachers by the National Board for Professional Teaching Standards and by the Interstate New Teacher Assessment and Support Consortium (INTASC) are powerfully suggestive of what can be done if we are serious about the assessment of quality teachers and their performance in classrooms. Such assessments not only determine mastery of subject matter content, but also assess how one responds to the complex problems and challenges that teachers face in their classrooms every day. Also important is the assessment of actual teaching performance in real classrooms through the use of videotapes and the analysis of student work.

How Do We Invest in Teachers?

If we take seriously the notion that teachers are the stewards of the young in our democratic society, and if we see teachers as playing very beneficial roles in society, then we must confront the question of our investment in teachers openly and honestly. The history of reforms for teacher preparation standards is a history of piecemeal reforms that are often short-sighted and subject to changing political and rhetorical forces. Quality is often sacrificed for expediency and low-cost alternatives. Budget crises and teacher shortages only acerbate the problem. We pay new teachers very little and provide limited incentive for their continuing professional development. We provide little mentoring for new teachers, and often give them the most difficult classroom assignments, saving the easier classrooms for the more experienced teachers. We isolate them in their classrooms and don't give them the opportunity and the time to interact with other members of their professional community. We treat teachers as glorified babysitters, as nonthinking factory workers in an assembly line of student production, and as cogs who can be given instructions and rotated around at will in the machine of large school bureaucracies. We drive many new, high-potential teachers out of the classroom if they resist this treatment. National estimates are that thirty to fifty percent of new teachers abandon the profession during the first five years of teaching. This is a very poor return on investment, both at the personal and societal level.

If, in fact, we want to have a quality teacher in every classroom, we have to rethink how we prepare teachers. We need to spend the money to recruit the best and the brightest into the profession. We must reconsider how we compensate and support teachers in their first years of teaching, and how we compensate and encourage outstanding experienced teachers to stay in our classrooms. There is no question as to what we have to do to produce quality teachers; *we know how to do it*. It is really a question of how much we are willing to invest to prepare quality teachers.

Sincerely,

Arturo Pacheco

RICHARD INGERSOLL

REVOLVING DOORS AND
LEAKY BUCKETS

Dear President :

Few educational problems have received more attention, and yet been more misunderstood, than the failure of our education system to ensure that elementary and secondary classrooms are all staffed with qualified teachers. Again and again, commentators and policy analysts have told us that our elementary and secondary schools are being confronted with severe teacher shortages. At the root of these problems, we are told, is a dramatic increase in the demand for new teachers primarily resulting from two converging demographic trends—increasing student enrollments and increasing teacher retirements due to a "graying" teaching force. Shortfalls of teachers, the argument continues, are forcing many school systems to resort to lowering their teacher qualification standards to fill teaching openings, inevitably resulting in the hiring of more and more underqualified teachers and lower school performance.

The prevailing policy response to these school staffing problems has been to attempt to increase the supply of teachers. In recent years, a wide range of initiatives have been implemented to recruit new candidates into teaching. Among these are career-change programs, such as the federally funded "Troops-to-Teachers" program, which aim to entice professionals to become teachers, and Peace Corps–like programs, such as the privately sponsored "Teach for America," a program that is designed to lure the best and brightest into understaffed schools. Some school districts have even taken to recruiting teaching candidates from other countries. Many states have instituted alternative teacher certification programs, whereby college graduates can postpone formal education training and begin teaching immediately. Financial incentives such as signing bonuses, student loan forgiveness, housing assistance, and tuition reimbursement have all been used to aid recruitment. The No Child Left Behind Act provides extensive federal funding for such initiatives.

The above efforts are highly worthwhile but, unfortunately, they will not solve the problem schools have staffing classrooms with qualified teachers. Indeed, a close look at the data shows these efforts are largely a case of a wrong diagnosis and a wrong prescription.

The best data to understand these issues come from the nationally representative Schools and Staffing Survey conducted by the National Center for Education Statistics, the statistical arm of the U.S. Department of Education. Begun in the late 1980s, this is the largest and most comprehensive data source available on teachers and the staffing of schools. Indeed, it was originally created because of a dearth of information on these very problems and issues.

What do these data tell us?

The data reveal that the conventional wisdom on teacher shortages is, in fact, partly correct. Consistent with shortage predictions, the data show that the demand for teachers has increased over the past two decades. Since the mid-1980s, student enrollments have increased, teacher retirements have also increased, most schools have had job openings for teachers, and the size of the elementary and secondary teaching workforce has increased. Most important, the data tell us that substantial numbers of schools have experienced difficulties finding qualified candidates to fill their teaching position openings.

After that, the data and conventional wisdom begin to diverge. The data also show that the demand for new teachers and subsequent staffing difficulties confronting schools are not primarily due to student enrollment and teacher retirement increases, as the conventional wisdom holds. Most of the demand for teachers and hiring is simply to replace teachers who recently departed from their teaching jobs, and most of this teacher turnover has little to do with a "graying" workforce.

Teaching is an occupation with relatively high annual turnover, especially compared to other kinds of professional work. Teaching is also a relatively large occupation. Teachers represent four percent of the entire civilian workforce. There are, for example, more than twice as many elementary and secondary teachers as there are registered nurses, and there are five times as many teachers as there are either lawyers or professors. The sheer size of the teaching force combined with its relatively high annual turnover means that there are large numbers of teachers in some kind of job transition each year. For example, the data establish that between the 1999–2000 and 2000–2001 school years, well over one million teachers—almost one third of this large workforce—moved into, between, or out of schools. The image that these data suggest is one of a "revolving door."

Of course, not all teacher turnover is a bad thing. Some degree of employee turnover is normal and beneficial in any workplace. Too little turnover of employees is tied to stagnancy in organizations; effective organizations usually both promote and benefit from a limited degree of turnover by eliminating low-caliber performers and bringing in "new blood" to facilitate innovation. But a "revolving door" is costly. In the corporate sector, it has long been recognized that high employee turnover means substantial recruitment and training costs and is both the cause and effect of productivity problems.

In contrast to the corporate sector, however, there has been very little attention paid to the impact of employee turnover in education. One notable exception was a recent attempt to quantify the costs of teacher turnover in Texas. This study concluded that teacher turnover costs the state hundreds of millions of dollars each year.

Some of the costs and consequences of employee turnover are more easily measured than others. One type of cost that is less-easily quantified includes the negative consequences of high turnover for organizational performance in work sites, such as schools, requiring extensive interaction among participants. The good school, like the good family, is characterized by a sense of belongingness, continuity, and community, and is especially vulnerable to teacher losses.

The data explain that another cost of high teacher turnover is the teacher shortage. However, while the teaching occupation, as a whole, has relatively high turnover, the data also reveal that the revolving door varies greatly among different kinds of teachers and different kinds of schools. Teaching is an occupation that loses large numbers of its new members very early in their careers—long before the retirement years. The data inform that after just five years, between forty and fifty percent of all beginning teachers have left teaching altogether. A number of studies have also found that the "best and brightest" among new teachers—those with higher test scores on the SAT and the National Teacher Exam—are the most likely to leave. Moreover, the data also show that the revolving door also varies greatly among different kinds of schools. High-poverty public schools have far higher teacher turnover rates than do more affluent schools. Urban public schools have more turnover than do suburban and rural public schools.

These data raise two important questions: Why do teachers depart at relatively high rates, and why are these rates so dramatically different between schools?

Contrary to conventional wisdom, the data attest that retirement accounts for only a small part—one eighth—of the total departures. Far more significant are personal reasons for leaving, such as pregnancy, childrearing, health problems, and family moves. These are a normal part of life and common to all workplaces. There are also two other equally significant reasons for teacher turnover—job dissatisfaction and the desire to pursue a better job inside or outside of the education field. Together, these two reasons are the most prominent source of turnover and account for over half of all departures each year.

Of those who leave because of job dissatisfaction, most link their turnover to several key factors: low salaries, lack of support from the school administrators, lack of student motivation, student discipline problems, and lack of teacher influence over school decision making.

What can federal policy do? One obvious strategy is to increase teacher salaries, which are, not surprisingly, strongly linked to teacher turnover rates. Recent national data (2003–2004) tell us that the average starting salary for beginning teachers is under thirty thousand dollars. But salaries are not the only source of the problem. This is important to recognize because increasing teacher salaries across the board is, of course, very expensive, given the sheer size of the teaching occupation.

A second strategy is to increase the support provided to teachers, especially for beginners. This might range from providing adequate amounts of classroom supplies to providing mentoring for new teachers. The latter is crucial. Life for beginning teachers has traditionally been described as a "sink or swim" proposition, and, as the data show, this is an occupation where large numbers of beginners do indeed sink in the first few years on the job.

A third strategy is to increase teachers' influence over school decision making and to address the all-important issue of how much input and autonomy teachers are allowed in their jobs. As I have shown in my book *Who Controls Teachers' Work?: Power and Accountability in America's Schools,* teachers have little say in many of the key decisions that directly affect their work, but they are, nevertheless, increasingly held accountable for the results. Notably, the data also indicate that there is significantly less teacher turnover in schools where teachers are allowed more influence over crucial decisions.

Traditionally, the management of schools has been under the jurisdiction of states and school districts and has been somewhat off-limits to federal policy. However, recent federal legislation, such as the No Child Left Behind Act, has steadily increased accountability for schools and teachers. Accountability for teachers is, of course, necessary but it is useful to remember one of the classic adages in management—employees should not be held accountable for things they do not control. If the new accountability measures only serve to increase pressure on teachers without providing commensurate increases in their autonomy and resources, then they may end up simply driving even more teachers out of the occupation.

Reduction of student discipline problems is a fourth factor tied to teacher turnover. Not surprisingly, many former teachers tell us this is one of the major reasons for their exits. Policymakers often bemoan the difficulty of confronting the seemingly intractable societal problem of disrespect for authority among youth. This may well be true, but the data tell us that schools vary dramatically in their degree of student misbehavior, regardless of the background and poverty levels of their student populations. Schools that do a better job coping with and curbing student misbehavior problems have significantly less teacher turnover. In this regard, one possible target of federal funds is alternative schools for problem students. These programs both help teachers by removing problem students from their classrooms, and help students by providing a second chance for those youngsters unable to fit into the regular public school program.

WHAT, THEN, CAN WE CONCLUDE FROM THE DATA about the causes and solutions to the teacher shortage? The data confirm that focusing all of our efforts on recruiting new teachers will not solve the staffing problems plaguing schools. The root of the problem is not shortages in the sense of too few teachers being produced; rather the root of the problem is largely turnover—too many teachers departing prior to retirement. Hence, the solution is not recruitment, but retention. In plain terms, recruiting thousands of new candidates into teaching will not solve the teacher crisis if forty to fifty percent of these new recruits leave the occupation in a few years, as the data tell us they do. The image that comes to mind is that of a bucket rapidly losing water because there are holes in the bottom. Pouring more water into the bucket will not be the answer if the holes are not first patched.

Of course, nothing in the data suggests that plugging these holes will be easy. But, the data do make clear that schools are not simply victims of inexorable societal demographic trends, and there is a significant role for the management and operation of these workplaces in both the genesis of, and the solution to, their staffing problems. Improving the workplace conditions in our schools, as discussed above, would contribute to lower rates of teacher turnover, which, in turn, would slow down the revolving door, help ensure that every classroom is staffed with qualified teachers, and ultimately increase the performance of schools. In short, the data give us a simple and clear message: If we want to ensure that every elementary and secondary classroom is staffed with a qualified teacher, we need to first improve the quality of the teaching job.

Sincerely,

Richard M. Ingersoll

Suggested Reading

Ingersoll, Richard M. (1999). The problem of underqualified teachers in American secondary schools. *Educational Researcher*, 28, pp. 26–37.

Ingersoll, Richard M. (2001). Teacher turnover and teacher shortages: An organizational analysis. *American Educational Research Journal*, 37(3), pp. 499–534.

Ingersoll, Richard M. (2003). *Who controls teachers' work? Power and accountability in America's schools.* Cambridge, MA: Harvard University Press.

Ingersoll, Richard M. (2003). *Is there really a teacher shortage?* Consortium for Policy Research in Education, University of Pennsylvania.

National Commission on Teaching and America's Future. (2003). *No dream denied: A pledge to America's children.* Washington, DC: Author.

PART FOUR
STANDARDS FOR ALL

SYLVIA BRUNI

CHOKING THE LIFE
OUT OF CLASSROOMS

Sylvia Bruni with her granddaughter, Victoria

Dear President,

What an awesome opportunity this is to write a letter to our next president, to send you an absolutely frank and personal message about public education in Texas—a state in crisis, as far as I am concerned. This letter is an account about what I have learned throughout a career that has spanned almost forty years, half of them directly in my own classroom and the other half working with the greater community of youngsters and their parents, teachers, and principals. This message is drawn from my experiences working with Texas educators and students, whose lives are now being more and more colored and shaped by an accountability system that is fast becoming the end rather than the means to better teaching and learning.

Mr. President, I tell friends that I was an "accidental" teacher. In the 1960s, I was a college girl, the proverbial first generation in my family to go on to college, and, quite frankly, my career goals were pretty simple. I majored in English because I loved to read and in

Spanish because I loved Mexico, and I was certain I was going to marry a Mexican and go on to live in that gorgeous and vibrant country.

Well, my plans took a one-hundred-and-eighty-degree turn when I met and fell in love with a local boy. I did what all good girls did in those days: I became a teacher. My life, my value system, and my view of the world were forever defined and enriched by that turn of events. The seventeen years I spent in my senior English classroom introduced me to the wonderful talents and capacity for discovery that my students brought to the classroom. Classrooms can be magical places, offering teachers and their students limitless opportunities to discover worlds of knowledge. Even more important, they are microcosms of the real world, where exploration and discovery occur, rich discussions and arguments take place, and good citizenship habits are shaped. Similarly, classrooms can be joyous and exhilarating places. That was what my classroom was for me and, I believe, for my students as well, during all those seventeen years of teaching.

The next twenty-two years have also defined me, but this collective experience has been a more sobering one. I left the public schools and spent seven years working with our local university. Here is where I began to discover seriously troubling realities. I learned that almost fifty percent of our Webb County residents over the age of twenty-five had no high school degree. I learned that forty-seven percent of this same population had a literacy level of one, meaning that they are unable to enter background information on a Social Security card application or locate eligibility information from a table of employee benefits. I discovered that our local university, an upper-level institution, was having great difficulty with its junior-level students, who could not cope with college-level courses. Equally troubling, our community college had enormous numbers of its students failing its entrance exams, forcing these same students to enroll in remedial reading, writing, and math courses. Years later, I would realize that the very same students whom I had been teaching in my senior English class had been the survivors and that fifty percent of their brothers and sisters had dropped out—fallen somewhere by the wayside sometime around their ninth-grade year.

Ten years ago, I came back to another public school system in my hometown, and here is where the story comes full circle. Just as I had discovered the vast potential and capacity that characterized my senior English students in my early teaching years, so have I now realized how seriously we have crippled that potential and capacity in these subsequent twenty years.

I came back to a public school system to find it gripped by a testing mandate that is literally choking the life out of our classrooms. That rich and stimulating curriculum that I had access to twenty years ago might still be on the books, but teachers now have little opportunity to tap into it. For example, those extended hands-on learning projects that made the medieval and Renaissance literary periods come alive for my students are rarely, if ever, the rule today. My students *lived* their curriculum and experienced the universal nature of good literature as they researched and sketched architectural renderings, composed original musical scores, and created portraits of haunting medieval figures. Through these types of hands-on experiences, they discovered that good literature was timeless in its relevancy to the everyday world that surrounded them. It was the most valuable and effective way of teaching and learning, especially for many of my students, who had come to my classroom table poor in their own worldly experiences. The hands-on learning activities that I had the time to lead them into helped them make the relevant connections that are essential for creating a lifetime of learning.

The assessment of what they had learned and how well they had done so was just as relevant in those earlier days, before *the test*. My students created portfolios of their own cumulative student work— their renderings, essays, compositions, performances, debates, and reflective essays. All of this was actual evidence of student learning.

Today's rigid emphasis on a state test makes this hands-on type of learning practically impossible. Learning is predicated, instead, on rigid timelines, on students digesting a fixed amount of facts and figures, and on a testing format that emphasizes memory and recall at the expense of critical thinking and thoughtful, purposeful learning. Then, we add to this narrow testing mix an assessment that is in a language that is often the second language of a student population whose English fluency is still very immature. Finally, we make the test a condition either for promotion to fourth grade or for graduation, and the testing scenario is now wrought with high anxiety. For many youngsters, this is a fatal mix.

Make no mistake about what I am claiming here: The emphasis placed on a single high-stakes test in Texas as the measure by which we hold our public schools, teachers, and students accountable is seriously flawed. It goes against all that we know about authentic and relevant assessment of student learning, and it has seriously weakened our capacity to prepare our children to become thoughtful, successful, and responsible citizens.

The evidence is all around us. Since the inception of the TAAS test, Texas continues to record startling drop-out rates, most recently ranging from thirty percent of its general student population to fifty percent of its minority student population. In February of 1999, the University of Texas reported to the Texas House Subcommittee on Education, complaining of "marked declines in the number of students prepared academically for higher education." Since 1982, when the first of the Texas tests was implemented, the rate at which Black and Hispanic students fail ninth grade has been steadily increasing, reaching as high as nearly thirty percent in the late 1990s. After George W. Bush became governor of Texas, the state's own college-readiness test, the TASP, showed a dramatic decrease—from 65.2 percent to 43.3 percent—in the numbers of test-takers passing all three tests in reading, writing, and math. In Texas, SAT scores, a barometer of sorts for college preparation, show no improvement in contrast to national scores. On the NAEP, another national test often used as a gauge of academic preparedness, the average statewide score gains in Texas surpassed those of the nation in only one of three comparisons—fourth-grade math. Even more astounding—in light of the amount of national acclaim given to the "Texas Testing Miracle"—is the fact that, while Texas NAEP scores are sluggish at best from year to year, TAAS gains are touted as greatly increasing from year to year. From 1994 to 1997, TAAS scores showed a twenty percent increase! A similar discrepancy appears between the scores of Whites and students of color, with the gap between the two on the NAEP widening, yet appearing smaller and decreasing greatly on the TAAS.

What could possibly be causing such dramatic differences in test score results? Consider the following facts: Hard data informs us that since the advent of TAAS, the number of children excused from taking the TAAS test on the grounds of a special education exemption has increased sharply—nearly doubling from 1994 to 1998. In fact, the number of youngsters being identified as special education students is, in some Texas communities, more than double the national norm. Also, even though fewer high school students are graduating (slightly less than seventy percent in the 1990s), there has been a subsequent sharp upturn in the number of GED test-takers. The 2000 Census data for my own border community, where minorities are a distinct majority of the population, shows that 45.2 percent of its adult population over the age of twenty-five has no high school diploma. Can we truly claim to be "leaving no child behind?"

So where do we go from here? What lessons have I learned from my own forty-some-odd years working with Texas schools, their teachers, and their children? What should the Texas experience teach us about what school reform and accountability should *really* be about? What can you, as our next American president, do to make a real difference? I would not have been able to tell you this years back, but it has become crystal clear today, as I've witnessed our world becoming more challenging and more diverse, and our school house more and more beset by forces that threaten, rather than support, our youngsters' access to successful futures.

Mr. President, help us regain the awesome power that lies within our public schools—the power to link young people to great learning experiences. Help us reclaim those classroom activities that ultimately shape young people into productive and healthy citizens, in every aspect of the word. Public schools should be, and can be, pathways that guide young people toward vigorous citizenship grounded in those democratic values that today, more than ever, are absolutely essential in our world. To get to the reality of good citizenship, we must provide a school house in which youngsters are engaged, inspired, and challenged. Our schools should be filled with classrooms where both essential basic skills *and* the greater intellectual and social skills needed for the burgeoning twenty-first century are the rule: cooperative team work, problem solving, fair play, self-expression, and assertiveness, among others. I want to see a return to classrooms where learning and motivation are intrinsically linked, and I want to assure that our educational system supports such classrooms and their teachers.

This is where you come in, Mr. President! Help us by becoming the lead advocate for those school practices that would ensure that schools that are pathways to great teaching, great learning, and great communities.

There is an enormous divide that separates those of us who teach, whether educator or parent, from those who set policy. If we are ever to truly reform our educational system, it must be done on the basis of what we know about good teaching and learning. School account-ability and development should not be predicated on rigid and narrow assessment systems that run so grossly against the kind of teaching and education that we know schools should nurture and strengthen. Help us facilitate the public dialogues that would bridge those gaps that exist today. There are critical issues that need to be explored: children's rights to fair and equitable assessment; high-stakes testing versus authentic assessments; issues regarding resources, equity, and a "dumbed-down curriculum" that concern so many of us who teach; and the equally worrisome role that partisan politics seems to play in these issues. Help us broaden that discussion and spur engagement within the greater community, which we sense is already sympathetic to public schools but is unsure about how to actively support them. Help the educators reclaim their voices, too. I speak for them as one who entered this profession "accidentally" and gradually grew in my own knowledge of what would make me a really wonderful teacher.

It has been this eventful journey that has made me realize, just as it has my countless other colleagues, that we need to lead a true reform of our public school system *now*! What Texas set out to do twenty-three years ago with the introduction of that first TAAS test was perhaps well intentioned. However, after years of rigid, high-stakes testing, and equally rigid and stifling test-prep lessons that are totally out of sync with what makes rich teaching and learning, the results absolutely cannot be claimed a victory, neither for our children nor for our state.

SO, I SAY TO YOU: COME TO TEXAS AND LEARN FROM OUR EXPERIENCE. Spend a day or two in our classrooms and visit with our students and our teachers. Meet and visit with my granddaughter, Victoria, a bright and clever little third grader who this past spring agonized over the advent of the third-grade TAKS test—the first one ever to hang the threat of retention over the heads of Texas third graders. Beginning several weeks before the test was first administered, Victoria, who was reading fluently in her kindergarten year, bit her fingernails down to the quick and cried for hours. She was fearful about failing—in spite of having tried all the test-prep strategies that consumed hours of her classroom time week after week. Eventually, Victoria passed the dreaded test, but not before it left its mark on her. At the tender age of nine, this child experienced the fear of failure, a fear she simply did not have the maturity to deal with!

Just as important, however, come and meet those intrepid and dedicated teachers and principals who can still be found scattered throughout our schools, braving and enduring the testing system while moving forward with marvelous teaching and assessment practices. They are too often the minority in what continues to be a test-driven Texas majority. The irony is that, as never before, we know and can speak about what makes for rich and relevant teaching and learning: lessons very much like those medieval literature experiences that my students and I so much enjoyed when I first began teaching. Yet we are starving in the midst of a teaching and learning feast, forced to forego the good stuff for the sake of a test-driven, tasteless curriculum.

Help us reset our learning course. Help us reclaim the teacher's voice so that it rings out not only in Texas but all across this country as well. What an awesome opportunity you have to really do it right!

Abrazos from Texas,

Sylvia Bruni

Note: In July, 2003, the *New York Times* reported the real story behind the "Houston Miracle." The turnaround of a poorly performing Texas school system, which was originally credited to high academic standards and close monitoring of performance on the high-stakes standardized test, turned out to be flawed. The reality pointed instead to the district's Enron-style accounting of the students who left the system. As a result, the state audit recommended lowering the ranking of fourteen of the sixteen schools from Best to Worst. This latest revelation came as no surprise to Texas educators.

EDWARD C. MONTGOMERY

WHAT MY STUDENTS
NEED TO KNOW

Dear President,

I am a teacher with almost twenty years of experience in the classroom teaching English and social studies from sixth through twelfth grade. There have been tremendous changes in curriculum during those twenty years, and we are teaching things never thought of at the beginning of my career. With the advent of the standards and assessment movement, education seems embroiled in a permanent discussion of what students need to know, what students need to be able to do, and how to measure those skills.

There is a need for a permanent discussion of standards, curriculum, and testing. More often than not, by the time we have curriculum in place in our schools, it is time to evaluate what we are teaching all over again—and this includes how to measure how well our students are learning.

In my home state of Nebraska, we are creating a dynamic system of standards and assessment that has no end, and this is as it should be. Our system demands constant reevaluation and revision.

No single test of student knowledge can last very long in a world full of so much change. Our system demands continual discussion among teachers, administrators, state department officials, and post-secondary institutions. We talk among ourselves, with other schools, and with educators across the nation. We discuss types of assessments, quality control of assessments, teacher training issues, and virtually any topic that has anything to do with good assessment. We share knowledge of the successes and failures we experience in trying to make the system work. We learn from each other and teach each other at the same time. Assessment in any district is really a product of the efforts of educators from across the state.

The system of assessment we have been developing in Nebraska comes from teachers. Teachers write the assessments that they use to test the state standards they teach in their own classrooms. All teachers follow the requirements found in the six quality criteria established by the state department of education, and there is substantial teacher development done by the state to ensure we understand the process of developing and documenting our assessment systems. The documentation required to verify any district's efforts is detailed and thorough, and we receive yearly feedback on our strengths and weaknesses in all aspects of assessment. Districts are rated in two categories: level of student achievement and quality of the assessment process in the district. Experts from individual districts, the state department of education, and educators from outside the state are used to ensure that our teachers are up-to-date and understand the requirements of Nebraska's system. Teachers may work within their own districts, within a service unit area, or in consortia of schools devoted to writing thorough assessments. Our assessments go through a very rigorous review on at least two levels: the local level and the state level. The review process is not punitive; rather, it provides feedback for constant improvement. New tests are not required every year, but we are expected to review our tests results every year and improve the tests if changes are needed.

One major advantage of our system is that the teachers running it get instant feedback about how well their classes are doing from the assessment. In larger districts, scoring is done in a central location, but in most schools scoring is done by the educators closest to the teaching and assessing process, which makes it possible to identify problems and to intervene quickly and effectively. They have the opportunity to remediate, reteach, and move forward instead of waiting for scores to come out after the year is over.

Our system says to the teachers of Nebraska, "We trust you." Three years ago, I despised the idea of assessment. Today, I run the system for my district and work in a new administrative position we didn't even have back then, in addition to my regular teaching duties. The key element that converted me was *teacher involvement*, which is something other systems lack. Under the system we have put into place in Nebraska, all variables are gone except "did the students learn it?" and "why or why not?" We cannot blame a state test imposed from above; we wrote the tests under the supervision of experts. We cannot say that the test does not fit our curriculum; our standards are embedded in the curriculum. We have achieved teacher accountability in a fair, forthright manner. As a teacher in Nebraska, it is *my* test delivered to students *I* taught and *I* am responsible for the outcome. As a result of this system, elementary teachers have been forced to delve deeper into specific subject areas and secondary teachers have been forced to examine new teaching methodologies.

Our assessment system is different from that of most states, yet it has been accepted by the federal Department of Education. I am not an expert on all of the assessment systems devised by the other 49 states, but I would recommend that all of them examine the way Nebraska has involved its teachers in standards assessment from top to bottom and from beginning to end. It is the most powerful tool for real school reform that I have ever seen.

A constant discussion of essential education means a constant disagreement among educators. This disagreement, however, forces teachers to identify and defend what they consider to be most important. It calls for data to support conclusions reached from intuition and from the heart. It means that educators will always have to justify what they are doing to the nation, to themselves, to parents, and, most importantly, to their students. The key to any good standards and assessment system is teacher involvement because teachers are the ones, in the end, who will make any assessment system a success or failure. We have that in Nebraska.

I do not, however, believe that our assessment system, or any assessment system, ensures that students will know all that they need to know when they graduate; there is such a wide world to see and my students need to know many different things.

I wonder: What could teachers across the nation, and perhaps the world, agree that all students *need* to know? Obviously, a basic knowledge of the "core" areas such as math, science, reading, and writing would be desirable. Life skills such as parenting classes or the "independent living" classes we offer in many districts might be essential. Some health knowledge would be good. Citizenship concepts necessary for the functioning of any democracy should be included in social studies classes. There are many subject areas that are important, but we are already having this discussion within the framework of standards and assessment. Each state continues to hammer out documents identifying essential knowledge, and I will take part in those discussions in my state, but what is the common thread among all of us? What do I want students to know well when they leave my classroom?

My students need to know that grades without knowledge mean nothing. With the mounting pressure to get good grades and to get accepted to prestigious colleges, I see students who care only about the grade and nothing about the knowledge the grade should represent. There are many complaints about the accuracy of assessment systems and standardized testing across the nation. Yet, what about the myriad of grading systems in the nation's primary, secondary, and post-secondary schools?

My students need to know that the grade they receive in class is an accurate representation of the knowledge they have attained. In order to achieve this, we need to establish a stronger link between scores received on state assessments and the scores achieved in the classroom. If students do not believe that their scores accurately represent their knowledge, they will have built-in excuses that they will use throughout their lives. Artificially high grades will either result in false confidence in students concerning their own abilities or the feeling that the grade is not worth anything because it really wasn't earned. If you want to attempt a major reform, link standards and assessment to classroom grading systems. Require that course grades be examined for correlation to assessment scores. To my knowledge, no one has yet examined the correlation of assessment scores to classroom grades; it is a field ripe for study. If we are teaching and measuring what we feel students need to know, then there should be a connection between classroom grades and assessment scores.

My students need to be lifelong learners. This is a catchphrase you hear often in education, one we all pay lip service to because we know there is no way to accurately measure it. I think I can produce a lifelong learner if I can teach a student to be confident in his/her ability to tackle life's problems and to accomplish any task encountered. We need an education system that produces confident young people capable of absorbing new knowledge and capable of using that knowledge to have productive, satisfying lives. You should demand a study to identify the qualities of lifelong learners and work backward to determine what created them.

Programs that encourage leadership and community involvement should be established in every school system. Surely, we want our students to be leaders and to be involved in their communities. Most of the leaders in my small community in Nebraska came straight from the classroom I am sitting in. We should invite these local leaders into every school and involve them in the educational process.

I want all of my students to know well that they are not the most important people in the world. In a world of instant gratification, most of my students have never learned that "service before self" can produce more happiness for them, and a better world for others, than all of the latest electronic gadgets ever invented. The success of our democracy demands that we consider the needs of the many before the needs of the few. We must create students who understand that they have a stake in this country and that they must consider the needs of their fellow citizens in everything they do in order to maintain a system that allows them to meet their own needs.

In my own state, American history and American government are not required classes. I am in favor of "local control," but I am sure I would be better able to produce students who are good citizens if my students were required to have some knowledge of their country's history and form of government. Is this kind of knowledge not as important as reading, writing, and mathematics? My students may or may not use their precalculus skills in life, but they will almost certainly be Americans for life. If the federal government wants to mandate certain things in education, consider mandating knowledge of our history, culture, and governmental systems.

Students need to be able to work together for the good of the whole. They must understand that they have a responsibility to their fellow students, neighbors, and countrymen. Unfortunately, my students live in a society that celebrates the success of the selfish individual. Publicize and encourage student participation in volunteer programs. Expand programs like AmeriCorps. Make community service a component in qualifying for federal student loans or Pell grants. Allow college students to work off student loans in programs like the old VISTA program. If you want a challenge, as president, strive to create a society in which the majority of citizens care more about each other than they do themselves. That society would be a true representation of what this county could be.

My students need to know that they are valued by their society. They need to believe that their school systems have their best interests at heart and not the interests of competing political agendas. I have heard that the best thing a father can do for his children is to love their mother. Perhaps the best thing we can do for our children is to love their teachers. Teachers are not valued by our society anymore. The last twenty years have been devoted to telling children and their parents everything that is wrong with our educational system instead of celebrating the many things that are right about it. If current legislation will work to identify *failing* schools it should give at least as much attention to recognizing *outstanding* schools.

I understand that numerous teachers across this country are not endorsed in the subjects that they teach. As president, examine why this happens. In addition to mandating that all teachers be endorsed in the appropriate subjects, help them become endorsed. A low-interest loan program for teachers seeking another endorsement might be a good first step. Loan forgiveness for teachers getting endorsements in critically short areas such as math, science, and special education might be another approach. There are literally thousands of good teachers out there, including the vast majority of teachers in Nebraska. Invite a teacher or two to the State of the Union address. Let the nation see examples of successful education and of successful educators. Create a society that once again values and rewards those who educate its children and you will be on the road to well-educated children.

Our children need to know that they live in a society that values them and their families. Let children learn that the government will support programs and opportunities that enable them and their parents to lead productive and happy lives, and then they will know something worth knowing. As president, ignore all of the discussion about assessments, all of the talk about whether to test or not to test, and think about the elephant in the corner of the educational room: The biggest factor in education achievement is socioeconomic status. For too long, this has been an excuse for children to be left behind, but we cannot allow this to go on any longer.

Current legislation is designed to ensure that no group is left behind by the educational system. On the other hand, what is our country doing to ensure that no parent or guardian is left behind? Striving to guarantee all children a quality education is a noble goal, but are we saying that a good education and good test scores are the only factors that will enable children to keep up? Students who come from a home life featuring alcoholism, joblessness, homelessness, drugs, abandonment, a single parent, or an income hovering around the poverty line are not worried about standards and assessments; they are worried about survival. Work to ensure that the parents of my students can earn a wage on which they can support themselves and their children. Guarantee that my students and their parents will receive adequate health care. Devise an economic plan that will reach the segments of our society most in need of "stimulation." Any attempt to improve student achievement without also improving the society that produces those students is doomed to failure.

IN SHORT, MR. OR MS. PRESIDENT, standards and assessments are needed. I will leave the arguments about the details to others for now. I can make almost any assessment system work if I have the right kind of students, and the right kind of students are a result of the right kind of society. Give me a society that values children and teachers. Create a society that supports and encourages families. Build school systems that never forget that their achievement statistics represent individuals who all have individual needs, hopes, and desires. Do these things, and I will give you students who know the important things and are capable of learning all they will ever need to know. My students need to know, more than anything else, that they live in a country that will help them see clearly who they are, show them who they could be, and help them to close the difference. If my students know these things well, we can work out the academic details.

Sincerely,

Edward C. Montgomery

W. James Popham

The No-Win
Accountability Game

Dear President:

Few Americans will deny that our nation's public schools urgently require improvement. However, few Americans realize that a test-based accountability strategy that originally intended to improve our schools is now having precisely the opposite effect.

Test-based educational accountability has been touted for more than 20 years as the key to sprucing up our schools. Such an approach to school improvement makes substantial sense, because the most important consideration in evaluating a school staff's success surely ought to be whether students have learned what they were supposed to. Because we can efficiently find out what students have learned by testing them, the logic underlying test-based educational accountability appears to be unassailable.

Unfortunately, the tests currently being used as the centerpiece of test-based accountability are the wrong ones. For educational accountability tests to function properly, the scores on those tests must reflect instructional quality. If students' scores are high, this should signify that instruction was effective. Conversely, if students' scores are low, this should indicate that instruction was ineffective. Yet today's accountability tests tend to measure not what students were taught in school but rather what those students brought to school. This is because students' scores on most of today's accountability tests are heavily dependent on students' inherited academic aptitudes and what a child has learned outside of school as a function of the child's socioeconomic status. Because such tests fail to measure how well students have been taught, these tests are *instructionally insensitive*. Using these tests at the basis for our system of educational accountability, therefore, will not improve America's public schools.

Throughout the United States today we can find educational accountability systems that can never work simply because the achievement tests they rely on are instructionally insensitive. It would be bad enough if such ill-conceived accountability systems merely failed to do a good school-evaluation job. But it's far worse than that: The use of inappropriate accountability tests frequently fosters classroom practices that harm children. For example, significant curricular content is often omitted, students are forced to take part in dreary "practice item" drills, and some teachers engage in score-boosting activities that are downright dishonest.

Teachers are currently under intense pressure to improve their students' scores on any test that is used to judge a school's success. As a result, many teachers understandably adopt classroom practices intended to raise their students' scores on these tests. However, if the accountability tests being used are *instructionally insensitive*, then teachers and schools don't stand a chance of being fairly evaluated. When these types of insensitive tests are employed in an accountability system, teachers soon discover that they have been forced to play a no-win accountability game. Desperate to boost their students' scores, such teachers often succumb to classroom practices that lower educational quality.

For one thing, many test-pressured teachers end up giving little or no instructional attention to any curricular content that's not likely to be included in the accountability test. On more than a few occasions, I have personally heard teachers from accountability-pressured states describe how, during the months immediately preceding the administration of state tests, they were required by their school administrators to give no instructional attention to *any* curriculum content not assessed by those tests. As a result of such test-triggered tunnel vision, children in these classrooms are denied exposure to more diverse and challenging curricular content. Such children are educationally shortchanged.

Another negative classroom consequence of instructionally insensitive accountability tests can be seen in the dramatically increased amounts of test preparation drilling we now find in many of our schools. Teachers, unable to raise their students' scores on these high-stakes tests, devote significant portions of their class time to seemingly unending "drill sessions" in which students must respond to testlike practice exercises. These drudgery-laden drills soon sap any pleasure students might otherwise derive from school. Try talking to any student who has been obliged to endure weeks of answering a never-ending stream of practice questions for these tests, and you'll find a student who regards school as anything other than exciting.

Even worse, some test-pressured teachers engage in test preparation practices or test administration practices that are downright dishonest. For example, test-preparation sessions might be employed featuring *actual* items that have been covertly copied from a *current* test form. Students who have been given an answer key for these "practice" items are clearly advantaged when the real accountability test is given. In addition, some teachers have been caught violating an accountability test's administration procedures by supplying their students with extra test completion minutes or by giving hints to students during the exam regarding which answers are correct. During recent years, the increasing prevalence of teachers' unethical score-raising tactics has forced almost all states to issue a list of verboten test preparation and test administration rules—along with the associated rule-violating penalties such as the loss of the teacher's job or license. If student cheating is wrong, then teacher cheating is surely inexcusable.

Unfortunately, these types of inappropriate classroom practices have been made more prevalent by the recent enactment of the No

Child Left Behind Act (NCLB). The accountability provisions of NCLB call for a marked expansion of state-level accountability testing in order for a state's schools to receive the funds provided by that federal statute. In brief, this important law requires annual appraisals of each public school's quality according to students' scores on a state's NCLB tests. NCLB does permit a modest number of state-by-state variations. For example, each state can select its own curricular aims, its own NCLB tests, and the levels of performance that the state considers acceptable on those tests. Nonetheless, there is no doubt that a national system of test-based educational accountability has now been federally imposed on America's public schools.

If the NCLB tests being used to evaluate a particular state's schools are instructionally insensitive, two bad things will happen. First, the state's schools will most likely be misevaluated—that is, ineffective schools will be considered effective and vice versa. A second, and even more negative, consequence is that many of the state's accountability-pressured teachers will adopt the kinds of educationally indefensible classroom practices I described earlier. Disturbingly, most of the tests that have been presently adopted by various states to satisfy the accountability requirements of NCLB do not effectively measure what is or is not being learned in a state's classrooms. As a consequence, such tests are corroding educational quality in those states.

There are two common types of instructionally insensitive NCLB tests. The first of these is the traditionally constructed standardized achievement test that has been widely used in the United States since shortly after World War I. During that conflict, one of the nation's first standardized tests, the Army Alpha, was administered as a screening test for potential officers to almost two million army recruits.

Today, our national standardized achievement tests are patterned directly after the Army Alpha. The function of these exams, as was true with the Army Alpha, is to compare an individual test-taker's performance with the performances of previous test-takers who are referred to as the test's "norm group." Interestingly, it is this overriding quest for comparative interpretations that makes today's accountability tests instructionally insensitive.

Achievement exams such as the Iowa Tests of Basic Skills, for example, perform an educationally useful function of comparing one student's performance to the performances of other students in that test's norm group. Such comparative interpretations are useful to both educators and parents. For example, when parents discover that their fourth-grade child has scored at the eighty-ninth percentile on a reading test, but at the twenty-third percentile on a math test, those parents can work with the teacher to deal with the child's low math performance.

When nationally standardized achievement tests are chosen to be a state's NCLB tests, new items are often added so that the test's content is more closely aligned to the state's approved curricular aims. However, in order for such traditional standardized tests to fulfill their comparative-measurement mission, test-takers' scores must be spread out reasonably well. To produce the needed degree of "score spread"—that is, a reasonable range of high scores, middle scores, and low scores—many items included in traditional standardized achievement tests are too closely linked to students' socioeconomic status or to their inherited academic aptitudes.

The developers of traditional standardized achievement tests have only a limited amount of time to test children, so the items in those tests must be very efficient in producing score spread. Because children's socioeconomic status and their inherited academic aptitudes are nicely spread-out variables, an item that is linked to either of those two variables will help produce score spread. For instance, one item in a current nationally standardized achievement test depends on the test-taker's familiarity with what fresh celery looks like. Clearly, children from affluent families are more likely to know what fresh celery looks like than children whose families are getting by on food stamps. Such a test item will produce score spread, but it has nothing to do with how well students have been taught. As a result, because of the way those items work, traditionally constructed standardized achievement tests tend to measure the makeup of a school's student body, not how effectively the school's students were taught.

A second type of instructionally insensitive "standards-based" accountability test is currently employed in many states. These tests are intended to measure students' mastery of a state's official "content standards"—namely, the skills and knowledge that students are supposed to learn in school. The shortcoming of such tests is that they attempt to measure far too many content standards. Although most states' official content standards have been determined by those states' own curricular specialists, such state-level curricular specialists almost always stake out far more content than could either be taught in a school year or tested during any reasonable test-administration session. In many states, a teacher must keep track of literally hundreds of these content standards. Most states' officially approved content standards are little more than well-intentioned curricular wish lists because the curriculum specialists who identified those content standards wanted the state's students to learn all sorts of wonderful things.

Because there are too many content standards to assess on any one test, it is impossible for teachers to know on which curricular targets they should focus their instructional energies. The consequence of such uncertainty is a gigantic guessing game in which a state's teachers try to foresee which state content standards will actually be measured on a given year's tests. Yet many of the state's teachers will guess wrong, and thus end up emphasizing content that is not tested. As a consequence, students' scores on standards-based tests often fail to accurately reflect a school staff's instructional success.

So far, I have suggested that test-based educational accountability, if implemented by using the types of flawed tests described above, is harming our schools rather than helping them. Moreover, the passage of NCLB has ratcheted up the accountability pressures on America's educators and, as a consequence, test-based educational accountability will have an even greater negative impact on schooling.

What, then, is to be done? The answer is simple. To make test-based educational accountability work the way that it is supposed to work, we must employ appropriate accountability tests. We need educational accountability tests that measure students' attainment of worthwhile skills and knowledge and that also help teachers to do a better job. We need tests that will provide accurate accountability evidence *and* support teachers' instructional efforts. If such tests are employed to fulfill NCLB's requirements, this significant federal legislation can have a decisively beneficial impact on our nation's public schools.

What would this type of "appropriate" NCLB test look like? Fortunately, we have excellent examples of such tests currently in use throughout this nation. One type of appropriate test is seen when educators assess students' composition skills by requiring students to generate actual writing samples. Writing-sample exams use teachable criteria in order to measure the powerful skill of writing. In other words, both teachers and students know what the key components of a well-written composition are. As a result of the teachers' and students' clear understanding regarding the attributes of this significant skill, children receive far better instruction in writing these days than was the case even a few decades ago.

Another example of the kind of really powerful skills an appropriate NCLB test might assess is a child's reading comprehension. This skill calls for a student to be able to read substantially different types of written materials (for instance, bus schedules, encyclopedia articles, or novels). Then, given the most common purposes that readers routinely use such materials for (e.g., being able to tell when a bus is going to arrive based on reading the bus schedule), students must demonstrate that they have comprehended what was read well enough to accomplish those purposes. Such a "purposeful reading" skill is another illustration of the kind of significant skills on which an instructionally *sensitive* NCLB test can be based.

Therein lies an important truth. Our educational accountability tests must measure a modest number of *the most significant skills* we want our students to master. If NCLB tests are supposed to assess students' mastery of reading and math, then only a small number of super-significant skills in reading and math should be assessed by those tests. As a result, teachers will not be overwhelmed by endless litanies of content standards and they will not have to guess about will be assessed. More importantly, since fewer skills (albeit significant ones) will be assessed, those skills can be *thoroughly* assessed. Thus, teachers, students, and parents can find out which skills a student has or has not mastered when the test's results are reported.

Because NCLB permits each state to identify the content standards its educators prefer, there is apt to be some minor state-to-state variation in the skills and knowledge that are assessed by NCLB tests. However, if state educators isolate a modest number of the most powerful content standards in reading and mathematics, we can expect that there will be substantial similarities in state-selected curricular aims. The really significant skills in reading and math should not vary all that much from state to state.

Accountability tests can be built that provide credible and accurate evidence of a school's effectiveness—and that also support teachers as they attempt to help their students to master truly significant skills. If such suitable tests are employed, then test-based educational accountability will benefit the students who attend our nation's public schools.

DEMOCRACY WILL NOT SURVIVE in any nation whose future citizens are poorly educated—and a poorly educated citizenry is what we will get if we impose a wrongheaded accountability strategy on our schools. Test-based educational accountability cannot work if it relies on inappropriate tests. A president who understands this situation—truly understands it—can set out to fix it. I truly hope you will.

Sincerely,

Jim Popham

PEDRO NOGUERA

GOING BEYOND THE
SLOGANS AND RHETORIC

Dear President

Despite all of its limitations, the passage of the No Child Left Behind Act (NCLB) by the Bush administration in January of 2002 was a significant achievement. For the first time in our nation's history, public schools are required to show evidence that all of the students they serve are learning. Although relatively little is being done to actually help schools achieve this goal, the fact that it has been enacted into law and has become the official policy of our country represents a considerable accomplishment.

For many years, the great shame of public education in the United States has been that large numbers of students attend schools that failed to provide them with even minimal skills. This is not because this great and powerful nation lacks the resources or the technical skills to educate all of our children. There is considerable evidence that we can make it possible for any child to learn under the right circumstances and if provided with all of the essential ingredients—competent teachers, adequate learning materials and facilities, and engaged parents. However, for too long, we have lacked the will to ensure that the circumstances and ingredients that we know are essential to promote high levels of achievement and learning are created for all children.

Certainly, some of our nation's achievements in education are impressive and worthy of praise. We send a greater percentage of our high school students to colleges and universities than any other nation, and our system of public education is by far the most democratic and accessible public institution in our society. Yet it is also true that large numbers of students languish in schools that do not provide them with intellectual stimulation and that fail to promote their academic skills and healthy social development. A disproportionate number of these students are poor, and many of them have not been exposed to the knowledge and skills that would make it possible for them to lead productive lives and obtain rewarding careers. Rather than serving as a vehicle that would make it possible to break the cycle of poverty, too often our schools have been complicit in the reproduction of poverty across generations.

Shortly after his election, President George W. Bush boldly told the nation that he intended to "leave no child behind." He and his administration promised to hold schools and students accountable to rigorous academic standards. What this has come to mean in practice is that failing schools are being pressured and publicly humiliated, and students are being held accountable for their school's failure through high-stakes testing.

To many, the slogans and rhetoric of NCLB sound like exactly what is needed to fix an ailing system. What sane individual could oppose an effort to demand greater accountability from an unresponsive, multibillion-dollar, publicly financed industry? Over the last ten to fifteen years alone, substantial investments of public and private funds have been provided to carry out various reforms, but still the system has proven almost immune to sustained improvement. For this reason, it is not surprising that NCLB has generated bipartisan support and is widely endorsed by corporate leaders, state officials, and the national media.

However, as is often true in matters related to social policy, there is a tremendous gap between the goals of NCLB and the process used to achieve them. States like Texas, Florida, California, and Massachusetts (among the first states to implement NCLB) rushed to declare victory in the struggle against mediocrity when NCLB was passed. Pointing to their tough new policies and rising test scores, these states claim progress is being made to improve public education even though they have done relatively little to actually improve schools. In poor communities, the old, persistent problems of overcrowded class-rooms, deteriorating facilities, and an insufficient supply of qualified teachers and administrators remain largely unaddressed. Not surpris-ingly, even as calls for closing the achievement gap take on an almost evangelical tenor, wide disparities in performance between the poor and affluent, and White and non-White students, remain, and, at times, grow more pronounced.

Of course, there are dissenters to NCLB and standards-based accountability, and it is my hope that our next president will be more responsive to the concerns that these dissenters have raised. I am one of many to point out that rising test scores do not necessarily mean that schools are improving or that students are learning more. However, amid all of the cheerleading for high standards, compelling evidence that NCLB has fallen well short of its goals has had little, if any, impact on official policy. Several researchers point out that many schools had found ways to raise test scores without improving the quality of teaching and without bettering conditions in the schools themselves. They do so by getting teachers to teach test-taking skills and by limiting the curriculum to material that would be covered on the tests. Some schools have also figured out that they can raise test scores simply by pushing out the neediest students who are likely to bring their scores down.

Despite evidence that the enactment of NCLB is not leading to large-scale improvement, criticisms of the policy are generally ignored. Instead of looking closely at how schools are responding to the new law, we pretend that it is possible to improve public educa-tion simply by applying greater pressure on schools. From their bully pulpits, politicians act as though they can raise standards simply by demanding that schools do a better job serving the needs of stu-dents. With slogans like "ending the tyranny of low expectations," they claim it is possible to produce greater equity in academic out-comes without taking any significant action to address the needs of poor children or to support the educators who work with them.

Enough time has lapsed since the enactment of NCLB for us to see that the vast majority of poor children in our country are still denied access to an education that would help them to escape pov-erty and to open doors of opportunity. This is not a small number of children. One out of five children in America is poor. One third of the children in the United States are enrolled in urban public schools—many of which are regarded as some of the worst schools in the nation. Poor children generally, and African Americans, Native Americans, and Latinos particularly, still lag behind on most measures of achievement, and many of the schools that serve them remain woefully inadequate to address this problem.

The massive cuts in spending that school districts were forced to undertake in 2003 as the federal government enacted the largest tax break in our nation's history, are only contributing to the further lack of progress in improving education. Faced with cutbacks caused by declining state revenues, many schools and districts feel compelled to eliminate subjects such as art, music, and even science if they are not covered on standardized tests. Some have eliminated field trips, recess, and physical education to increase the amount of time avail-able for test preparation. Rather than taking steps to ensure that stu-dents in failing schools are taught in enriched learning environments where they are exposed to creative and effective teachers and stimu-lating curricula, the narrow pursuit of higher test scores has reduced the focus of education in many schools to test preparation.

Even before our nation's recent fiscal crisis, it was clear that policymakers were failing to tackle the most important issues facing public education. Our next president will need to recognize that the toughest and most controversial educational issues have always been related to the ways social inequality shapes and limits educational opportunities. Getting serious about improving public education will require that we tackle these issues head-on.

In most parts of the United States, we continue to spend less on the education of poor children than we do on middle-class and

affluent children. Consistently, we give the most privileged—those
who have the most in terms of personal resources—the very best in
public education while we provide substantially less to those with
the greatest needs and relegate them to the least desirable schools.
It is still true that, in many parts of the country, poor children are
more likely to attend schools with fewer qualified teachers and inferior facilities. Even when poor and minority students are enrolled
in more affluent schools, they are more likely to be excluded from
honors and gifted and talented programs, and to be overrepresented
in special education and remedial classes. Getting serious about
improving public education will require that we truly embrace the
vision of Horace Mann, who called for public schools to serve as the
"great equalizer of opportunity."

Opposition to standards-based reform should not be equated
with a desire to return to the time when it was possible for students
to graduate from high schools with meaningless diplomas, or when
too many schools showed little interest in promoting higher levels
of learning and achievement. There is nothing wrong with establishing academic standards and testing students to see if they have
met those standards. The main questions are: Will we allow the tests
to determine what students are taught, and will we use the results
of tests to punish failing students or to provide them with greater
academic support? What about the most troubled schools? Do we
simply pressure and threaten them with state takeovers if they fail to
show progress, or do we take the steps necessary to make it possible
for them to improve? Finally, and perhaps most importantly, how do
we reconcile the drive toward greater equity in academic outcomes
with the deeply held belief that all students are not equal? How do
we accept the fact that producing greater achievement for all students
places our educational goals in conflict with our economic goals,
which operate on the assumption that there will always be inequality
in wages and opportunities?

If you, as our next president, are serious about improving public
education and are willing to ensure that all children—regardless of
their race, culture, immigration status, and wealth—have access to a
quality education, here are some steps that you will have to take in

order to end the cycle of reform and failure and to produce lasting progress in public education.

Respond to the Nonacademic Needs of Poor Children

If we want to ensure that all students have the opportunity to learn, then we must ensure that their basic needs are met. This means that students who are hungry should be fed, that children who need coats in the winter should receive them, and that those children who have been abused or neglected should receive the counseling and care that they deserve. Removing lead paint from old apartments and homes and providing students in need with eyeglasses and dental care are both examples of the necessary steps that must be taken to ensure that students have the opportunity to learn. Although the law was called "No Child Left Behind," many of these needs have been ignored, and, consequently, many children have been left very far behind. Addressing these needs will require the development of a more comprehensive social policy because it is neither fair nor reasonable to expect schools to serve these needs on their own. We are a wealthy nation, and, like other affluent nations, it should be possible for our government to ensure that all children have access to the basic services they need so that they can concentrate on learning in school.

Hold State Governments Accountable for Maintaining High Standards in Schools

Just as we do for the maintenance of highways and the public water supply, we should ensure that common standards of education are upheld at all public schools. A recent ruling by the New York State Court of Appeals will require that state to ensure "a meaningful high school education" to all of its students. Despite the ambiguity of this charge, it is a step in the right direction. Unlike the state of Florida, which affixes letter grades to schools as a symbol of the quality of education provided there while doing practically nothing to improve them, state governments should be required to do more. No students should be allowed to attend schools staffed by unqualified teachers or to learn in buildings that are falling apart. *State governments should be required to establish minimal operational standards for public schools, and they should be held accountable for the quality of education provided to all children.*

Focus on the Problems Facing Low-Performance Schools

There are a few things we already know about low-performance schools:

- They tend to be racially and/or socioeconomically segregated.
- They often lack essential resources.
- They tend to suffer from a dysfunctional culture where low expectations for students, lack of order and discipline, and poor professional norms are common.
- Such schools also tend to have high turnover among staff, particularly among administrators.

Schools like these need help, not humiliation. They need adequate funding so that they can attract and retain highly skilled professionals. They also need assistance in devising and implementing intervention strategies. States should set up intervention teams comprised of skilled educators who can be deployed to work closely with troubled schools.

Make Schools More Responsive to the Parents and Families They Serve Through the Enactment of Systems of Mutual Accountability

One of the reasons why schools in middle-class communities tend to perform well is that the parents of the students they serve feel entitled to insist upon high-quality education. Poor parents are much more likely to defer to the decisions made by the professional educators who serve them, and are more likely to keep their children in the schools that they are assigned to, even if they are not happy with the education their children receive there. NCLB allows parents to remove their children from failing schools, but it does not provide them with funding for transportation to new schools or access to information on superior alternatives. The only way to ensure that poor parents are treated as valued education consumers is for districts to devise strategies to ensure that the concerns and satisfaction of parents are taken into account in the school's operations. This requires the development of systems of mutual accountability in which the responsibilities of schools, parents, and students are clearly spelled out so that all can be held responsible for their role in the educational process. Site councils, like those in Chicago, that require parents to be involved in decision making, and the development of formal contracts between parents and schools that establish norms and expectations for all parties (including students), are some of the ways that this can be done.

Implement Diagnostic Assessment to Strengthen the Link Between Teaching and Learning

Instead of using standardized test results for ranking purposes, we should use those test results to figure out how to help students in need. Typically, state exams are given in the spring and the results are not available until the fall. By this time, students have been assigned to new teachers and, in some cases, new schools. Such an approach limits the possibility that the data generated from these tests could be used to provide teachers with an accurate sense of the academic needs of students. It also makes it difficult to use data from tests to make modifications in instruction.

Diagnostic assessments administered at the beginning of the school year can provide schools with a clearer sense of the strengths and weaknesses of students. Such an approach makes it possible for schools to monitor student performance over time and to measure the performance of students in relation to established standards. Provided with a clearer and more accurate sense of the learning needs of students, schools would be in a better position to make informed decisions about curriculum and instruction and how best to utilize supplemental resources (e.g., Title I funds and grants). Schools should strive to ascertain how much academic growth occurs over a course of a year so that they can determine whether the approaches they utilize to support teaching and learning are effective. This requires treating assessment as an ongoing process of evaluating student knowledge and ability, not through the administration of more standardized tests, but through the meaningful analysis of student work. Such an approach would also make it more feasible to hold teachers accountable for the growth in knowledge and skills that they produce among their students during the course of a school year.

Build Partnerships Between Schools and the Communities They Serve

Schools serving poor children and poor communities will often need additional help in meeting their needs. In many communities, help could be provided by health centers, community agencies and non-profits, churches and local government, and even private businesses and corporations. Organizations and institutions that have a vested interest in the health and well-being of the communities in which they are located should be the natural partners of schools. Some of these organizations may have no prior experience working with schools, and they may need to be persuaded to play a role in supporting public education and to do more than simply making token donations. Strategic partnerships with outside organizations will need to be developed to provide schools with the technical support, material resources, and personnel that are required to make it possible for them to meet the needs of students.

There is evidence that NCLB has succeeded in forcing some schools that were previously complacent to become much more serious and deliberate in how they approach teaching and learning. However, pressure alone will not produce substantial improvements in public education, particularly in communities with the greatest concentrations of poverty. Schools serving poor children need help and, thus far, the advocates for standards-based reform have not displayed a willingness to provide the help that is needed.

IT IS NOT FAIR OR REASONABLE FOR OUR SOCIETY to expect schools to solve the problems facing young people—especially those from poor families—without help. Educators must call attention to the great injustice of such an expectation while simultaneously doing all they can to improve their schools. It is also not realistic to assume that all children will achieve at high levels, graduate from high school, and enroll in college. Our society will never be Lake Wobegone where "all children are above-average." But we *can* make sure that all children receive a sound basic education that provides them with the skills they will need to lead productive lives, and with the knowledge they will need to participate in a democratic society.

Most of all, you, as our next president, must realize that the future of our society will ultimately be determined by the quality of our public schools. This simple fact has been ignored for too long, and we have suffered the consequences of our neglect. Finding ways to fulfill the great promise and potential of American education is the task before us. For the sake of the country, our kids, and our future, I hope that we can meet this challenge.

Respectfully,

Pedro Noguera

JEANNIE OAKES &
MARTIN LIPTON

"... AND EQUAL
EDUCATION FOR ALL"

Dear Ms. or Mr. President

Americans want a society where everyone is able to reap the benefits of their ability, hard work, and persistence. Inherited wealth, family connections, or being of the "right" social group or race should not constrain or advantage anyone in the pursuit of prosperity and fulfillment. Of course, we recognize that this has not always been the case; at times, unfair advantages have been built into culture and law. But we like to believe that most of that unfairness is behind us. Gone are the days when most people believed that genetic differences resulted in immutable distinctions between those who could accomplish and deserve great things and those who must be satisfied with less. Today, many educators commit their lives to providing better opportunities to children with the fewest material and inherited advantages. Why? Because we believe there are no limits on what children from any group can achieve.

Yet American schooling does continue to favor children from privileged families. Although low-income and minority families have the same desire for their children to do well in school that those who are more advantaged have, far fewer children from these disadvantaged groups are given the tools necessary to transform their hard work and desire into economic and academic success.

Stated plainly, poor and minority students go to schools that are not as good as the schools that more privileged students attend. This is not an indictment of the teachers and others who work at these schools; their achievements are significant. However, across the country, there is a predictable pattern: Poor and minority students have fewer opportunities to learn. Sure, it's possible to point out the exceptions. And from these exceptions, it's possible to mount all kinds of arguments that if *some* kids and teachers can rise above the odds, *everyone* can. Not so, Mr. or Ms. President. Exceptions are just that—unusual occurrences that defy the trend. The historical trend— the undeniable trend—is that poor and minority students have fewer opportunities to learn in American schools than the other students with whom they must compete in the marketplace of higher education and better jobs. That's the way it has always been in America, that's the way it is today, and that's what has to change.

The next president faces two challenges before addressing the apparently straightforward goal of the No Child Left Behind Act. The first challenge is that much of the nation simply does not know that schools are unequal. It's a lesson they have to learn. The second challenge is that many people believe that if inequalities exist, they don't matter. Unless the next president can "teach" the nation that inequality exists and that it *does* matter, policies to improve and reform public schools will be thwarted at every turn.

Teaching Americans That Inequality Exists

Why is the inequality lesson so tough to teach? First, because the facts about unequal resources are kept well hidden. Second, because no one likes an unpleasant lesson. Americans are so committed to the principle of equality that they are hard-pressed to accept inequalities when someone points them out. Also, people who are prosperous rightly credit American society and values for contributing to their prosperity, and they are reluctant to speak ill of the country and values to which they owe so much. They also might worry that equality might cause them to lose their advantages. If school inequalities are forcefully pointed out—thrust in our face, so to speak—we blame "those kids," or their parents, or teachers, or the teachers' unions, or sloppy management, or low expectations, and so on. It's less common for Americans to identify what should be the more obvious culprit: Students who achieve less in school do so, in large part, because they get fewer of the basic resources they need for achievement. They do not have up-to-date materials for learning, highly qualified teachers to learn from, and healthful and secure facilities in which to learn.

Teachers, materials, and facilities—it's not rocket science. These tangible and measurable school resources are only the starting point of a good education, but without these basic resources, millions of American students are "nonstarters." The next president must put off the temptation of getting entangled in the high-stakes testing frenzy and relying on "marketplace" initiatives such as vouchers, incentives, competition, privatization, and so on. None of this can possibly matter if Americans aren't taught the hard facts of students' unequal opportunities to learn that result directly from unequal access to qualified teachers, useful materials, and adequate facilities. If some American children have inadequate schools, it simply will not do to say that they deserve those schools because their parents or communities didn't compete well enough in the educational marketplace. This will be a tough argument to sell to Americans because people who believe that these problems are the "natural" result of competition or birthright will accuse you of "throwing money at the problem" when you talk about providing the tangible and material resources that children lack in schools.

For example, schools serving African American and Latino students typically offer fewer advanced classes and have fewer and more outdated textbooks, materials, and science laboratories. Their school buildings are older, in greater disrepair, and far more likely to be crowded, unhealthful, and uncomfortable. Their teachers are more likely to have less experience, to not have their state's highest teaching credential, or to not have a degree in the subject they teach. In racially mixed schools, low-income students and students of color are placed disproportionately in low-level programs. Once placed, they have less access to knowledge and powerful learning environments. Therefore, they don't learn as much as comparable students in more enriched settings, and they don't qualify for college. When schools do not support children's health, learning, and guidance needs, middle-class families can often supplement or negotiate for what's missing; poor families can't.

An important dimension of your challenge, Mr. or Ms. President, is that Americans tend to believe that if they have the advantages of good schooling, it is because they deserve those advantages. But to say that also implies that if some students don't have the basic foundational opportunities of schooling it's because they *don't* deserve them. And we know that this is simply not true. This type of thinking is painfully similar to America's discriminatory past and continues to promote sorting according to power, privilege, race, and social class.

Helping Americans understand that fundamental inequalities— not just hard work and intelligence—influence which students do and do not achieve at school requires strong presidential leadership. There is no better platform than the presidential bully pulpit to unsettle Americans' complacency about the fairness of their schools.

Teaching Americans That Inequality Matters

Teaching that inequality does matter should be even easier than demonstrating that inequality exists. It's close to unbelievable that a president would have to take on this task in a democracy that's now in its third century. Yet powerful groups in America *are* successfully advocating that very same inequality-doesn't-matter position. A small but influential group of analysts has argued that basic school resources really don't matter. As a result, many Americans question whether low-status students of color could actually profit from better schools. In fact, the analysts argue that schools, in general, matter little and that ensuring that all students have basic resources is counterproductive to good schooling. Their analyses ignore the massive amount of empirical evidence that basic school resources such as qualified teachers, textbooks, facilities, and college preparatory classes are fundamental to learning and achievement.

It is significant that these analysts are largely supported by the same think tanks that also promote privatization of schools, vouchers, and get-tough reward-and-punishment schemes for getting low-resource schools to shape up. These folks argue that the best way to improve schools is to use market mechanisms to motivate teachers and students to work harder. They have already convinced many federal and state policymakers to simply set standards, administer tests, and hold students and schools accountable through incentives such as public rankings, rewards, sanctions, and school choice without regard to equal access to basic resources. This logic underlies the substance, if not the sentiment, of No Child Left Behind.

These advocates for test-only accountability rely on narrow arguments to prove that concerns about shortages and inequalities are misplaced. There are many problems with the science behind their "resources-don't-matter" arguments, and their analyses have been criticized repeatedly as conceptually and methodologically flawed by some of the nations' most prominent scholars—including leading economists who study education. In the end of course, these analysts blame students, their families, their communities, and their cultures for their low achievement. They fail to sort out the highly correlated effects of background and schools. Poor students and students of color attend schools with fewer school advantages. More advantaged students attend more advantaged schools. To determine with any confidence whether families or schools cause achievement, we'd need to randomly assign students to good and bad schools. Of course, families of advantaged students would never stand for such an experiment because *they* know that schools matter.

In sum, the president must not get distracted by statistical manipulations that defy both sound research methods and common sense. Only a president can lead all Americans toward realizing the Constitution's guarantee of the rights of all students to education on equal terms.

*Teaching Americans to Identify, Value, and Guarantee
Educational Opportunities*

Public schools remain our best hope for achieving a free and democratic society where all have decent lives and rich opportunities. But for schools to work honestly toward that goal, America's leaders—including our next president—have to teach Americans that opportunities are not a prize for being successful, but are a guarantee that everyone has the essentials on which to build success.

A first step is to expand state standards and accountability systems to include opportunities to learn. Such systems should include measures of how students perform on tests that are closely aligned with the state's standards (as required by No Child Left Behind), along with other important outcomes such as school attendance, promotion and graduation rates, course-taking patterns (higher- versus lower-level mathematics, AP courses, and so forth), the percentage of students completing all courses required for state university eligibility, the percentage of students taking college entrance exams, and the percentage actually going on to college.

But you can't stop there. These kinds of data only tell the states how the kids are doing; they don't tell anyone how the *states* are doing! If the United States was losing a war, our commander in chief would not be satisfied with monthly reports telling about lives lost and projections for battle victories. You would ask about weapons and materials, about the condition of the soldiers' equipment, and about whether military leaders are getting the best intelligence and training. You would want to check if America had the *appropriate* and, at the very least, the *basic* opportunities needed to win. Similarly, schoolchildren need basic opportunities to learn.

Although the specific opportunity to learn standards and accountability indicators might vary from state to state, at a minimum they *must* include the following:

Access to high-quality teachers. This includes student–teacher ratios; the percentage of fully credentialed, board-certified teachers; availability of specially trained teachers for students still learning English; and required standards-based teacher professional development.

Access to books and other learning materials. This includes ratio of library books to students, ratio of course-specific textbooks to students, ratio of students to computers, and ratio of students to Internet-accessible computers.

Adequacy of school facilities. This includes overcrowding in classrooms, access to clean and well-maintained bathrooms, availability of functional heating and cooling systems, presence of lead paint, and so on.

Availability of a college preparatory curriculum. This includes the number of college preparatory and advanced courses offered and the number of sections available.

The usefulness of even these minimal opportunity standards is obvious and could target quick action directed at patterns of much lower achievement when combined with data on inferior resources, inadequate facilities, and less-qualified teachers. Such data would also enable educators to reflect on goals and to communicate with their communities.

Simply collecting information about opportunities to learn and making the information public could mobilize states and the federal government to provide some of the resources that students need for learning. However, information is easily ignored by short-sighted people who do not see immediate benefits to themselves. Therefore, opportunity to learn standards must be a part of the states' and the federal government's overall accountability system. For the states, such an educational accountability system would specify the responsibilities of all of the appropriate adults—from the governor down to the classroom teachers—who are accountable to children, families, and communities for the things over which these particular people have control.

The ideal accountability system is one that is reciprocal—that is, it includes a two-way flow of accountability information. In addition to local officials communicating performance expectations and over-seeing adequate performance and learning conditions, accountability systems must also ensure that state officials have the necessary infor-mation to craft effective policies that address systemic shortcomings on the local or state levels. Moreover, accountability must also mean that communities and citizens hold states accountable for adequate and equitable education.

States could also explore the use of a corps of local "inspec-tion volunteers." Parents, grassroots groups, or local experts could monitor and report on the conditions in schools while calling in more highly trained monitors for particular needs. This is not a completely untried idea. In New York State, School Quality Reviews have not only provided valuable information that could be used with test scores to base school evaluations, but have also been cost-effective. These School Quality Reviews involved local people from multiple perspectives and with stakes in education (educators, busi-nesspeople, and parents) in assessing school quality, and they did not drain state resources by requiring state employees to conduct the reviews.

Acting on their common interest in quality education, orga-nized parents are better positioned to demand good service from schools and to hold them and the state accountable when their expectations are not met. However, local engagement in reciprocal accountability must be supported with mechanisms that organize and keep parents and community members informed about their rights and responsibilities. This will require technical assistance, translation services, child care, and active support from community-based organizations. Churches and community groups that possess strong ties with communities, especially with recent immigrants, are often well positioned to provide training and to facilitate com-munication between parents, local schools, and the state education bureaucracy.

THE SPECIFIC REMEDIES AND MORE COMPREHENSIVE REFORMS suggested here are not radical. There is nothing groundbreaking about giving kids books, qualified teachers, and adequate facilities. Framing an accountability system that holds state and local officials responsible for providing these basic educational tools is not only "sensible" and managerially sound, but leaders across the state and nation have made calls to make accountability the cornerstone of education policy reform and practice. The recommendations in this letter do not aim at creating a cookie-cutter to stamp out identical schools, they do not encourage a leveling-down of opportunity and quality, and they do not regulate professional decisions about how educators teach children. Sadly, they are not even aimed at meeting the worthy and still-neglected goal of bringing exemplary, high-quality education to *all* children. Rather, the modest goal of what is proposed here is to bring the worst schools up to a standard of common decency and to do so expeditiously.

Sincerely,

Jeannie Oakes

Martin Lipton

THOMAS SOBOL

A PRESIDENT WHO "GETS IT"

Dear Madam President

Pardon me, Madam President, if I begin this letter somewhat informally, but hey, I'll bet they were destroyed when you decided to use your maiden name! That and the Mexican poncho you wore at the inauguration were two highlights for me. It's so wonderful to have a president who *gets it*! Especially when it comes to kids. You know what it means to leave no child behind—you have to worry about it every time you drive the family to the mall or the soccer field! You don't rely on scores from an end-of-the-year test to see if Tommy and Rosie were in the car—either they are or they aren't—every trip. Our kids are so lucky to have you in charge of their education!

The thing is, although they've given you to work with may look terrific, it will be a bear to live with in the long run. The No Child Left Behind Act promises that all our children will learn better each year and that the "achievement gap" between different portions of the population will disappear. It also implies that all this can be done without significant new resources. It claims that all we need to do is make teachers and students more accountable and they'll shape up and start achieving like they've never achieved before!

Among other things, the NCLB act assumes that:

- We can improve schools through a top-down program dictated by state legislatures and the federal government.
- This program should consist essentially of standards, annual testing, and accountability.
- The program should apply in equal measure to all students, regardless of background, ability, or aspiration.
- Teachers and other school workers know how to teach such a program and will be more inclined to do so if they are held more accountable.
- Students can and should make measurable progress on standardized tests administered on an annual basis.
- The time, capacity, and financial resources now available are sufficient to do the job.

With all respect, Madam President, as someone who wishes you well, I hope you take a hard look at these assumptions. Because if they're right, we will all be happy; but if they're wrong, as so many of us strongly believe, we're heading for a giant mess—*on your watch!*

The good news is that the standards movement, of which NCLB is a part, is making a positive difference for some students in some places. For some, the movement promotes clarity of purpose, quality of work, equity of expectations, and consistency of approach across schools and school districts. The bad news is that for many other students in many other places, the movement is narrowing the curriculum, imposing a stifling uniformity of practice at a time when we should be discovering new ways to use our miraculous new learning technologies, and punishing students and teachers for failing to achieve what we have not given them the means of achieving. No wonder there is such a backlash against the standards movement developing across the country!

Consider, Madam President, what we are trying to do. We are attempting something no other large and diverse society has ever done: to educate *all* of our children and young people to high academic standards. Despite the seeming assurance of our policy pronouncements, it is not entirely clear that we know how to do this. And it is certainly clear that we cannot achieve this ambitious goal unless we develop the capacity to do so, provide the resources that are required, and take the time that is needed. We would not invade Europe or Iraq without training our troops and providing them with the supplies and equipment they need to be successful, and we should attempt nothing so bold and fundamental in our schools without providing what is needed there, as well.

Some people will tell you that money doesn't matter. They will produce impressive regression equations purporting to show that increased spending on education does not produce increased results in our schools. They will argue, by implication if not directly, that our problems are stupidity and laziness, not resources. I am so glad that you have family experience in the matter. You know that when the roof is leaking and the toilet is overflowing, you have to pay money to have these things fixed—even if the kids won't be better or smarter as a result. The same logic applies to schools. If you increase spending to fix the roof and the toilet, you don't expect students' SAT scores to shoot up. But the roof and the toilet must still be fixed. It is a matter of decency.

There are some areas where you need to spend money to improve the quality of schools and the education they provide. You can't reduce class size without hiring more teachers and using more space, and teachers and space cost money. You can't create new preschool programs without hiring new staff, and hiring staff costs money. You can't expect teachers to teach the new curriculum effectively until they have mastered it, and time for professional development costs money. Yet, reducing class size, making good preschool programs available to all children, and providing teacher training have all been linked to improving student learning. The critics are right when they say that money alone will not solve our problems, but they need to understand that, although more money on its own is not sufficient, it is necessary. The question is not whether we need more money; the question is how we can most effectively spend the money that we need.

And how much money do we need? You are right to ask that question, Madam President, and I wish I had a simple answer for you. It is difficult to estimate of what it will cost to fund NCLB adequately at the federal, state, and local level. In recent years, some of us have argued for the implementation of "opportunity-to-learn" standards—standards that specify the conditions and resources students and schools need to meet the new learning standards. We haven't gotten very far. I guess it's easier for politicians to advocate high standards for others to meet than to find the means to give them the resources they need to do so.

Anyway, I don't yet have a firm answer to your question. However, help is on the way, provided you are willing to regard anything from the courts as helpful. Over the past decade or so, there has been a wave of "adequacy" cases in the courts (usually state courts). Essentially, plaintiffs in such cases cite the state's duty (under the education clause of the state's constitution) to provide an adequate public education for its youth. They then show evidence that this duty is not being met—that many students are not receiving the education to which they are entitled. Such suits are not brought on equity grounds, as many were in the 1970s, 1980s, and 1990s. The issue is no longer whether a state's system for financing public education is *fair*; the question is whether it is *adequate* to meet the state's legal duty to provide an appropriate education.

Such lawsuits have been litigated (or are being litigated) in more than two dozen states, with mixed results. Collectively, however, they are moving us closer to a shared understanding of the kind of education the law requires, what conditions are necessary for students to acquire this education, what the cost of providing these conditions may be, and what remedies are most effectively applied if a state is found delinquent in its duty.

In *Campaign for Fiscal Equity, Inc. v. the State of New York*, New York State's highest court ruled that under the state's existing funding system, "New York City schoolchildren are not receiving their constitutionally mandated opportunity for a sound basic education." In today's society, the court held, a sound basic education is defined as a "meaningful high school education." The measure of such an education is the state's own learning standards. In order for students to meet these standards, schools must receive sufficient funding to ensure quality teachers, reasonable class sizes, adequate school facilities and classrooms, and up-to-date libraries and computers, among other things.

On April 1, 2007, the state legislature voted to enact the 2007–2008 Education Budget and Reform Legislation, allocating an unprecedented increase of $1.76 billion in education aid for the 2007–2008 fiscal year, bringing total funding to $19.64 billion. The law also established new transparency and accountability measures in the distribution of funds and school finance reform. More importantly, this year's budget bill includes a four-year commitment to increase annual state school aid by seven billion dollars by the 2010–2011 school year. From this process, the nation should learn much about the nature and costs of the educational reforms NCLB is pursuing.

I understand, Madam President, that state court decisions are not binding on the federal government. But I respectfully hope that they will help you see clearly the way to your own duty. First, the federal government should increase its share of public education funding. The NCLB Act creates a pervasive—some would say intrusive—role for the federal government in what traditionally have been state and local affairs. Richard Elmore of Harvard has called NCLB "the single largest, and single most damaging, expansion of federal power over the nation's education system in history." It is not right for the federal government to impose such demands and leave most of the financial burden to others that are less able to pay.

Second, we hope that your administration will help the states develop opportunity-to-learn standards that spell out the conditions and resources that must be in place if students are to learn and grow

as we would wish them to. We accept today's zeal for accountability. But just as our government seeks to hold students and teachers
accountable for results, so should our government be held accountable for carrying its share of the load. In our democracy, it is not
enough that people be accountable to the government; government
must be accountable to the people.

Third, I hope that your administration will assist states in
defining and meeting their educational obligations. We need less
"Do this . . ." and more "Here are some things you might try. How
can we help?" Public education has always been close to the people,
and we'd like to keep it that way. We want to think of our federal
government as an ally in educating our children, not as a distant
regulatory agency whose demands get in our way.

Finally, Madam President, I hope you will display a certain openness of mind when it comes to educational issues. There is no one
best way to teach and no one best way to learn. As you well know,
what works best for Tommy may not work for Rosie. Orthodoxy in
matters of curriculum and instruction is misplaced in a democracy.
One of the things our public schools have done well is to permit a
healthy diversity of people, ideas, and methods. As our population
changes, we must remain open to that diversity. It is what our country is about. So use your vast influence to bring us together, so that
we may understand our differences and our commonalities more
fully. Don't divide us along a set of ideological fault lines. Our goal is
standards, not standardization.

THANK YOU FOR TAKING THE TIME to read this letter. Give my best to
Tommy and Rosie. I know you'll keep each of them in mind as you
develop policy for all our children!

Sincerely,

Tom Sobol

PART FIVE
EDUCATION FOR ALL

U.S. Senator John Glenn &
Leslie F. Hergert

The Civic Mission
of Schools

Dear President,

In December 2000, just after the tumultuous presidential election, we were privileged to hear two Philadelphia middle school students and their teacher describe a project they designed on the census. The project was undertaken as part of the students' social studies and English language arts program, but their work took them far outside the usual textbooks. In addition to learning about the history and purpose of the census, the students organized and implemented information campaigns to convince their families and neighbors that answering the census questions would not "get them in trouble" but rather would bring needed funds and services to their neighborhood. The students made presentations to church and community groups, created and aired public service announcements, and in other ways promoted an accurate count of their neighborhood for Census 2000. The students appeared to be typical urban kids, a little shy about speaking to a group of adults, and yet they had made a profound difference in their community. Ultimately, their inner-city neighborhood had the most complete census count of any in the city. The project made civic education come alive for these students. It was academics in action.

As we listened to their story, we thought about our own experiences with civic participation in different ways and different eras. One of us served as a Marine pilot, an astronaut, and a U.S. Senator; the other was one of the first VISTA volunteers, and, more recently, organized community conversations among immigrants and citizens about what it means to be an American. We both still get a thrill when we go into the voting booth. We learned, growing up, that our democracy depends on the participation of all citizens.

Today, American citizens are more educated than ever before—a larger percentage attends school longer—yet civic involvement is on the wane. As adults' civic involvement has declined, so has that of the nation's youth, and at even sharper rates of decline. Numerous studies have documented youth's low voter participation rate, negative opinion of elected officials, and general alienation from government and politics. Young people have learned apathy, not engagement.

For our democracy and economy to survive in the twenty-first century, we must reverse these trends. We call upon the next president to reclaim the public purpose of education and include preparation for citizenship as an important goal of education.

Recent education reforms have focused on standards and accountability. While much in these reforms is admirable, the emphasis on testing has narrowed the focus of schooling to topics that can easily be measured on machine-graded tests. The best civic education, like the lessons we both learned from our teachers and adult leaders, cannot be measured by multiple-choice questions alone. Civic education is about learning both the history and principles of the past, as well as the can-do spirit we need for the future.

To correct our course, we must do two things. First, we must explicitly embrace civic education as an essential purpose of education. We must go back to our roots. More than half our state constitutions explicitly tie education to citizenship. Nationwide, we have recognized that for a democracy to work its citizens must be educated, thoughtful, and involved. To implement this ideal, we ask the next president to include the civic purpose of education as part of the public dialogue about education reform, to expand the definition of *student achievement* to include students' community contributions, and to support the nation's schools to develop students as citizens. Explicit commitment to the civic purpose of education is essential to revive democratic involvement among our youth.

Second, we must provide all students with the kind of education experience the Philadelphia students had, the experience of service-learning. The National Commission on Service-Learning defines *service-learning* as *a teaching and learning approach that integrates community service with academic study to enrich learning, teach civic responsibility, and strengthen communities*. When students apply what they learn in the classroom to better their community, their active engagement reinforces classroom learning, gives it purpose, and generates an enthusiasm for more learning. Service-learning embodies the ancient Chinese proverb: "I hear, I forget. I see, I remember. I do, and I understand."

We must ensure that all of our students "do" and "understand." The National Commission recommended that every American student should participate in a high-quality service-learning project each year from kindergarten through twelfth grade. We must realize that goal.

Service-learning has a unique potential to revitalize students' interest in their communities and public service. While many American youth are currently alienated from government, they are increasingly involved in community service. They also volunteer in record numbers for the armed services, AmeriCorps/VISTA, and local causes and organizations. Recent studies found that more than half of young people had engaged in volunteer work during the previous year, and that they found their volunteer experiences stimulating and rewarding.

Through service-learning, we can capture this enthusiasm for community service and direct it toward active citizenship. Service-learning involves students directly in civic activities. It connects directly to traditional American values, drawn from our many contributing cultures, of giving back to the community and joining together to make our communities and our country work. And it taps the inner need that has caused young people to respond so strongly when they are called—as they have done in World War II, the war on poverty, and the recent war on terrorism. The backdrop of recent civic events demonstrates vividly the critical need to teach students the importance of voting, that all votes count, that we must work to ensure that there are qualified political candidates with many views, and that collaboration to solve community problems is essential.

We need to teach youth that their contributions are needed not only in times of crisis, but as a regular and ongoing part of life in a democratic country. We all have the responsibility to attend to our democratic traditions and keep them strong. Without active citizenship, we are in danger of losing our freedoms and our strength. Educating youth for citizenship should be the job of all teachers, not just those who teach history, social studies, and civics.

When teachers link service activities with the academic curriculum through service-learning, they are teaching civic values. At the same time, they deepen academic learning and make it meaningful to students. A river cleanup reinforces biology lessons. Students who interview the residents of a nursing home and publish books of their stories expand their language arts skills. And they also learn qualities of responsibility, teamwork, and problem solving. They learn that they can make a difference in their community and what it takes to do so.

The two of us drew on different experiences and interests as we examined service-learning. Senator Glenn's commitment to improving science and math education arose from his concerns, documented by the Third International Mathematics and Science Study that, although our children begin their education leading others around the world in math and science understanding, they rank close to *last* in these fields by high school graduation. These concerns fueled his interest in projects where students use math and science skills to measure water quality, construct buildings and playgrounds, create nature trails, and care for the land. Through such projects, students learn that math and science are not just abstract principles confined to textbooks, but are the real knowledge and skills that launch astronauts into space and power all our technological advances. Too often, our students sit and listen to a teacher lecture. We need to teach our students, not only the "what" of math and science, but the "how," "why," and "why should I care." Service-learning supplies those missing pieces.

Dr. Hergert's work in adolescent literacy has shown that all students—but teens especially—need to be able to connect reading and writing with life. They need to be engaged in reading and see the purpose in reading and writing. Service-learning projects where students write books for younger children, exchange letters with senior citizens, and research information to solve community problems provide these opportunities. Young people, even those who do not enjoy reading, become engaged in learning more about the people and situations they encounter. Students who interview community elders and write their stories—whether the elders are grandparents or the famous Tuskegee Airmen—learn the value of listening, writing, reading, and much more. They become involved in something greater than themselves.

Service-learning deepens skills in critical academic areas such as literacy, math, and science, and at the same time develops the civic attitudes and skills students need to contribute to democratic government and problem solving. Students enjoy the experience of helping others and "feel good" when they do so. Service-learning moves these positive feelings of individual satisfaction to deeper analysis of the causes and solutions of the problems and situations that youth encounter. They learn to appreciate the complexity of situations, to resolve differences and conflicts, and to determine when and how they can help. They become active citizens.

The time has come for U.S. schools to embrace service-learning as an essential ingredient of the education we want and need for our children. With minimal federal funding, service-learning has spread to thirty-two percent of American schools. Impressive though this number is, most students remain untouched by the benefits of service-learning. The National Commission on Service-Learning has challenged the country to ensure that every student in kindergarten through high school participates in quality service-learning every year as an integral part of the American education experience. We ask the next president to take up this challenge and to provide critical personal and federal support so that all children can learn citizenship by doing citizenship. What should the next president do?

Lift up the civic purpose of education and the important role schools play in developing citizenship knowledge and skills. In speeches about education, recognize the role schools play in preparing young people for active citizenship as well as the workforce. Advocate for schools to incorporate civic knowledge, skills, and actions as a "renewed basic" that all students must learn.

Expand the definition of student achievement to include students' community contributions. Student achievement is measured primarily by standardized tests. Such tests are one important measure of students' learning, but they should never be the only measure. Students can and should demonstrate learning in a wide variety of ways. In order to highlight civic learning, schools should value the contributions students make to their community.

Increase federal policy, program, and financial supports for service-learning. Federal support conveys a national commitment to active civic education of our young people. In addition, federal funding acts as an incentive to leverage support at the state and local levels, where responsibility for education lies, to fund schools to train teachers, provide transportation and supplies, and coordinate connections with community partners. Furthermore, the federal government should support and orchestrate high-quality professional development and conduct research studies on the impact of service-learning.

THE LANGUAGE OF DEMOCRACY AND CIVIC ENGAGEMENT has been conspicuously absent from speeches about school change. Perhaps this is because the adult population is losing a sense of the common good. We ask the next president to ignite the nation's tradition of commitment to the common good, to our democratic traditions and can-do spirit, and to help kindle those values in our young people. We need these values, these beliefs, and most important, these actions, more than ever.

Sincerely,

Leslie F. Hergert   John Glenn

Suggested Reading

National Commission on Mathematics and Science Teaching for the 21st Century. (2000). *Before it's too late.* Washington, DC: U.S. Department of Education.
National Commission on Service-Learning. (2002). *Learning in deed: The power of service-learning for American schools.* Newton, MA: Author.

THEODORE R. SIZER

WHAT WE ALL WANT FOR
EACH OF OUR CHILDREN

Dear President,

Congratulations on your election. Your work on behalf of the American people will now begin. Education—meaning what happens in schools and colleges, both real and virtual—is certain to find an early place on your agenda. Your aides will soon barrage you with data: current and projected student enrollment in schools; graduation rates; projected supply and quality of professional staff; budget estimates arranged in various patterns; test scores on a range of subjects from algebra through literature to science, with international comparisons; lists of influential professional leaders and their political supporters; samples of curricula; intricate charts of the federal, state, and local education apparatus; and much more. All this may be unfamiliar to you and overwhelming in its bulk. The temptation to hand these numbing piles of information quickly back to your aides and to request that they advise you on their meaning will be strong.

I ask you, however, to resist this temptation. The issue of education touches more of your fellow citizens—particularly the young, who are our most vulnerable citizens—than almost all other policy areas. At the start of your tenure I beg you to take a step back, to put aside the familiar political and bureaucratic ways of addressing education policy, and to look afresh at what might and must be at its core if education is to improve our children's futures and the state of our democracy.

To guide your reflection, I suggest that you ponder fully what you want and hope for your own children and grandchildren. Education policy must have a child's face, and what better faces with which to begin than those of your own offspring? You will find that what you devoutly wish for each of your own children, born and yet to be born, is probably quite similar to what all parents and grandparents wish for their children. To the greatest possible extent, education policies in a humane democracy should emerge from such wishes, messy and vague though they may often appear.

We all want our offspring to be themselves, one by one, none exactly like any other, each reveling in and prospering from the best of his or her passions and worthy commitments. I am sure that each of your children is special to you; and surely it is thus in every American family. No parents see their child as merely a faceless part of some age cohort. Even the young, themselves, will at some moment point out to us elders, politely or impolitely, *I am someone!* And good for them. We would have it no other way. Especially in America.

At the same time, we want each of our children to be principled, to make wise choices and to respect those of others, and to behave toward others as they would have others behave toward them.

We want each of our children to have as fair a chance in life as any other child and to be as good and effective as they can be.

We all want each of our children to grow into constructive self-sufficiency, aware that life is demanding and there is no such thing as a free lunch. At the very least, every child must be able to read, communicate, and master essential mathematics, and must be flexible in the use of those skills that not only equip each of them to compete but also keep them from dependence on others. Without exception, each needs the basic tools of life: acceptance of endless change and the habit of responding judiciously to the unexpected.

We all want our offspring to be aware of the world and its history and to be in awe of its dimensions, yet unafraid. The past rarely teaches; but it always suggests possibilities as well as explanations of why things—cultural, artistic, spiritual, and physical—might be as they are. We want our children to be questers, people who are in the habit of asking, with sincere respect, the question *why?*, and who are in the habit of trying, in an informed fashion, to find the answer.

We all want our children to be people who at once follow the law and ever try to improve it. We want them to feel the security of a healthy community, the obligations of engagement and reciprocity among its members, and the inevitable need for restraint.

We want them to find happiness in the use of their minds and bodies. We want them to find joy in the taking of responsibility. We want them to be in the habit of constructive activity, whether at work or at play.

Too often in the past, your predecessors' administrations have started with *means* rather than *ends*, because such is familiar and easy. We rush to categorize and simplify—ninth graders, special needs youngsters, academically talented youngsters, and the rest—rather than address the more demanding task of universal personalization within demanding but broad common objectives. Today, too many of us worship standardization—one curriculum, one textbook, one test, one score, one class size, one measure of qualification, one hierarchy from valedictorian to presumed doofus—because it provides a veneer of fairness. However, such standardization undermines your and my wish that each of our children be treated with the respect that his or her *individuality* deserves, no more and no less. In order for us to nurture our children's diverse talents and interests and to provide them with the greatest chance of future success and fulfillment, individualized and personalized treatment must itself be a standard in educational practice and the concept of fairness in education must reflect the reality of idiosyncrasy. We expect no less in medicine and law, where professionals deal with cases on a one-by-one basis. Yes, there are patterns, but patterns should not morph into strict universal expectations. Patterns are a place to start; they are guideposts rather than hitching posts.

When your aides return with a short list of initiatives that emerge from the pile of data on education, I beg you to require them to justify whatever they recommend against the following list of questions:

Is this policy fair and equitable? Does every affected child gain an equal chance to its anticipated benefits? Does it provide all children with a fair chance for happiness and fulfillment and allow them to be as good and effective as they can be?

Does this policy explicitly or implicitly extend each child's independence by assuring his or her mastery of the basic skills and habits that life in our society requires?

Does this policy honor individual differences among our young citizens and, indeed, build on them? Does this policy protect or extend each child's own unique worldview, opening for each avenues that were earlier unrecognized or closed? Does this policy enrich the diverse culture of our nation?

Does this policy reinforce, by example as well as direction, the functioning of democracy for and among the young?

Your aides will chafe at such a list. Still, insist on it. Do not let its complexity and imprecision, both practical and political, dissuade you. Be impatient with those who will suggest that these concerns are merely sentimental froth and that they are impossible to make into "programs." Ask of each of them: *Would you want anything less for each of your own beloved kids?* Making things personal makes them real.

Ultimately, it is the American people who will judge you, not your aides or other politicians. I believe that the American people are ready for a fresh look, a fresh voice, fresh approaches, and fair policies that rest on bedrock democratic principles, however loosely, even sentimentally, defined. The people are ready for talk about education that is both straight and sensitive. Persist with this approach and you will start a happy revolution in our vast, paralyzed, defensive, inequitable, and yet well-meaning system of formal schooling, a revolution that most of America's citizens profoundly desire.

Good luck. And never be too busy that you forget even one family birthday.

Sincerely,

Ted Sizer

MICHELLE FINE, APRIL BURNS, &
MARÍA ELENA TORRE

POSTCARDS FROM AMERICA

Dear President,

Congratulations on the election.
We are delighted that you have
captured the hearts and minds of
the American people. We worry,
though, that you have inherited a nation damaged by systematic
disinvestment in public schools, a democracy fractured by unequal
education. We write to you as social psychologists who have, over
the past five years, collaborated with, interviewed, and surveyed more
than seven thousand youth and young adults across the United States
about social (in)justice in their schools and in our nation.

In the midst of our travels between California and New York, we
have asked middle and high school students attending under-resourced
schools to paint a picture in words of their ideal school, and we've
heard chilling reminders of how dire the situation is in some schools:

> If I could have my ideal school, I guess I would have seats on the
> toilets and enough paper in the bathroom to clean yourself.
> —*Sarafina, the daughter of migrant workers in California*

᪥

I'd like a teacher who really knows math and knows how to teach it. All through high school, I don't think I ever had a teacher really qualified in math. When I heard there was a Math Regents test, I knew I wasn't prepared. So I left. No diploma. [Jacob's high school of approximately three thousand seven hundred students had two certified math teachers.]
—*Jacob, an African American junior from the South Bronx*

We have sponsored youth research camps in New York, New Jersey, and Delaware to create a cadre of high school youth researchers able to study "the gap" within and across their schools; conducted focus groups with nearly two hundred elementary, middle school, and high school students from across the nation; and surveyed just over seven thousand middle and high school students about social (in)justice in America and in their schools.

In this letter we are drawing from this rich pool of material from poor, working-class, middle-class, and elite youth—young adults from Watts, the South Bronx, suburban Delaware, the Lower East Side of New York City, Kensington in Philadelphia, Westchester County in New York State, Chicago's South Side, Essex County in New Jersey, South-Central Los Angeles, and the Bedford Hills Correctional Facility for Women in New York State. They are African American, Latino, Asian American, and White. They are straight and gay. Some of them have disabilities. Some live in the wealthiest zip codes in America and some survive the dorms of group foster homes.

In many ways, these young people have much in common. Almost all plan to attend college (96.9 percent), care a lot about their grades (90.1 percent), and say that attending a racially mixed school is important (76.2 percent). In a single voice, they despair over the sustained racial and class inequities that define life in America today (91.4 percent). Nevertheless, despite high aspirations and common values, fifty years after *Brown v. Board of Education* (1954) some are on a non-stop elevator to success while others are forced to take the stairs.

I think we're starting at different points. I think a White student gets a head start whereas someone else started back there and if you run fast enough, you can catch up. If you don't catch up or don't know how, you stay there. Even if the White kid isn't motivated, I still feel that the whole school experience . . . it's different. I thought maybe I'm being paranoid because I'm just ultra-sensitive to this, but I don't think so. So many other people notice it. Even White people that I know.

—Shivon, an African American high-achieving junior

These are the young women and men whose fathers, brothers, mothers, and sisters serve in our military, languish in our prisons, chair international corporate boards, clean our streets and our hotel rooms, own two homes, left their children years ago, volunteer in our schools, live in shelters, sit on school boards, teach in our classrooms, hold greencards, and fill our churches and mosques and synagogues praying for a better tomorrow.

When we asked youth of privilege to explain their academic success, they told us, with a blend of pride and ambivalence, about a series of academic supports privately supplied by families and educators that enabled them to sustain their competitive edge:

My neighbor is a freshman who has a ninety-nine average in biology and she has a private tutor for that. Imagine [what it's like] for a kid who doesn't have a ninety-nine average and who doesn't have the money to put into that. . . . Maybe you need to have a job every day after school. Even beyond high school, you're limited by what college you can go to depending on what you can pay. And it puts severe limitations—especially in a community where the playing field is so uneven—because you're either getting so much because of the money or so little. If everyone is just working on their own merit, then it would be a lot different than people who can get all this extra help compared to kids who can't.

—Casey, the White daughter of Ivy League educated parents.

In this volume, we have crafted a set of postcards, e-mails, and memos from these young people, written from their own words, to convey their concerns over the state of public education and social (in)justice in America. They, like we, worry that democracy is fundamentally threatened by unequal education. They narrate vividly their passions, their commitments, and the broken promises. The words of these young people haunt and inspire because they yearn for a nation that does not yet exist.

> I like to think we are where we are because we worked hard . . . but there is also this sinking feeling that you are where you come from and that no matter what the country's standards are, you still have your background as the dominating force of who you are.
> —*David, a White AP student from suburban New York*

We write toward a vision of leadership because we believe these students deserve nothing less. Bishop Desmond Tutu once said: "If you are neutral in situations of injustice, you have chosen the side of the oppressor. If an elephant has its foot on the tail of a mouse and you say you are neutral, the mouse will not appreciate your neutrality."

In prophetic harmony, James Baldwin wrote: "People who shut their eyes to reality simply invite their own destruction, and anyone who insists on remaining in a state of innocence long after that innocence is dead turns himself into a monster."

Innocence, in U.S. public education, is dead.

Case in point: In our travels we had the opportunity to speak with one hundred and two students who were involved in a class action lawsuit regarding inadequate schooling, *Williams v. California* (the case was settled in 2004). These students attend schools with more security guards than advanced placement courses, more metal detectors than encyclopedias, more surveillance than care, and more long-term substitute teachers than qualified educators. They attend the kind of schools most poor children attend regularly—the kind of schools most middle-class parents forbid their children to walk past.

We met Charisse and Thomas, two California students who spoke unknowingly in the tongues of Tutu and Baldwin about their education:

> The teachers . . . one minute they're there . . . and then they're gone the next week. And you try to find out where the teacher went and they say, "you just sit outside." We asked the security guards to bring us the principal. . . . They told us to wait and they left. And they didn't come back. They forgot about us. We ain't getting no education by sitting outside.
> —*Charisse, a young woman who attends a high school where over one third of the teachers are long-term substitutes*

> The people in the state capital just look at this city like it's a shithole. They see teenagers as future inmates, not worth the investment. . . . Sometimes I think, "Is anyone really listening to us?"
> —*Thomas*

Across the nation budgets are thin; but the pain, the deprivation, and the human costs are by no means evenly distributed. In the spirit of Desmond Tutu, the mice are getting mad and are taking to the streets. In the absence of leadership, we sacrifice our children and our future. Our democracy is wilting.

Sincerely

Michelle Fine

April Burns

María Elena Torre

The Bronx, New York
May 2001

Dear Mr. President:

MY NAME IS ASHLEY and I'm an eighth grader from the Bronx, New York. I live near Yankee Stadium. I'm writing because I can't decide where to go to high school. The New York City Department of Education's information on high schools in the Bronx is really depressing. I just learned that schools in the suburbs receive something like sixteen thousand dollars per student compared to our eight thousand dollars per student! City schools are really in bad shape. If we need more, how come we get less? I really want to finish high school and go to college, but look at these numbers!

Where would you tell your daughter to go if *you* lived in the Bronx?

Please write back to me,
Ashley St. Pierre (For more information, see *http://www.cfequity.org*)

Brown 50 Years Later . . .
Segregation Within the "Desegregated" Suburbs

> It just breaks my heart that I can walk down the halls of this building, look in, and know what level class it is by who's in the classroom. If it's all White with one or two awkward-looking Black kids, it's AP. If it's all Black, it's probably special education.
> —*Kantara, an African American, academically successful*
> *sophomore addressing faculty in her "desegregated"*
> *New Jersey high school, August 2003*

> I get really tired of being the only Black person in my most advanced classes. Even if you're strong, you get really intimidated. I sketched a portrait of what it feels like; it's entitled "Hunting Bison." (See figure on next page.)
> —*Emily, a multiracial senior in a "desegregated" New Jersey high school*

Figure 1. Hunting Bison

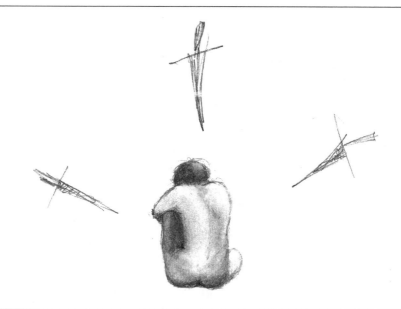

In North Carolina, I never thought about race, now I'm very conscious of it. I'm the Black kid. I'm the Black kid. I'm the Black kid. . . . I'm taking a lot more AP classes. I'm the only Black kid and that's why it's so stressful for me. . . . Why am I the only person to speak from this group? A lot of times that's very hard for me just to sit there—even though I know that these are cool people. . . . But, still, I'm the only Black kid. And that bothers me."

—Solomon, an African American student
in suburban New York

DID YOU KNOW? Of the 3,799 New York and New Jersey suburban students surveyed, sixty percent of White students and Asian students take AP and honors classes—almost twice the rate of African American students (thirty-eight percent) and four times the rate of Latino students (fifteen percent).

DID YOU KNOW? For those students with college-educated parents, the gap was sustained: seventy-four percent of Asians, sixty-five percent of Whites, forty-three percent of African Americans, forty-two percent of African Caribbeans, and thirty-five percent of Latinos with college-educated parents were enrolled in AP/honors classes.

To: New President
From: Stephanie Kern, Senior Class President, Fairway High School
Subject: How do we measure merit?

I HOPE IT'S OK TO E-MAIL YOU. I wanted to write you from one president to another. I'm the senior class president of Fairway High School, and, ever since the 1997 Supreme Court decision about affirmative action, I've been thinking about how we measure merit and about whether it's really fair. The dictionary defines *merit* as "a reward or honor given for superior qualities or conduct." I work hard in school, but I've also had a lot of help—SAT prep courses, chemistry and math tutors, and special brush-up sessions. As class president, I had the opportunity to look over the data we collected from the surveys in our school and in the other districts, and you can definitely see the differences in opportunities. We found, for example, that across schools—*and even in the same desegregated school*—White and Asian American students are almost twice as likely as African American, Afro Caribbean, and Latino students to be in AP/honors classes and to take SAT prep courses. We also found that Black and Latino students are about twice as worried as White and Asian American students that financial problems and high-stakes testing could keep them out of college.

When I compare myself to other students in this school, it sometimes feels like—with all the support I get from my teachers and counselors—there's a floor that I can't fall through. Even when I filled out my college applications, I was able to check "legacy" twice because my mother went to Cornell and my father went to Columbia. Isn't this affirmative action for White people? The playing field is so obviously uneven. I know it's an uphill struggle to change things, but right now it feels like we're on a treadmill walking in place instead of running up the hill.

It may sound weird, but it seems to me that if we were serious about making things more equal for all students, wouldn't we get rid of levels, give all schools the same amount of money to spend per student, offer free SAT prep classes (or just stop using the SAT, since we know it's full of bias), move the best teachers to the students and schools who need them most, and have more needs-based scholarships rather than "merit-based" ones? I'm not sure exactly what to do first, but I know it's time to act. Thanks for listening.

I look forward to your advice,
Stephanie Kern

Dear Mr. President:

TODAY'S *New York Times* REPORTS that the 2003 Math Regents scores for juniors and seniors were tossed out because almost two out of three test-takers failed. Didn't the commissioner also throw out the scores when students in Westchester suburbs did poorly on the Physics Regents?

Don't get me wrong, I think this is great, but I'm noticing a pattern. When rich students or White kids or students in the suburbs fail the Regents, you determine that the tests are invalid and scores are discounted, but when poor kids or Black and Latino urban students fail in huge numbers, you declare that these same tests are reliable measures of accountability and we are denied our diplomas. Please explain.

Sincerely,
Jose Miguel Gonzalez
Brooklyn, New York
(For more information on high-stakes testing and its impact on African American and Latino students see *http://www.fairtest. org*.)

Dear President,

I WAS NINE YEARS OLD when my mother gave me a book by Frederick Douglass and I learned that literacy meant freedom from slavery. Today, I write to you as an inmate at a correctional facility for women near the Canadian border, concerned about the absence of educational opportunities for women and men in prison. I was transferred here from a prison in Bedford Hills, New York, where I spent eight years working in the learning center, attending college, tutoring, and participating in a collaborative research project that documented the impact of college on women in prison (see *http://www.changingminds.ws*). With reincarceration rates of inmates being between forty and sixty percent, I bear witness that the revolving doors fling wide open for all who leave the prison system—especially those with no education.

I live now in a prison without college in a dorm with twelve women. The other morning I sat on my bed circling the room with my eyes, gazing closely at my peers. They are very young. Many have been abused, were drug addicts, and/or have lived in poverty. I wondered how they got here. In between my quiet thoughts, I heard a loud roar, "ON-THE-COUNT!" I scurried to my feet, searching for my hot pink slippers. The officer counted us, in silence. We were all there. Afterward, some of the women went back to watching television, others played cards; very few opted to read or write. Few know how. I struggled and wondered why. I myself desperately try to fight the feeling of a life without hope. Everyday I read the dictionary and try to learn one new word to stay alive. I am refusing to go back to a life where I assumed I had no choices. I look at these women and feel anxious and afraid. How is it possible that we are willing to throw these lives away?

In 1994, there were three hundred and fifty college-in-prison programs in the nation. In 1995, there were eight. Once President Clinton signed the Violent Crime Control Act, an era of "get tough on crime" prevailed, and prisoners were no longer eligible for Pell grants. Ironically, research consistently demonstrates that educational programs like college-in-prison lower recidivism rates. In our study, *women who participated in college while in prison were four times less likely to be reincarcerated than comparable women not in college.* Participation in college reduced reincarceration rates from 29.9 to 7.7 percent.

Access to college for women in prison often means that a woman does not have to return to an abusive relationship, substance abuse, boosting, picking pockets, a life of poverty, or breaking the law. As one woman we interviewed told us, "When I started going to college that was, like, the key point for me of rehabilitation, of changing myself. And nobody did it for me, I did it for myself. . . ." (Roz entered prison at twenty-three and is now a college graduate serving fifty years to life). Our study confirmed what scores of other studies had found: College-in-prison programs positively impact prisoners, the children of prisoners, peace in the prison environment, transitions back home, and even save taxpayer dollars.

So on behalf of the two million women and men behind bars, I urge you to have the courage to restore the once common college-in-prison programs. A friend in Bedford once said that college-in-prison is like a light to redirect ourselves in a very dark place. As you enter office and strive to build a stronger, more democratic nation, please allow this light to shine. Thank you.

Very sincerely yours,
Iris
84D26727

Suggested Reading

Clark, D. (1991). *Analysis of return rates of the inmate college program participants.* Albany, NY: New York State Department of Correctional Services.

Lockwood, D. (1988). *Prison higher education, recidivism, and employment after release.* Unpublished manuscript, Utica College of Syracuse University.

Tracy, C., & Johnson, C. (1994). *Review of various outcome studies relating prison education to reduced recidivism.* Hunstville, TX: Windham School System.

Sources

Fine, M., Torre, M. E., Boudin, K., Bowen, I., Clark, J., Hylton, D., Martinez, M., Roberts R., Smart, P., & Upegui, D. (2001). *Changing minds*. New York: The Graduate Center of the City University of New York (*www. changingminds.ws*). A participatory-action research project focused on the impact of college-in-prison programs on women, their children, the prison environment, reincarceration rates, and tax expenditures.

Fine, M., Burns, A., Payne, Y., & Torre, M. E. (October 1, 2002). *Civic lessons*. UCLA's Institute for Democracy, Education, & Access. Williams Watch Series: *Investigating the Claims of Williams v. State of California*. Paper wws-rr003-1002. (http://repositories.cdlib.org/idea/wws/wws-rr003-1002) Expert testimony for *Williams v. California*, drawn from focus group interviews and surveys with 102 California elementary, middle, and high school students attending schools with inadequate facilities, undercredentialed faculty, and insufficient instructional materials.

The Opportunity Gap Project. Michelle Fine, Principal Investigator; María Elena Torre, Project Director; with Janice Bloom, April Burns, Lori Chajet, Monique Guishard, Yasser Payne, Tiffany Perkins-Munn, and Kersha Smith. Funded by the Rockefeller Foundation with Leslie Glass and Spencer support. This project involves a two-year participatory youth research design in which a diverse collective of youth researchers, drawn from urban and suburban schools, created a survey on youth perspectives on schooling and social justice (n = 7,049 students across 15 schools districts), conducted focus group and individual interviews with youth across urban and suburban lines (n = 94 youth in focus groups), cross-visited schools, generated original research on questions of statewide finance inequity, tracking, and differential suspension rates by race/ethnicity. A detailed description of the study design can be found in Torre, M. E., & Fine, M. (2003). Youth researchers critically reframe questions of educational justice. *Harvard Evaluation Exchange*, 9 (2), pp. 6, 22. Preliminary analyses can be found in Fine et al. (2005). *Dear Zora: A Letter to Zora Neale Hurston Fifty Years After Brown*. Teachers College Record.

MAXINE GREENE

LEARNING TO COME ALIVE

Dear President:

I am sure that, like most of us, you are interested in education for democracy as much as you are in education for its own sake. Clearly, that means something more than an emphasis on skills or even basic literacy, important as these skills are. Education for democracy has to do with the deliberate nurture of *reflectiveness, curiosity, imagination,* and what has been called "a passion for the possible."

Those involved in teaching and learning cannot be expected simply to comply with what is taken for granted. In classrooms, situations must be created that provoke questioning and that move students to go in search of meanings that they can achieve for themselves. In this search for meaning, a capacity must be developed that calls for students to look through a range of perspectives: those of the various disciplines, those of the diverse human beings they are bound to meet in the course of their lives, and those derived from their own life experiences. The point I am making is that a mode of aliveness must be encouraged; democracy, or what has been called "a community always in the making," cannot be attained by the passive, the careless, or the thoughtless. What must connect us all are the values by which we choose to live together: fairness, equality, regard for others, and the sense of our being the initiators of our own lives.

For the student, there must be a continual awareness of perceptions only partially visible, of doorways still to be unlocked. It is through the arts that students can experience this awareness, as they are exposed to multiple vantage points. Imagination sets the mind in motion when, in a quest for understanding, it reaches out toward what might be. This is one reason for placing the arts in a central place where education is concerned. *Alternative pathways open new modes of questioning, of confronting, of resolving. The arts must never be merely decorative.* Literature, drama, film, music, painting: Each has the power, when grasped by consciousness, to radiate through experience, moving from memory to meanings. When we are engaged, we are alive to the presence of an art form—whether it is a Rilke poem, a Cezanne mountain jutting outward and opening a field ordinarily closed, or a Toni Morrison novel grounded in the earth and revealing something never suspected before. Some art forms shed a remarkable light; others immerse us in the shades of darkness. But, again, they bring us a heightened sense of existence if we take the time to experience them as meaningful.

The arts, as you may recall from your own experience, provide moments of freedom and presence that bring together not only the past and the present, but also the inside and outside as people begin to realize that education and schooling are human creations that are always in the making. *They are ways of coming alive just as learning is a matter of coming alive and becoming different*—even for those who prefer to remain in the familiar, despite its deficiencies and lacks.

Personal and social education can communicate that individual fulfillment depends a great deal on being a *member*—a participant— in shared undertakings and concerns. It seems evident that someone like you, Mr. President, who has long since consciously chosen to take an active part in public life, has discovered the importance of collaboration, joint activity, cooperation, and communion within a public space. Educators and policymakers must become aware of the

ways in which such collaborations may lead, in time, to the emer-
gence of an articulate public to which our political representatives
cannot but be moved to respond. This is at the heart of educating for
democracy.

Teachers may find themselves changing as more challenges are
posed by the increasing demands of diversity. There are unfamiliar
cultures to be understood and unfamiliar notions of what learning
should entail. Customary objectives must be reexamined. Teachers
must ask themselves what they do in classrooms and other spaces
where students gather. Even what has long been believed to be
effective teaching must be reexamined. Criticisms have been raised
of practices that seem too relativistic or too fundamentalist. Some
argue vehemently for a stress on content and contextual learning, as
in history; others insist that history is "now," and should be taught
with reference to contemporary questions and from many different
points of view. Some believe that we must teach toward the dominant culture, others talk about the need for a delayed recognition
of the silenced voices of people excluded by history and the social
sciences—women, persons of African ancestry, former slaves, Native
Americans, and newly arrived immigrants.

What are teachers to think of as accomplishment? Should the
emphasis be on assimilation and socialization, or should the focus be
on a regard for differences instead? For all of the present-day insis-
tence on "uniform curriculum" and on the right of administrators and
officials to shape curriculum, decide on assessment, and announce
standards, the practicing teacher within the classroom today has to
make existential choices at particular moments of classroom life. This
means choices made on the teacher's own responsibility, with all the
anxiety that comes from there being no "right answer." However,
teachers who communicate a sense of open possibility are often able
to make their feelings contagious and to enlist their students in the
pursuit of meanings that belong to the realm of possibility. When
this happens, apathy as well as passivity are overcome. On their own
initiative, students may view themselves as beginners who are ven-
turing into an unknown land. Upon entering, some students may be
shocked into a new awareness, a new recognition of injustices. Some

students may try to find out what can be done to involve members of the public in protest or reform. Still other students may seek ways in which they can offer help without demeaning those in need. Again, it is a matter of choosing a way of acting and of being. This is a reasonable expectation for learning at a time when public spaces need to be opened and people need to be willing to risk taking action in an uncertain and unpredictable world. As Emily Dickinson wrote, "Imagination lights the slow fuse of possibility;" surely some sense of the possible must infuse our commitment to learn.

Education, when examined from without, deals with trends and tendencies rather than personal choices. Rules, regulations, and instructions are intended to avoid predicaments, and those who look at schooling from a distance are convinced that they do so. When viewed from within, however, no rule book or set of prescriptions can determine what ought to be done at particular moments in the classroom. We have discovered by now that no two classroom situations are precisely alike and, obviously, no group of young people is composed of identical individuals. Not only must the teacher improvise, he or she, more seriously, must choose an approach, a series of practices, a set of gestures, and even a tone of voice in response to what a particular situation seems to demand.

This mode of thinking can only be found if education is viewed not from the outside, but from within, from the vantage points of the teachers, learners, parents, and members of a community. Yet many people, when they pay attention to education, focus upon a school *system* and come to identify the system with schooling. The system is an institution comprised of a set of offices, bureaus, and meeting rooms where policy for the schools is made and rules and regulations are defined. Prescriptions for curriculum and subject matter are handed down a ladder of authority to those who are concerned with an area of practice. Those who are instructed to comply with it in classrooms (teachers and others) are seldom consulted or informed in advance. Hierarchical, and in many ways impersonal, the controls are experienced as they typically are in bureaucracies: as "rule by no one." There is rarely any certainty with regard to who is making decisions and who takes responsibility. Personal choice and the idea of reaching beyond what is known, play little, if any part, in systems devoted to meeting mechanistic needs.

There is no question that public education requires many varieties of leadership and organization. Yet, if there is to be a proper regard for principles such as equity and respect for others, if there is to be at least some commitment to freedom of thought and speech, then those in authority must first be conscious of the importance of such norms. Even this does not ensure its inclusion in the curriculum any more than it ensures that "no child will be left behind," despite all the talk of literacies and technological expertise.

Mr. President, we hope you can reach back and recall the moments of aliveness and surprise you experienced in your own education. Even as you deal with policy and programs, we hope you can view education with memories of your own beginnings and your own initial plan of living. With you, we will reach forward toward what cannot be measured or defined with any certainty. And that may be the wonder of it: We can become alive as never before to visions of what we might be and of what is forever not yet. Only then will educating for democracy become a realized possibility.

In anticipation,

Maxine Greene

KEN ROLLING &
SANDRA HALLADEY

VOICES CLOSEST TO THE
ONES WE LOVE

Ken Rolling

Sandra Halladey and her
two children, Emma and William .

Dear Sir or Madam

We write this letter on behalf of parents
whose children attend public schools
in communities across the nation. Our
work through the organization Parents
for Public Schools expands parents' roles in improving the quality of
all public schools. We implore you to listen to the voices and ideas
of parents and students in all of your deliberations about improving
and preserving public education in this country. We are the voices
closest to the schools we love, and we have the highest expectations
for their improvement.

Our families—children and parents alike—benefit most directly
from excellent, democratically managed schools, and we bear the
lifelong consequences when our public schools fail. We know better than most the successes and challenges the present system faces
because our children are in the schools every day.

We are committed to public schools as the bedrock of our democratic society. This commitment challenges all attempts to abandon public schools. If public schools are not good enough for our own children,

why should they be acceptable for anyone else's? It is a sad reflection on our cities that twenty to thirty percent of school-age children attend private school. Public schools must be a viable option for all. Access to an excellent education must not be tied to family income. We want what is best for all children as they learn the importance of contributing to a caring and just local, national, and even international community.

Free and open public schools are the only institutions in our country that offer access to full participation in our democracy. Our public schools should exclude no one who is willing to learn or participate. We intend to guard that opportunity even as we work to prepare parents adequately for involvement that goes beyond the homework table or the bake sale. However, for parents to take responsibility for their part in shaping the best schools possible, we must be included at the decision-making table.

Research repeatedly demonstrates that schools and school districts do better when parents are engaged as equal partners in the decision making that affects their children and their schools. We are our children's first teachers, we know our children better than anyone, and we have much insight to offer if given the opportunity to share our knowledge. Unfortunately, too few schools and districts actively seek to involve parents in the education process. We ask you to put the public back into public education by creating opportunities for all citizens to engage in public school improvement and reform. Only through this richer level of engagement will parents and the public at large better understand their vital connection to quality public education.

As the leader of the greatest nation in the world, you must use the bully pulpit of your office to speak about the value of public education and to energize the country to take note and participate in its improvement. We urge you to use the power of the presidency to highlight the many successful efforts to improve education in our public schools—successes that defy all excuses—so that they will be duplicated in other schools. Set our society on a positive course toward providing good schools for all students.

Mr./Madam President, we ask you to support our efforts to improve public schools for all students in rural, urban, and suburban communities across the country by focusing on the following:

Require that federal agencies, committees, and other rule-making bodies involve significant numbers of public school parents in their deliberative and decision-making processes. If you want parents to support regulations, policies, and financial decisions affecting public education, then let us work with you to shape these decisions. Effective parent engagement is not extra work; it is a necessary component of improved teaching and learning. Invest in the training of parents and educators for this responsibility.

Demand that public schools teach the children who actually live in their communities and not the students they wish they had. When parents send children to school, we ask that they be accepted, respected, and taught with equal commitment to each student. As our country becomes more diverse, we need to understand differences in cultures, values, and learning styles. Public schools must model mutual respect for all individuals so that students learn how to live and work in a world as varied as ours has become.

Recommend that educators see the whole child and that they take note of who their students are, where they come from, and what their families' experiences are. Encourage and support community-based programs that connect students and families to local resources through public schools, thus keeping children and families involved in school and learning.

Look for ways to increase financial and human resources aimed at improving our public schools. No matter how we interpret the data, our schools are lacking in both money and personnel. Many communities should be ashamed of the conditions they provide for teaching and learning. Our country must act on its commitment to public education and increase the resources dedicated to public schools at the local, state, and federal levels. Every school needs access to the resources and assistance necessary to develop the best teaching and learning experiences possible. Only when schools have these adequate resources (not luxuries) can we hold them accountable for improvements.

Look at the tremendous federal government outlays to schools of education at colleges and universities across this country and demand that those investments—our tax dollars—be directly linked to the improvement of public schools. These institutions of higher learning have absorbed uncounted millions of federal dollars—for example, in research grants—but those dollars are not tied to improving public education for all students. Criteria for awarding grants to any institution of higher learning should include requirements that the institution demonstrate how its research will directly improve public schools for all students in its community and beyond.

Reexamine the meaning and purpose of the reauthorization of the Elementary and Secondary Education Act, known as No Child Left Behind. NCLB has been misappropriated by partisan political forces to "dumb down" our learning expectations to one-size-fits-all standardized tests. Remove the crippling emphasis on punishment that frustrates positive learning. Instead, rekindle our public schools' commitment to help all children learn by supporting the many successful programs already in use—programs that both meet students' learning needs *and* take them to higher academic achievement. Examples of such programs can be found in the many successful efforts across the country to create small schools that are proven to reach and teach students more effectively. Other effective approaches include the implementation of improved professional development programs that help teachers successfully challenge their students to learn.

Use your influence to help America understand what it takes to improve this country's public schools and the public education experience for all students. We know how to teach every child in America already. What this nation lacks is the equitable distribution of resources and the public will to implement these programs everywhere. We parents know how many years it takes to nurture and rear caring, contributing citizens for this country. We expect patience and determination from our communities and our struggling schools.

Use your leadership from the oval office to open our public education system to include family learning centers where we can learn with our children. While we are gravely concerned about the education our children are getting, many parents are also concerned about their own lack of education in these times of rapid changes in the employment world. Public schools can provide new learning opportunities for any citizen willing to take advantage of the offerings. We need public schools to once again take their position as the cornerstone of a healthy community.

Abandon the illusion of vouchers as a tool for school improvement. Vouchers will not fix our schools; they simply let schools and communities off the hook. Help us share a common vision backed by hard work, adequately trained and supported professionals, and community involvement to fix our schools.

WE EXPECT NOTHING SHORT OF HIGH STANDARDS and accountability at every level of our public school system—for the students who walk through the school doors, their families, teachers, principals, superintendents, school boards, and elected public officials. But we must balance that accountability with the flexibility of local control so that parents, along with educators and the community, determine the best educational opportunities for their students.

Do this for every school and every student: Make certain the playing field is level with resources. Parents want to know that you see success as inevitable and will not accept failure as an option.

Our nation looks to your leadership to ensure that all children can be educated well in a publicly funded school system. To accomplish this, a new commitment to parent involvement is required. Encourage us. Join us. Together we can make it happen.

Sincerely,

Ken Rolling   Sandra Halladey

A NATION OF LEARNERS

Dear Mr. President,

As a parent and a former teacher, I am writing to ask you to use your bully pulpit to reinvigorate the national discussion on education in this country and open it up to new voices. As both a long-time grassroots organizer and a citizen who cares about the vibrancy of our civil society, I believe it is imperative to America's future and prosperity that you do so.

For too long, the debate on improving our children's learning has centered around a narrow field of insiders—many of whom have little day-to-day experience in educating young people. Parents, children, and others who have a wealth of knowledge and experience in this field have been shut out of the discussion about kids and learning. It's time to have the politicians in Washington and the lawmakers in the state house move over and let the people who know best how to create success for kids in schools—parents, teachers, and students—lead the discussion on improving schools so that our children can really learn.

At no other time in our country's history has it been so important to have America be a nation of learners. Learning is the fuel that allows our communities to grow and to adapt to changes, as well as to solve emerging problems. Our public education system was created so that everyone in this country would have an opportunity to learn. All of us have a stake in a healthy public education system. So why not engage all of us in making decisions about our public education system? Engaging new voices in a genuine exploration of how to ensure success for every child will lead to a new and greater understanding of the changes we need, as well as a nationwide commitment to making these policy changes.

If you are truly committed to creating the best education system in the world, you will work to ensure that there are real ways for parents and students to have an impact on education in their communities. This simple step of involving those most affected by these decisions does not cost a dime.

The current education policy, as embodied in the No Child Left Behind Act, limits the ability of educators, administrators, and local school boards to use their expertise to create schools that will best meet the needs of their local students. While the No Child Left Behind Act may have been a well-intentioned effort to raise standards and accountability, it is hurting children across the country by refusing to recognize their uniqueness and diversity. Instead of engaging students in learning, it actually has resulted in kids being pushed out of schools and has pitted parents against teachers, and teachers against administrators. Worst of all, the students' learning is often geared to the test, not to the kind of skills that will prepare them for the lifelong learning they will need to succeed in a constantly changing world.

Rather than meeting the promise of closing the achievement gap, No Child Left Behind is widening that gap as districts, under tremendous pressure to show progress on tests, push growing numbers of students out of the system into an educational limbo. They have neither passed nor failed, they have just simply become "invisible." This is a tragedy. We as a nation cannot tolerate losing the potential that these "invisible" children represent. No Child Left Behind is causing thousands of young people to see themselves as failures, and they are now truly left behind any promise of good jobs and a bright future. The harsh consequences for these young people can only be imagined, but I assure you the cost to their communities and our country will be profoundly real.

Public education is in crisis, yet real results can be achieved and will be achieved because parents and students are no longer willing to leave the task to others. All across this country, people are organizing. They are seeking out educators and researchers who know what works and what does not. Parents for Public Schools, for example, has organized chapters of parents who have worked with school officials to strengthen their local public school systems. The Parent Leadership Training Institute (PLTI) in Connecticut has trained parents to become advocates for their children by teaching them to become practiced change agents in their community. One PLTI graduate created the first after-school program in a large housing complex in Stamford, Connecticut. Another adapted some of the PLTI techniques to increase attendance by fifty percent at PTO meetings.

There are answers to the questions of how to solve the problems of student achievement, a shortage of quality teachers, and a growing discontent that our children leave the education system less prepared than they should be.

I know that by engaging new voices in the education policy arena you can change the way these problems are seen and, in doing so, make breakthrough policy changes on these issues and more. We lived for five decades on the brink of nuclear confrontation. Citizens built bridges and literally tore down walls that separated East and West, ending the Cold War. As both a founder of a local campaign to protect the citizens of Denver from plutonium at Rocky Flats and as a founder and international representative for the Nuclear Freeze movement, I was there in the midst of these changes. Politicians were the last to see the changes coming, but the people of Europe and local communities throughout this country had a vision beyond mutual assured destruction (MAD), the official "security policy" for half a century. That vision of a peaceful end to the Cold War became reality and smart world leaders accepted its inevitability and ushered in a new world order. New and different dangers persist, but the face of global politics was changed from the bottom-up.

More recently, families and patients whose lives are most affected by policies about medical research have organized to ensure increased funding for medical research and have kept narrow, partisan politics from determining the future of stem cell research. These families, fueled by their hope for a cure, share a vision of lives unmarred by debilitating diseases such as Alzheimer's, Parkinson's, and juvenile diabetes, to name a few. Their voices, experiences, and determination are the most powerful assets they have to shape the future. When the Juvenile Diabetes Research Foundation (JDRF) wanted policymakers to understand the critical need to find a cure for juvenile diabetes, JDRF families organized a Children's Congress so that children could share their personal stories about the disease. The power of child delegates telling members of Congress and administration officials in their own words what they endure on a daily basis with the disease and their dreams of a cure helped pave the way for a solution on the research issue that was above the partisan fray of Washington, D.C.

To borrow a phrase, policy is too important to be left to the "experts." Isn't this what a democracy is all about, anyway? If leaders want positive, lasting results for our country, they will encourage and allow citizens who pay taxes to have a say in the policy decisions that affect them.

I would like to propose a three-step plan to put the public back into the discussion of our public education system.

First, we must commit to engaging new voices and to improving education for all kids in this country. As president, you should organize forums around the country to address these three basic questions:

- What kind of education do we want for all of our children?
- What changes could we make to get that kind of education for all children?
- How do we ensure that the voices of parents, teachers, students, and people who care deeply about public education influence the decisions made at the local, state, and national levels?

You will be surprised at how much information you will get from these forums—not the least of which are concrete ideas and models for success that have already been created. Go out among the people and mine the richness of this country for the wisdom, innovation, and problem solving that we need. Ask that local officials attend the forums, and hear firsthand the concerns of citizens in their community. Make sure that some of the forums are broadcast so that the broadest possible audience can participate in the conversation. In order to shine a spotlight on these forums, host a White House Town Hall and invite a wide range of stakeholders—especially parents and students—to come together to have a *new* conversation about education in this country. The answers that emerge from these forums would provide the roadmap for local, state, and national leaders to create policies that truly meet the needs of *all* children.

Second, you must do more to engage students in this national discussion. Visit more schools and talk to children about the importance of education in their roles as citizens of this country. Ask them to tell you about their best moments in school. Solicit pictures, stories, essays, speeches, plays, or poems from students in all grades. Inspire and encourage them to share their insights, ideas, and dreams about learning and school. There is no doubt that they have insights about how to create schools where learning flourishes and where they will thrive. By asking the children, *and listening to them*, we would learn firsthand what works.

Third, challenge governors and mayors to find their own ways to create opportunities for citizens to have a larger role in developing education policy. Urge them to ask for regular parent meetings with superintendents, or to work with local radio stations to hold a monthly question-and-answer session between school officials and parents. Challenge local school board officials to create a governance role for parents in their schools.

I BEGAN WRITING THIS TO YOU AS A PARENT who knows from talking to other parents that there is a hunger for a new debate on education, one that acknowledges the importance of having our children experience the joy of learning. I end this letter knowing, as a grassroots organizer, that the parents and students of this country are now mobilizing to create this new national discussion. The changes they seek are inevitable. They are as inevitable as the changes that eventually brought down the Berlin Wall and those that changed the face of South Africa. People have been stirred to action by their own experience of education and by the disillusionment in the faces of their own children, who have lost the joy of learning.

People know that better, more responsive, and more responsible schools are possible. They may be difficult to build, but they are possible. The only missing ingredient is the political will of elected leaders. The smart and true leader of our country will encourage the wisdom and experience of these citizens. The president will harness their creativity and dedication to renew the nation's commitment to our kids and to their future as lifelong learners and educated citizens. If you only do one thing to strengthen our democracy and to prepare the country for a new global role and a secure place in the global economy, you will help change schools for kids.

Sincerely,

Pam Solo

ELIZABETH DeBRAY-PELOT

CRAFTING LEGISLATION

Dear Mr. / Mrs. President,

By now, your party will have crafted a set of education policy proposals, some of which are undoubtedly in competition with those of the opposing party. They will have been touted in your stump speech and perhaps will survive as major priorities of your administration. But whether you are an advocate for vouchers and privatization, for test-based reforms, or some mix of both, I'd like to offer some advice on how you can make the legislative policy process in Congress a less divisive and more inclusive one than it was during the last Elementary and Secondary Education Act (ESEA) reauthorization.

What do I mean by "inclusive"? Isn't it the prerogative of the president and the majority party in Congress to pursue their legislative agendas? Yes. A heightened partisan tone in current education policy debates is inevitable, as the Republicans gained a new advantage with the passage of No Child Left Behind. But let me give several examples of what I mean by inclusiveness. Back in 2001, the partisan tone was at such a fever pitch that the policy process pushed right past the suggestions of researchers, who drew on data from North Carolina and Texas to question the efficacy of the single-test accountability model that would label most schools as "needing improvement," and state legislators, whose main membership association protested what it saw as the flaws in such a system. There was only one congressional hearing in the Senate for NCLB in 2001, and Secretary of Education Rod Paige was the sole witness. Interest groups such as teacher and administrator membership associations were termed the "blob"—"big learning organization bureaucracy"—by committee staff. These groups were viewed as representing the educational "status quo" and were accused of blocking "true" education reform for decades. Meanwhile, new players, mainly center-to-right think tanks, business groups, and organizations advocating for poor and minority students, gained an ear with members of Congress and their aides.

None of this is surprising. The old coalitions of education lobbyists, Democratic committee staff, and presidential administrations of the 1970s and 1980s were bound to have been transformed by the Republicans' consistent majority leadership since 1994. As education became a far more visible issue for both governors and the president during the 1990s and moved far higher on the list of voters' concerns, Republicans naturally sought a platform beyond shutting down the Education Department. Faced with passing an omnibus education bill in 1999–2000, the Republican majority in Congress was more apt to consult with ideologically aligned think tanks than with practitioner groups.

Too often, this partisanship has not encouraged an environment in which tough questions about the unintended consequences of NCLB's policies could be posed—questions concerning high school completion rates, student retention, curriculum narrowing in high-poverty schools, effects of testing on limited English–proficiency students, White flight from integrated schools under public school choice, and so on. The passage of NCLB has led many state and local leaders and school administrators to be out-and-out hostile to whatever regulations make it through Congress without their consultation. It is always important to question in whose interests a particular group is speaking, but the exclusion of practitioners in the development of NCLB is making it much harder to solve problems of practice.

So I think that one of your most important responsibilities, both on the campaign trail and in your future dealings with Congress on education policy, is to cultivate an environment where difficult, substantive questions about policy are raised openly and directly. When working with Congress to craft legislation that will affect high-poverty schools, it will be critical for you and your advisors to consult the research community. Summon those who know the most about what Title I schools are like and about the conditions of teaching and learning inside them—those who have spent the past several years studying NCLB's effects at ground level. Also, seek out and listen to those who understand how the broader social policy context affects the "achievement gap," which many contributors to this volume have emphasized. Think tanks are far more prominent players in policy now, and will be issuing sparring reports with numerous new policy recommendations. Just bear in mind that many reports published by think tanks across the ideological spectrum that are touted as "research" are often not research at all, but rather are heavily ideologically based policy positions. Surround yourself with advisors who can discern the difference.

Another important point to remember is that you will be more effective in crafting legislation if you or your advisors negotiate with the education committee members in the party opposing you. NCLB's passage, although a compromise, did not change the core beliefs and ideologies between the two parties on education. Many conservative members still despise the universal testing provisions as intrusive federal intervention in state matters; most Democrats want to see higher funding levels for the bill's programs. By the time of your inauguration, the two parties' positions will likely have hardened even further.

Another component that was missing from the last ESEA reauthorization was adequate time. The bill that became NCLB went into the conference or resolution phase in the summer of 2001. After September 11, the president placed enormous pressure on the four committee leaders to get the bill out of conference and back to the floor as quickly as possible. Interest groups representing practitioners were not able to see and react to the testing and accountability provisions of the bill. Although this rushed conference phase did secure the president and Congress a domestic victory, the price was that numerous policy details about the "workability" of the accountability system were never adequately addressed. Not wanting to be viewed as "anti-accountability," most members of Congress voted in favor of the bill with minimal to no knowledge about what its provisions would mean for real schools. As chief executive, you have the power of the bully pulpit to strongly encourage House and Senate leaders to give adequate consideration to questions of capacity.

Since our federal education system is still implemented by state and local authorities, you and your staff would do well to seek out and listen to their concerns. Meet with teachers, administrators, local citizens, and parents in both big cities and rural areas to gain a reliable picture of what the law actually means at ground level. State education administrators have been stretched to the breaking point both financially and energy-wise, over the past six years. No matter what new set of education policies Congress enacts, if state officials do not have the required technical and fiscal capacity, they cannot be meaningfully implemented. As for the public, NCLB is not the only educational concern in their mind, as I am sure you found out on the campaign trail. Citizens will want to weigh in about the rising cost of a college education and access to high-quality preschool programs, special education services, and workforce training.

I AM NOT SUGGESTING THAT YOU or anyone else can take party politics out of education policy. I do, however, think that it is possible and necessary for the president to set a tone of open inquiry, making it clear that legislation can and should be developed with due deliberation over the complexities of both policy implementation and effects. One way to accomplish that is to organize forums where the viewpoints of both NCLB advocates and dissenters may be heard, and, in turn, to try to sway Congress to take the same approach. As I write, the legislative agenda in the 110th Congress has broadened beyond the debate over the NCLB reauthorization to include national standards and the competitiveness agenda; and the number of interest groups and institutions attempting to be "players" in the policy process has grown significantly. Such competing agendas and disparate voices are healthy for the democratic process. I hope that you will embrace the principles of openness and inclusiveness as you seek to enact your own education agenda.

Sincerely,

Elizabeth De Bray-Pelot

Schools That Work for
All Children

Linda Darling-Hammond

Dear M. President,

Congratulations on your decisive victory. I know that your pledge to be a true education president made a big difference in getting out the vote. Americans have been saying for years that education is their number-one domestic priority and that investing in quality teaching is their number-one solution to the problems we face in our schools. Voters clearly believe you mean it when you say you will ensure that all children are served by caring, competent, and qualified teachers working in schools that are organized for success.

To meet the goals you have laid out, we will have to tackle some tough problems, including persistent inequalities that plague our schools, and we will need to invest in federal policies—like those we already have in place for medicine—to create a well-prepared teaching force for *all* students, not just those in the most well-to-do districts. Finally, we will need to restore sensible systems of accountability to our schools, supporting ambitious learning for all students by using standards and tests to improve teaching rather than to punish kids.

The Social and Economic Challenges We Face

More than ever before in our nation's history, education is the ticket not only to economic success but to basic survival. As you well know, the skills needed to succeed in today's economy are much greater than they were even two decades ago when your youngest son graduated from high school. Today, nearly seventy percent of all jobs require the higher levels of knowledge and skill once reserved for the education of the very few, and only about ten percent of jobs are available to low-skilled workers. Whereas a high school dropout had two chances out of three of getting a job twenty years ago, today he has less than one chance in three, and the job he can get pays less than half of what he once would have earned.

Because the economy can no longer absorb many unskilled workers at decent wages, lack of education is increasingly linked to crime and welfare dependency. Unfortunately, as a nation, our investments have tipped much more in the last two decades toward incarceration rather than education. During the 1980s and 1990s, national spending for corrections grew by over nine hundred percent, while prison populations nearly tripled. During the 1990s, there were more African American citizens in the criminal justice system than there were in college. During the same period, per pupil spending for schools grew by only about forty percent in real dollar terms, and less in cities, which have fallen further behind their suburban neighbors in acquiring the resources to educate a growing population of students, more of whom speak little English, live in poverty, lack health care, and have special educational needs.

Children who receive inadequate education are increasingly unlikely to be able to become productive citizens, yet many schools—especially those that serve large numbers of students of color—lack the courses, materials, equipment, and qualified teachers that would give students access to the education they will need to participate in today's and tomorrow's world. More than half the adult prison population has literacy skills below those required by the labor market, and nearly forty percent of adjudicated juvenile delinquents have treatable learning disabilities that went undiagnosed and untreated in the schools. In short, because we did not invest enough in their education, we have had to pay at least five times as much each year to keep them in jail.

Solving these problems will depend in part on a major overhaul of the federal No Child Left Behind Act (NCLB), so that it achieves its goals of improving underperforming schools, rather than inadvertently undermining our public education system. Although well-intentioned, it has become clear that NCLB will, in the next few years, label most of the nation's public schools "failing," even when they are improving in achievement. This will lead to reductions in federal funding to already under-resourced schools, and it will sidetrack funds needed for improvement to underwrite transfers for students to other schools. Furthermore, the incentives that NCLB creates to boost average school scores are likely to exacerbate the current surge in grade retention, drop-out, and push-out rates for low-income, "minority," and special needs students. If left unchanged, NCLB will deflect needed resources for teaching and learning to ever more intensive testing of students, ranking of schools, busing of students, and lawyers' fees.

Now don't get me wrong, I have nothing against lawyers. Some of my best friends (and my dear husband) are members of the bar. However, I would much rather see schools invest in children than in attorneys, whose bills already amount to hundreds of millions of dollars for lawsuits that defend states against pleas for equitable funding for students in under-resourced schools. Some of these suits also argue for protection from the consequences of state tests that deny many of these same students diplomas—and entry into the labor market—when they have not been offered the most basic conditions for learning.

We cannot long sustain a society that is so deeply divided in opportunity as the one we are now creating—one in which a large share of the population cannot find a way to contribute. At the most pragmatic level, there were twenty workers for every person on Social Security in 1950, but there will be only three such potential workers in 2020. We need every citizen to be prepared as a full participant, and, of course, that is what every child wants to be. For both moral and fiscal reasons, we cannot afford any more lost children in America.

You might be asking why we are in this situation and what we should do about it. Although the problems are complex, many of the solutions are straightforward for a president who understands what is going on and is committed to doing the right thing. First, we need to understand and address the underlying inequalities in our funding systems for schools. Second, we need to build an accountability system that helps schools improve and ensures that students get the learning opportunities they deserve. And finally, we need to support the provision of highly qualified teachers to all schools just as we support the training and distribution of doctors to all communities.

The Problem of Educational Inequality

Few Americans are aware that, unlike most countries that fund schools centrally and equally, the richest U.S. public schools spend at least ten times more than the poorest schools; these disparities contribute to a wider achievement gap in this country than in virtually any other industrialized country, as well as the inability of many children to make a living, pay taxes, and become solid members of the community. I am convinced that if Americans knew about this, they would not stand for it. I think we understand that our public education system exists to ensure that all people can become productive members of this society. And we know that Thomas Jefferson was right when he said, "A people who would be ignorant and free wants what never was and never will be." This drives our national commitment to public education. It should also drive the reforms that you seek.

Ten years ago, we talked about how deeply distressed you felt when you read Jonathan Kozol's *Savage Inequalities*, replete with examples of schools that lack the basics of a sound education. Those disparities have not lessened in recent years. Across the country, schools that serve large numbers of low-income students and students of color have larger class sizes; fewer teachers and counselors; and fewer and lower-quality academic courses, extracurricular activities, books, materials, supplies, computers, libraries, and special services. Because it is hard for many of us whose children receive the best of education to imagine what school is like for students who do not, I'd like to share with you a short description of Luther Burbank school, which serves low-income students of color in San Francisco and is one of many schools attended by children who are plaintiffs in *Williams v. California,* an equal educational opportunity lawsuit:

> At Luther Burbank school, students cannot take textbooks home for homework in any core subject because their teachers have enough textbooks for use in class only. . . . Some math, science, and other core classes do not have even enough textbooks for all the students in a single class to use during the school day, so some students must share the same one book during class time. . . . For homework, students must take home photocopied pages, with no accompanying text for guidance or reference, when and if their teachers have enough paper to use to make homework copies. . . . The social studies textbook Luther Burbank students use is so old that it does not reflect the breakup of the former Soviet Union. Luther Burbank is infested with vermin and roaches, and students routinely see mice in their classrooms. One dead rodent has remained, decomposing, in a corner in the gymnasium since the beginning of the school year. The school library is rarely open, has no librarian, and has not recently been updated. Luther Burbank classrooms do not have computers. Computer instruction and research skills are not, therefore, part of Luther Burbank students' regular instruction in their core courses. The school no longer offers any art classes for budgetary reasons. Two of the three bathrooms at Luther Burbank are locked all day, every day. The third bathroom is locked during lunch and other periods during the school day, so there are times during school when no bathroom at all is available for students to use. Students have urinated or defecated on themselves at school because they could not get into an unlocked bathroom. . . . When the bathrooms are not locked, they often lack toilet paper, soap, and paper towels, and the toilets frequently are clogged and overflowing. . . . Ceiling tiles are missing and cracked in the school gym, and school children are afraid to play basketball and other games

in the gym because they worry that more ceiling tiles will fall on them during their game. . . . The school heating system does not work well. In winter, children often wear coats, hats, and gloves during class to keep warm. Eleven of the thirty-five teachers at Luther Burbank have not yet obtained regular, nonemergency credentials, and seventeen of the thirty-five teachers only began teaching at Luther Burbank this school year (*Williams v. State of California*, Superior Court of the State of CA for the County of San Francisco, 2001, Complaint, 58–66).

Most Americans would be surprised that this kind of school setting is a reality for hundreds of thousands of children in the wealthiest nation on earth. It should be no surprise that the low-income and minority students at Luther Burbank and schools like it achieve at low levels and often fail state-imposed tests, ending their school careers with less opportunity to play a productive role in society than when they began as eager kindergartners. A new generation of equity lawsuits has emerged in Alabama, California, Florida, New York, South Carolina, and elsewhere to try to correct this unfair situation. In 2004, the highest court in New York ordered the state to provide more equal resources; however, the outcome in other states is still unclear. Children should not have to wait for expensive lawsuits to wend their way through the courts in order to have a reasonable chance at a decent education in the United States of America. They need your leadership on this agenda.

There are at least two things that you, with help of Congress, can do about this. First, you can rekindle the federal commitment to schools in cities and poor rural areas—investing in programs like those that were in place during the 1970s, when we began to close the spending gap and the achievement gap for low-income children. At that time, before budget cuts sliced the federal share of education funding from more than twelve percent to only half that level, funds were targeted to needy schools for teacher training and recruitment, magnet schools, preschools, after-school programs, and special education supports. Although some complain about the ineffectiveness of federal programs, the evidence shows that efforts providing quality preschool, effective reading programs, and stronger teacher training made a difference in educational opportunity and achievement for urban and poor rural schoolchildren. Fully funding federal programs that support these high-yield investments under No Child Left Behind, Head Start, and the special education provisions of IDEA would go a long way toward allowing schools to meet the needs of their children and the expectations of our society.

In addition, you can work to amend the No Child Left Behind Act so that standards for equitable educational opportunity are tied to standards for learning. Test score results should be published alongside indicators of learning opportunities: the availability of qualified teachers, appropriate courses, materials and equipment, and necessary services. States should be asked to show progress in assuring that, while schools and students are expected to meet standards of learning, they also have an equitable "opportunity to learn."

Reforming Accountability

You can also lead Congress in rethinking what accountability ought to mean under the No Child Left Behind Act, which has waylaid the "standards-based" reform movement that began in the early 1990s. Since 1990, virtually all states have created new standards reflecting what students should know and be able to do, new curriculum frameworks to guide instruction, and new assessments to test students' knowledge. Advocates of these reforms have hoped that setting standards would mobilize resources for student learning—including high-quality curricula, materials, and assessments tied to the standards; more widely available course offerings that reflect the high-quality curricula; more intensive teacher preparation guided by related standards for teaching; more equal resources for schools; and more readily available safety nets for educationally needy students.

This comprehensive approach has been followed in some states and districts, including Connecticut, Kentucky, Maine, Maryland, Minnesota, Nebraska, North Carolina, Vermont, and Washington, among others. In these cases, thoughtful assessments have been tied to investments in improved schooling and teaching. These efforts have begun to improve student achievement while enhancing teaching and increasing educational opportunity. Many of these states created sophisticated assessments that measure critical thinking and real performance in areas such as writing, mathematical and scientific problem solving, and research. They developed their systems carefully over a sustained period of time and have used them primarily to inform ongoing school improvement—including curriculum changes, professional development, and additional investments—rather than to punish students or schools.

Much of this effort threatens to be undone by NCLB. The biggest problem with NCLB is that it mistakes measuring schools for fixing them. It sets annual test score goals for every school—and for subgroups of students within schools—that are said to constitute "Adequate Yearly Progress." Unfortunately, the targets—based on the notion that one hundred percent of students will score at the "proficient" level on state tests by the year 2010—were set without an understanding of what this goal would really mean. One researcher has calculated that it would take schools more than one hundred years to reach such a targets in all content areas if they continued the rate of progress they were making in the 1990s.

More problematic is that NCLB requires that schools be declared "failing" if they fail to meet these targets for each subgroup of students. It requires the largest gains from lower-performing schools, ignoring the fact that these schools serve needier students and are generally less well-funded than those serving wealthier and higher-scoring students. Some estimates indicate that well over half of the nation's schools will be declared "failing" in the next few years under NCLB's current definition, even many that already score high and those that are steadily improving from year to year. According to NCLB, students must be allowed to transfer out of "failing" schools at the school's expense, schools stand to be reconstituted, and states and districts stand to lose funds based on these designations. Ironically, states that use more ambitious tests and have set higher standards for themselves will have more schools designated as "failures" even though they actually perform at higher levels. Some believe that this Alice in Wonderland process of labeling most public schools as "failing" will lead to a nationwide voucher proposal, inviting parents to bail out of public schools for private schools that are not even held accountable to the same measures.

One of the first perverse consequences of NCLB is that many states have formally lowered their standards in order to avoid having most of their schools declared failing. Another perverse consequence is that states that have worked hard to create forward-looking assessment systems during the 1990s have begun to abandon them, since they do not fit the federal mandate for annual testing that allows students and schools to be ranked and compared.

Finally, the federal mandate is likely to exacerbate the negative side effects of high-stakes testing that have increasingly emerged in states that attach rewards and sanctions to students' scores on standardized tests, such as grade promotion and graduation for students; merit pay awards or threats of dismissal for teachers and administrators; and bonuses or loss of funding, accreditation, or reconstitution for schools. In states where "high-stakes testing" is the primary reform, thousands of students who have failed tests for promotion and graduation have been denied diplomas and held back in grade—a policy that has consistently been found to increase drop-out rates without improving achievement—without having received adequate teaching, texts, curricula, or other educational resources. In these states, two-way accountability does not exist: The child is accountable to the state for test performance, but the state is not held accountable to the child for providing a basic level of education.

Recent studies have found that systems that reward or sanction schools based on average student scores (rather than looking at the growth of individual students) create incentives for schools that push low-scorers into special education so that their scores won't count in school reports, retain students in grade so that their grade-level scores will look better, exclude low-scoring students from admissions, and encourage such students to leave schools or drop out. Rising drop-out rates in Georgia, Florida, Massachusetts, New York, and Texas have been tied to the effects of grade retention, student discouragement, and school exclusion and transfer policies stimulated by high-stakes tests.

Although the hope is that such carrots will force schools to improve, this does not necessarily occur. Last year, we learned that the "Texas Miracle," which was the model for No Child Left Behind, boosted test scores, in part, by keeping many students out of the testing count and by making tens of thousands disappear from school altogether. At Sharpstown High School in Houston, a freshman class of one thousand dwindled to fewer than three hundred students by senior year, and—like many high schools in Texas—the miracle is that not one dropout was reported. In Texas, fewer than seventy percent of White students who enter ninth grade graduate from high school four years later, and the proportions for African American and Latino students are under fifty percent.

The consequences for individual students can be tragic, as most cannot go on to further education or even military service if they fail to graduate. The consequences for society are even worse, as more students are dropping out of school earlier without the skills to be able to join the economy. In Massachusetts, for example, drop-out rates have skyrocketed as its exit exam requirements went into effect in 2003. Not only did the state go from having one of the top cohort graduation rates in the nation (nearly eighty percent) to one of the lowest (close to sixty percent), but students have been dropping out much earlier—some with only a seventh- or eighth-grade education—and few are returning to school. Many are losing touch with their futures.

Take, for instance, the case of twenty-year-old Tracey Newhart of Falmouth, Massachusetts, who left school without a diploma because she could not pass the exam on repeated attempts. Although Newhart has Down syndrome, a chromosome disorder that causes mental retardation, last year she beat local caterers and won an award in a cooking competition. Having worked hard to pass her classes throughout fifteen years of school, she had pinned her hopes on attending culinary school. Her dream dashed, Tracey joined four thousand three hundred other Massachusetts seniors who failed the exam after multiple attempts—forty percent of whom are special needs students, along with an estimated seventeen thousand students who had already dropped out of school since ninth grade, discouraged by their inability to pass the single high-stakes test that determines whether they can join the labor market and go on to become productive citizens in life.

In addition to the limits of punishments for motivating students, sanctions for low-scoring schools appear to reduce the likelihood that the schools can attract and keep qualified teachers. For example, Florida's use of aggregate test scores—unadjusted for student characteristics—to allocate school rewards and sanctions led to reports that qualified teachers were leaving the schools rated D or F in droves, to be replaced by teachers without experience or training. As one principal queried, "Is anybody going to want to dedicate their lives to a school that has already been labeled a failure?"

As president, you will need to lead the process of amending NCLB so that states have flexibility and encouragement to keep using thoughtful performance assessments and so that tests are used appropriately for informing curriculum improvements, but not for punishing students or schools. Annual progress should be evaluated with "value-added" measures showing how individual students improve over time, rather than school averages that are influenced by changes in who is taking the test. Schools that are struggling should receive help to strengthen their staffs and adopt successful programs.

Just mandating high-stakes tests does not provide what parents and children would call genuine accountability. Obviously, students will not learn to higher levels unless they experience good teaching, a strong curriculum, and adequate resources. Most of the students who are struggling are students who have long experienced suboptimal schooling and students who have special learning needs that require higher levels of expertise from teachers. Because this nation has not yet invested heavily in teachers and their knowledge, the capacity to teach all students to high levels is not widespread. Only by investing in strong teaching can we improve the instruction of students who are currently struggling to learn; adding tests and punishments will not do the trick.

Ensuring Qualified Teachers

One of the greatest shortcomings of the schools serving our neediest students is that they typically have the least-experienced and least-qualified teachers, even though such students need our most skilled teachers if they are to learn what they need to know. Although recent studies have found that teacher quality is one of the most important school variables influencing student achievement, teachers are the most inequitably distributed school resource. Although states do not allow the hiring of doctors, lawyers, or engineers who have not met licensing standards, about thirty states still allow the hiring of untrained teachers who do not meet their certification standards, most of whom are assigned to teach the most disadvantaged students in low-income and high-minority schools while the most highly educated teachers are typically hired by wealthier schools.

In states that have lowered standards rather than increasing incentives to teaching, it is not hard to find urban and poor rural schools where one third or more of the teachers are working without training, certification, or mentoring. In schools with the highest minority enrollments, students have less than a fifty percent chance of getting a mathematics or science teacher with a license and a degree in the field that they teach. Thus, students who are the least likely to have learning supports at home are also the least likely to have teachers who understand how children learn and develop, who know how to teach them to read and problem solve, and who know what to do if they are having difficulty.

Studies of underprepared teachers find that they have difficulty with curriculum development, classroom management, student motivation, and teaching strategies. They tend to revert to rote learning strategies such as workbooks and reading kits that require little planning, and are less likely to use strategies that have been found to be more effective, such as hands-on manipulatives and problem solving in math, laboratory work in science, and integrated reading and writing strategies using a wide variety of reading materials in language arts. With little knowledge about how to teach effectively, these teachers are less able to plan and redirect instruction to meet students' needs. They are also less likely to see it as their job to do so, often blaming the students if their teaching is not successful.

One of the great ironies of the federal education programs designed to support the education of low-income students and those requiring special education, compensatory education, or bilingual education services is that poor schools have often served these students with unqualified teachers and untrained aides, rather than the highly skilled teachers envisioned by federal laws. The very purpose of the legislation—to ensure greater opportunities for learning for these students—has often been undermined by local inability to provide them with teachers who have the skills to meet their needs.

It is no exaggeration to say that our nation is at a crossroads. We are currently developing a sharply bimodal teaching force, just at a time when researchers and policymakers have recognized the crucial importance of teacher quality. While some children are gaining access to teachers who are more qualified and better prepared than in years past, a growing number of poor and minority children are being taught by teachers who lack training and are sorely unprepared for the task they face. This poses the risk that we may see heightened inequality in opportunities to learn and in outcomes of schooling, despite the apparent drive to raise standards and to extend opportunity.

Thus, one of the most important aspects of No Child Left Behind is that it requires all schools to provide "highly qualified teachers" to all students by 2006. This requirement—that all teachers be fully certified and show competence in the subject areas they teach—is intended to correct this longstanding problem. And it is a problem that can be solved. What often looks like a teacher shortage is actually mostly a problem of getting teachers from where they are trained to where they are needed, and keeping teachers in the profession once they enter, especially in central cities and poor rural areas. As my friend Richard Ingersoll has written to you, with more than thirty percent of beginners leaving teaching within five years, and low-income schools suffering from even higher turnover rates, producing more teachers—especially through fast-track routes that tend to have high attrition—is like spending all our energy filling a leaky bucket rather than patching the holes.

We need to understand this problem if we are to solve it. There are actually at least three or four times as many credentialed teachers in the United States as there are jobs, and many states and districts have surpluses. Not surprisingly, however, teachers are less likely to enter and stay in teaching positions where salaries are lower and working conditions are poorer. They are also more than twice as likely to leave if they have not had preparation for teaching and if they do not receive mentoring in their early years on the job. These are issues that can be addressed by policy. States and districts that have increased and equalized salaries to attract qualified teachers, created strong preparation programs so that teachers are effective with the students they will teach, and provided mentors have shown how we can fill classrooms with well-prepared teachers.

But solving this problem everywhere requires a national agenda. The distributional inequities that lead to the hiring of unqualified teachers are caused not only by disparities in pay and working conditions, but also by interstate barriers to teacher mobility, inadequate recruitment incentives to distribute teachers appropriately, and fiscal conditions that often produce incentives for hiring the least expensive rather than the most qualified teachers. And while the nation actually produces far more new teachers than it needs, some specific teaching fields experience real shortages. These include teachers for children with disabilities and those with limited English proficiency, as well as teachers of science and mathematics. Boosting supply in the fields where there are real shortfalls requires targeted recruitment and investment in the capacity of preparation institutions to expand their programs to meet national needs in key areas.

You can help the federal government play a leadership role in providing an adequate supply of well-qualified teachers just as it has in providing an adequate supply of well-qualified physicians for the nation. When shortages of physicians were a major problem more than forty years ago, Congress passed the 1963 Health Professions Education Assistance Act to support and improve the caliber of medical training, to create and strengthen teaching hospitals, to provide scholarships and loans to medical students, and to create incentives for physicians to train in shortage specialties and to locate in underserved areas. Similar federal initiatives in education were effective during the 1960s and 1970s but were eliminated in the 1980s.

We need a federal teacher policy that will:

1. *Recruit new teachers* who prepare to teach in high-need fields and locations, through scholarships and forgivable loans that allow them to receive high-quality teacher education and pay back their subsidies with service in K–12 schools.
2. *Strengthen teachers' preparation* through incentive grants to schools of education to create professional development schools, like teaching hospitals, to train prospective teachers in urban areas and to expand and improve programs to prepare special education teachers, teachers of English language learners, and other areas where our needs exceed our current capacity.
3. *Improve teacher retention and effectiveness* by ensuring they have mentoring support during the beginning teaching stage when nearly one third of them drop out.

FOR THE COST OF ONE PERCENT OF THE BUSH ADMINISTRATION'S TAX CUTS in 2003 or the equivalent of one week's combat costs during the war in Iraq, we could provide top-quality preparation for more than one hundred and fifty thousand new teachers to teach in high-need schools and mentor all of the new teachers who are hired over the next five years. With just a bit of focus and a purposeful plan, we could ensure that all students in the United States are taught by highly-qualified teachers within the next five years. Now that would be *real* accountability to children and their parents.

I know this is what you came to Washington to do, and I trust you'll stay the course. Our children need you there.

Sincerely,

Linda Darling-Hammond

ORGANIZATIONS FOR PARENTS, EDUCATORS, AND ACTIVISTS

The Forum for Education and Democracy (www.forumforeducation.org)

The Forum for Education and Democracy supports research, publications, and action projects that promote the democratic purpose of public education. The forum works on behalf of a system of public education that is vibrant, equitable, and consistent with a belief in a government of, for, and by the people. The forum believes in and works for schools that nurture in all children the habits of heart and mind that make democracy possible and aims to re-center the democratic purpose of our public schools.

The Center on Education Policy (www.cep-dc.org)

The Center on Education Policy is a national, independent advocate for public education and for more effective public schools. The center helps Americans better understand the role of public education in a democracy and the need to improve the academic quality of public schools. The center does not represent any special interests but, instead, tries to help citizens make sense of the conflicting opinions and perceptions about public education and create the conditions that will lead to better public schools.

The Children's Defense Fund (www.childrensdefense.org)

The mission of the Children's Defense Fund (CDF) is to ensure every child a Healthy Start, a Head Start, a Fair Start, a Safe Start, and a Moral Start in life and successful passage to adulthood with the help of caring families and communities. CDF provides a strong, effective voice for all the children of America who cannot vote, lobby, or speak for themselves, and pays particular attention to the needs of poor and minority children and those with disabilities. CDF encourages preventive investment before they get sick or into trouble, drop out of school, or suffer family breakdown.

The Civil Rights Project/Progecto de Derechos Civiles (www.civilrightsproject. harvard.edu)

The Civil Rights Project (CRP) is a leading organization devoted to civil rights research. It has found eager collaborators among researchers nationwide, and wide open doors among advocacy organizations, policymakers, and journalists. Focusing initially on education reform, it has convened dozens of national conferences and roundtables; commissioned more than three hundred new research and policy studies; produced major reports on desegregation, student diversity, school discipline, special education, dropouts, and Title I programs; and published seven books, with four more in the editing stage. CRP has initiated joint projects across disciplinary and institutional lines at universities, advocacy organizations, and think tanks throughout the country. CRP directors and staff testify and provide technical assistance on Capitol Hill and in state capitals. Its research has been incorporated into federal legislation, cited in litigation, and used to spur congressional hearings. The CRP is in the process of relocating from Harvard University to the University of California in Los Angeles.

The Public Education Network (www.publiceducation.org)

Public Education Network (PEN) is a national association of local education funds (LEFs) and individuals working to advance public school reform in low-income communities across our country. PEN's network of LEFs operates in thirty-four states, the District of Columbia, and Puerto Rico, and serves 11.5 million students—that's twenty-two percent of America's public school population—in eighteen thousand schools in more than one thousand six hundred school districts in low-income areas. In addition, PEN's international affiliates serve more than seven million children in Mexico, Peru, and the Philippines. PEN seeks to build public demand and mobilize resources for quality public education for all children.

Parents for Public Schools (www.parents4publicschools.com)

Parents for Public Schools is a national organization of community-based chapters working in public schools through broad-based enrollment. Invigorated by a diverse membership, the group's proactive involvement helps public schools attract all families in a community by making sure all schools effectively serve all children. Parents for Public Schools believes that quality public education is vital to our democracy and to America's future

JOINT ORGANIZATIONAL STATEMENT ON THE NO CHILD LEFT BEHIND ACT

(See www.fairtest.org for more information on the statement. Original statement issued on October 21, 2004, and then updated on August 25, 2006.)

The undersigned education, civil rights, children's, disability, and citizens' organizations are committed to the No Child Left Behind Act's objectives of strong academic achievement for all children and closing the achievement gap. We believe that the federal government has a critical role to play in attaining these goals. We endorse the use of an accountability system that helps ensure all children, including children of color, from low-income families, with disabilities, and of limited English proficiency, are prepared to be successful, participating members of our democracy.

While we all have different positions on various aspects of the law, based on concerns raised during the implementation of NCLB, we believe the following significant, constructive corrections are among those necessary to make the Act fair and effective. Among these concerns are overemphasizing standardized testing, narrowing curriculum and instruction to focus on test preparation rather than richer academic learning; overidentifying schools in need of improvement; using sanctions that do not help improve schools; inappropriately excluding low-scoring children in order to boost test results; and inadequate funding. Overall, the law's emphasis needs to shift from applying

sanctions for failing to raise test scores to holding states and localities accountable for making the systemic changes that improve student achievement.

Recommended Changes in NCLB

Progress Measurement

1. Replace the law's arbitrary proficiency targets with ambitious achievement
   targets based on rates of success actually achieved by the most effective
   public schools.
2. Allow states to measure progress by using students' growth in achievement as well as their performance in relation to predetermined levels of
   academic proficiency.
3. Ensure that states and school districts regularly report to the government
   and the public their progress in implementing systemic changes to enhance
   educator, family, and community capacity to improve student learning.
4. Provide a comprehensive picture of students' and schools' performance
   by moving from an overwhelming reliance on standardized tests to using
   multiple indicators of student achievement in addition to these tests.
5. Fund research and development of more effective accountability systems
   that better meet the goal of high academic achievement for all children.

Assessments

6. Help states develop assessment systems that include district and school-
   based measures in order to provide better, more timely information about
   student learning.
7. Strengthen enforcement of NCLB provisions requiring that assessments
   must:
   • Be aligned with state content and achievement standards;
   • Be used for purposes for which they are valid and reliable;
   • Be consistent with nationally recognized professional and technical
     standards;
   • Be of adequate technical quality for each purpose required under the Act;
   • Provide multiple, up-to-date measures of student performance, includ-
     ing measures that assess higher-order thinking skills and understand-
     ing; and
   • Provide useful diagnostic information to improve teaching and learning.
8. Decrease the testing burden on states, schools, and districts by allowing
   states to assess students annually in selected grades in elementary, middle
   schools, and high schools.

Building Capacity

9. Ensure changes in teacher and administrator preparation and continuing professional development that research evidence and experience indicate improve educational quality and student achievement.
10. Enhance state and local capacity to effectively implement the comprehensive changes required to increase the knowledge and skills of administrators, teachers, families, and communities to support high student achievement.

Sanctions

11. Ensure that improvement plans are allowed sufficient time to take hold before applying sanctions; sanctions should not be applied if they undermine existing effective reform efforts.
12. Replace sanctions that do not have a consistent record of success with interventions that enable schools to make changes that result in improved student achievement.

Funding

13. Raise authorized levels of NCLB funding to cover a substantial percentage of the costs that states and districts will incur to carry out these recommendations, and fully fund the law at those levels without reducing expenditures for other education programs.
14. Fully fund Title I to ensure that one hundred percent of eligible children are served.

We, the undersigned, will work for the adoption of these recommendations as central structural changes needed to NCLB at the same time that we advance our individual organization's proposals.

Advancement Project
American Association of School Administrators
American Association of School Librarians
American Association of University Women
American Counseling Association
American Dance Therapy Association
American Federation of School Administrators
American Federation of State, County, and Municipal Employees
American Speech-Language-Hearing Association
Annenberg Institute for School Reform
Asian American Legal Defense and Education Fund

ASPIRA
Association for Supervision and Curriculum Development
Association of Community Organizations for Reform Now
Association of School Business Officials International
Big Picture Company
Center for Community Change
Center for Expansion of Language and Thinking
Center for Parent Leadership
Children's Aid Society
Children's Defense Fund
Church Women United
Citizens for Effective Schools
Coalition of Essential Schools
Commission on Social Action of Reform Judaism
Communities for Quality Education
Council for Children with Behavioral Disorders
Council for Exceptional Children
Council for Hispanic Ministries of the United Church of Christ
Council for Learning Disabilities
Cross City Campaign for Urban School Reform
Disciples Home Missions of the Christian Church (Disciples of Christ)
Division for Learning Disabilities of the Council for Exceptional Children
Education Action!
FairTest
Forum for Education and Democracy
General Board of Church and Society, The United Methodist Church
Hmong National Development
International Reading Association
International Technology Education Association
Japanese American Citizens League
Learning Disabilities Association of America
League of United Latin American Citizens
Ministers for Racial, Social and Economic Justice of the United Church of Christ
National Alliance of Black School Educators
National Association for the Advancement of Colored People
NAACP Legal Defense and Education Fund
National Association for Asian and Pacific American Education
National Association for Bilingual Education
National Association for the Education and Advancement of Cambodian,
    Laotian, and Vietnamese Americans

National Association for the Education of African American Children with
  Learning Disabilities
National Association of Pupil Service Administrators
National Association of School Psychologists
National Association of Social Workers
National Coalition for Asian Pacific American Community Development
National Coalition for Parent Involvement in Education
National Conference of Black Mayors
National Council for the Social Studies
National Council of Churches
National Council of Jewish Women
National Council of Teachers of English
National Down Syndrome Congress
National Education Association
National Federation of Filipino American Associations
National Indian Education Association
National Indian School Board Association
National Korean American Service & Education Consortium
National Mental Health Association
National Ministries, American Baptist Churches, USA
National Reading Conference
National Rural Education Association
National School Boards Association
National Urban League
Native Hawaiian Education Association
People for the American Way
Presbyterian Church (USA)
Rural School and Community Trust
Service Employees International Union
Sikh American Legal Defense and Educational Fund
School Social Work Association of America
Social Action Committee of the Congress of Secular Jewish Organizations
Southeast Asia Resource Action Center
Stand for Children
Teachers of English to Speakers of Other Languages, Inc.
United Black Christians of the United Church of Christ
United Church of Christ Justice and Witness Ministries
Women's Division of the General Board of Global Ministries, the United
  Methodist Church
Women of Reform Judaism

ABOUT THE EDITOR
AND CONTRIBUTORS

Sylvia Bruni has served seventeen years as a senior English teacher and twenty-three years as a gifted/talented program coordinator, elementary campus principal, director of curriculum and instruction, university administrator, and college professor. As Administrative Assistant for Special Programs, she is the chief advocate for Laredo ISD on legislative, governance, and community issues that are of critical importance to the district. Ms. Bruni has also served as chairperson for a number of civic groups, among them United Way of Laredo, the Laredo Gateway Rotary Club, Leadership Laredo, Mi Laredo Goals for the 90s, AVANCE, a Family Support Program, and the International Children's Advocacy Center. Most recently, she has been named to the state education committee of the League of United Latin American Citizens (LULAC). Just as important, she has raised not only three children—Selina, Anita, and Tony—but also two of her five grandchildren, Ashley and Victoria.

April Burns is a doctoral candidate in Social Personality Psychology at the Graduate Center of the City University of New York. She is a recipient of a Spencer Foundation Discipline Based Studies Fellowship in Education for Social Justice and Social Development. Her research focuses broadly on issues of privileged consciousness, ideology, and the psychology of social class. Current projects include an investigation of academically successful youths' understanding of—and sense of social responsibility for—race and class-stratified differences in educational outcomes, or what has been called the "minority achievement gap."

Louis B. Casagrande joined the Children's Museum in 1994 as president. Previously, he had spent twenty years at the Science Museum of Minnesota, where he developed numerous major exhibitions, supported a broad range of community and statewide collaborations, and helped to create the award-winning Museum Magnet School with the Saint Paul School District. At the Children's Museum of Boston, he has continued to develop innovative collaborations among communities, schools, and the Museum, including the creation of the Harcourt Teacher Leadership Center, an expanded Early Childhood

Center, and new exhibitions on theater arts, environmental sciences, and world cultures. He is married to Julie Petty Casagrande, a former Spanish teacher at Brookline High School, MA. They have two grown children.

William H. (Bill) Cosby, Jr.'s educational journey:
Elementary: Mary Channing Wister Elementary School
Junior High School: Fitzsimmons Junior High School
High School: Central High School, class #204, class #205, class #206, class #207; transferred to Germantown High School—dropped out.
Post–High School: U.S. Navy, Hospital Corpsman, Physical Therapy, GED.
Undergraduate: Temple University, B.A.; simultaneously granted high school diploma, Central High School, retroactive to class #204
Graduate: University of Massachusetts, Amherst, School of Education, Master's, 1972; University of Massachusetts, Amherst, School of Education, Ed.D., 1976
Postgraduate: Still studying with Dr. Camille Cosby

Linda Darling-Hammond is Charles E. Ducommun Professor of Education at Stanford University School of Education. She has served as executive director of the National Commission on Teaching and America's Future, which produced the widely cited blueprint for education reform *What Matters Most: Teaching for America's Future*; chair of New York State's Council on Curriculum and Assessment; and co-chair of California's Task Force on Professional Development. Darling-Hammond's research, teaching, and policy work focuses on educational policy, teaching and teacher education, school restructuring, and educational equity. Among her more than two hundred publications is *The Right To Learn*, recipient of the 1998 Outstanding Book Award from the American Educational Research Association and *Teaching as the Learning Profession*, which was awarded the National Staff Development Council's Outstanding Book Award in 2000.

Elizabeth DeBray-Pelot is an Assistant Professor in the Department of Lifelong Education, Administration, and Policy in the College of Education, University of Georgia. She received her Ed.D. in Administration, Planning, and Social Policy from the Harvard Graduate School of Education in 2001. Between 2002 and 2005, she was a Fellow in the Advanced Studies Fellowship Program on Federal and National Strategies of School Reform at Brown University, research assistant with the Consortium for Policy Research in Education from 1997 to 2001, and research associate with the Civil Rights Project at Harvard University from 1998 to 2002. Her major interests are the implementation and effects of federal and state elementary and secondary school policies and the politics of education. She has authored articles on school desegregation, school choice, high schools' organizational response to accountability policies, and compensatory education. Dr. DeBray-Pelot served as program analyst in the Office of Educational Research and Improvement (OERI) from 1992 to 1996. She is author of *Politics, Ideology, and Education: Federal Policy During the Clinton and Bush Administrations*, which analyzes the politics of the reauthorization of the Elementary and Secondary Education Act in the 106th and 107th Congresses. She was a 2005 recipient of the National Academy of Education/Spencer Postdoctoral Fellowship, which is currently supporting her research on education interest groups, think tanks, and Congress.

Lisa Delpit is an Eminent Scholar and Executive Director at Florida International University's Center for Urban Education and Innovation. Dr. Delpit received a MacArthur "Genius" Fellowship in 1990 for her work to improve educational outcomes in low-income schools and communities in the United States and abroad. She is the author of several books, including the award-winning *Other People's Children*, as well as a number of other publications. She has received the Harvard University Alumni Award for Outstanding Contributions to Education, The Children's Television Network's first annual Sunny Days Award for Outstanding Contributions to Young Children, and numerous other awards for her dedicated work for those children who are least well-served by our educational system.

Rosa Fernández, was born in La Vega, Dominican Republic. Her experiences at Manhattan International High School, a small public high school in New York City, led to her serving on a new school planning team for New Century High Schools in the Bronx. She has collaborated with What Kids Can Do, Inc., on *The Schools We Need: Creating Small High Schools That Works for Us* and *First in the Family: Advice About College from First-Generation Students*. She organized a symposium with national education leaders on public education, school reform, and the 2004 presidential elections. She is a senior at Wellesley College and intends to go on for her doctorate in Latin American history.

Michelle Fine is the Distinguished Professor of Social Psychology, Women's Studies, and Urban Education at the Graduate Center of the City University of New York. She has been funded by Rockefeller, Spencer, Ford, Pew, Leslie Glass, and Open Society to study how youth view distributive and procedural justice in schools, prisons, the economy, and in local communities. She is interested in the relation of scholarship and activism.

John Glenn has devoted his life to public service. He was the first American astronaut to orbit the Earth in 1962, for which he received the Space Congressional Medal of Honor. In 1974, he was elected to serve in the U.S. Senate. In 1992, he became the first popularly elected senator from Ohio to win four consecutive terms. Senator Glenn again made history in 1998 when he returned to space aboard the shuttle Discovery, making him the oldest person to fly in space. His deep commitment to education and involving youth in public and community service inspired the formation of the John Glenn Institute for Public Service and Public Policy at Ohio State University. He has served as Chair of the National Commission on Mathematics and Science Teaching for the 21st Century and the National Commission on Service-Learning.

Carl Glickman is Scholar-in-Residence in the Educational Administration and Policy program at the University of Georgia. He began his career in 1968 as a Teacher Corps intern in the rural south and later became principal of award-winning schools. During his career at the University of Georgia, he founded the Georgia League of Professional Schools, a nationally validated network of K–12 schools devoted to democratic learning for all students. In 1997, he received the "University Professorship" for bringing "stature and distinction" to the mission of the University, and, in a separate honor, students selected him as the faculty member who had "contributed most to their lives, both inside and outside the classroom." Carl is a founding member of the Forum for Education and Democracy (www.forumforeducation.org) and serves on the steering committee of the National Campaign for the Civic Mission of Schools (www.civicmissionofschools.org). He has authored thirteen books on school leadership, educational renewal, and the moral imperative of education. Carl and his spouse Sara reside in Athens, Georgia, and spend summers with their children and grandchildren in St. Albans Bay, Vermont.

John I. Goodlad is professor emeritus at the University of Washington and president of the nonprofit Institute for Educational Inquiry in Seattle. He has completed a Ph.D. degree at the University of Chicago; held professorships and administrative positions at Agnes Scott College, Emory University, the University of Chicago, and the University of California at Los Angeles; wrote, edited, or coauthored some three dozen books; and received twenty honorary doctorates and various other awards due, in part, to his long career in the advocacy and support of public education. Two children, Paula and Stephen, joined him and his wife Lynn early on. Lynn is still patiently waiting for that promised summer of relaxation and has come to the conclusion that the Golden Years are an oxymoron.

Maxine Greene is Professor of Philosophy and Education (Emerita) at Teachers College, Columbia University and Philosopher in Residence at the Lincoln Center Institute for the Arts in Education. Presently, she teaches classes under the auspices of the City University Graduate Center and the Foundation for Social Imagination in the Arts and Education. She is a past president of the American Educational Research Association, the American Educational Studies Association, and the Philosophy of Education Society. She has written about one hundred articles and forewords as well as six books, most recently *The Dialectic of Freedom* and *Variations on a Blue Guitar.*

Sandra Halladey is the mother of two children who attend public school in San Francisco, CA. A native of England, Sandra graduated from the University of Sussex. After graduation, she volunteered in number of nonprofit organizations and worked in the nonprofit sector. When her first child reached pre-school age, Sandra became involved with public school enrollment, school reform, and related issues. In 1999, she founded the San Francisco chapter of Parents for Public Schools. Currently, Sandra works for San Francisco State University. Improving public education is a family priority. Her husband, Paul, an artist, is committed to ensuring that public school students have opportunities to work with professional artists.

Karen Hale Hankins teaches first grade in Athens, GA. She also teaches graduate courses at Piedmont College. In addition to teaching, which she says feeds her need to be an actor, she is also a writer. Her recently published book, *Teaching Through the Storm: A Journal of Hope*, recounts a difficult yet hopeful year she spent with one particular first-grade class. She enjoys public speaking and storytelling. She and her husband, Brad, have four wonderful children and two spectacular grandchildren. She lives within walking distance of her parents, her school, her church, and her writing mentor.

Leslie F. Hergert was the director of the National Commission on Service-Learning. Currently, as a senior project director at Education Development Center, Inc., she works on leadership development efforts in urban school districts and develops and evaluates civic education curricula. Prior to coming to EDC, Dr. Hergert developed and led multistate schoolwide change programs and taught graduate courses in educational leadership. She earned a doctorate from Harvard Graduate School of Education in administration and social policy in 1994, and from 1966 to 1967, she served as one of the early VISTA volunteers in Carrollton, GA, and Miami, FL.

Asa G. Hilliard III–Nana Baffour Amankwatia II is the Fuller E. Callaway Professor of Urban Education at Georgia State University. He has helped to develop several national assessment systems, including a proficiency assessment of professional educators and developmental assessments of young children and infants. Dr. Hilliard has consulted with many leading school districts, publishers, public advocacy organizations, universities, government agencies, and private corporations on valid assessment, African content in curriculum, teacher training, and public policy. Several of his programs in curriculum assessment and valid teaching have become national models. Dr. Hilliard has served on such boards as the Agency for Instructional Technology, Zero to Three, the Public Education Fund Network, the American Association of Colleges for Teacher Education, the Far West Regional Laboratory for Educational Research and Development, and the Center for Applied Linguistics.

Richard Ingersoll, a former high school teacher, is currently Professor of Education and Sociology at the University of Pennsylvania. Professor Ingersoll's research is concerned with the management and organization of elementary and secondary schools and the character and problems of the teaching occupation. Dr. Ingersoll has done extensive research on the problems of teacher shortages and underqualified teachers and has been invited to present his research to numerous federal, state, and local legislators and policymakers, including the congressional hearings on teacher policy held by the U.S. House of Representatives in 1998; the National Commission on Mathematics and Science Teaching for the 21st Century in 1999; the Science and the Congress Briefing in 2000; and the 2001 congressional seminar for new members of the House of Representatives. In 2004, he received the Outstanding Writing Award from AACTE for his book, *Who Controls Teachers' Work?: Power and Accountability in America's Schools,* which looks at how much control and accountability are exerted over teachers and their work in schools and what impact this has on school performance.

Jacqueline Jordan Irvine is the Charles Howard Candler Professor of Urban Education in the Division of Educational Studies at Emory University in Atlanta, GA. Her specialization is in multicultural education and urban teacher education, particularly the education of African Americans. Her books include *Black Students and School Failure, Growing Up African American in Catholic Schools, Critical Knowledge for Diverse Students, Culturally Responsive Lesson Planning for Elementary and Middle Grades, In Search of Wholeness: African American Teachers and Their Culturally Specific Pedagogy,* and *Educating Teaching* *for Diversity: Seeing with a Cultural Eye.* In addition to these books, she has published numerous articles and book chapters, and presented more than two hundred papers to professional education and community organizations.

Jim Jeffords spent thirty-two years in Congress, including three terms in the Senate. Jeffords championed legislation to strengthen our nation's education system and increase opportunities for individuals with disabilities. He also chaired the Senate Environment and Public Works Committee from 2001 to 2002, and served as the committee's ranking member. Jeffords also served as a member of the Senate Finance Committee; Senate Veterans' Affairs Committee; Special Committee on Aging; and the Senate Health, Education, Labor, and Pensions Committee, which he chaired from 1997 to 2001. Jeffords was one of six founders of the Congressional Solar Coalition, and was the Chairman of the House Environmental Study Conference from 1978 to 1979. In recognition of his achievements, Jeffords received many prestigious awards, including being named Legislator of the Year by *Parenting* magazine in 1999 and being awarded the Sierra Club's top honor in 2002. Jeffords is a black belt in tae kwon do and enjoys cross-country and downhill skiing. He lives in Shrewsbury, VT, with his wife, Elizabeth Daley. He has two children, Leonard and Laura.

Lilian G. Katz is Professor Emerita of Early Childhood Education at the University of Illinois (Urbana-Champaign) where she is also codirector of the ERIC Clearinghouse on Elementary and Early Childhood Education. She is a past president of the National Association for the Education of Young Children, and is editor of the first online peer-reviewed early childhood journal, *Early Childhood Research & Practice.* Dr. Katz is the recipient of many honors, including two Fulbright Awards (India & New Zealand), an Honorary Doctor of Letters degree from Whittier College in California, and an honorary Doctor of Philosophy from the University of Goteborg in Sweden. In 1997, she served as Nehru Professor at the University of Baroda in India. In 2003, Dr. Katz was appointed Visiting Professorial Fellow at the Institute of Education, University of London, UK. Professor Katz and her husband, Boris, have three grown children, four grandsons, and one granddaughter.

Reynold Levy is the president of Lincoln Center for the Performing Arts. He formerly served as president of the International Rescue Committee, a senior officer at AT&T, and president of the AT&T Foundation, as well as the executive director of the 92nd Street YMCA. He has also been a trustee of the Manhattan Theatre Club, the Independent Sector, and the Nathan Cummings Foundation, among many other nonprofit institutions.

Martin Lipton is a communications analyst at UCLA's Institute for Democracy, Education, and Access. He is the author, with Jeannie Oakes, of *Becoming Good American Schools* (winner of the 2001 AERA Outstanding Book Award) and of *Teaching to Change the World*.

William J. Mathis was a National Superintendent of the Year finalist in 2003 and was the Vermont Superintendent of the Year for 2002. He serves on the board of directors of the American Education Finance Association, is an education policy research fellow with Arizona State University, and serves as a senior fellow of the Vermont Society for the Study of Education. Previously, he was president of the Vermont Superintendents' Association. Currently, he is superintendent of schools in Brandon, VT. He has published or presented more than one hundred research papers, policy briefs, newspaper columns, and monographs and has been invited to speak to groups around the nation. Active in school finance matters, he has worked on assessment and funding systems in a number of states, and teaches educational finance at the University of Vermont.

Deborah W. Meier has spent four decades working in public education as a teacher, writer, and public advocate on behalf of democracy and equity. She began her teaching career as a kindergarten and Head Start teacher in Chicago, Philadelphia, and New York City schools. In 1974, she began Central Park East Elementary School in East Harlem, the first of a network of small New York City public schools. In 1985, she founded Central Park East Secondary School in which more than ninety percent of the entering students went on to college. She is a founding member of the Coalition of Essential Schools. In 1987, she was the recipient of the MacArthur Award. Meier is on the editorial board of *Dissent* magazine, *The Nation*, and the *Harvard Education Letter*, and she writes and speaks extensively on educational issues. She is a board member of the Association of Union Democracy, Educators for Social Responsibility, the National Academy of Education, and a founding member of the National Board of Professional Teaching Standards, among others.

Edward C. Montgomery graduated from the University of Nebraska-Lincoln in 1979 with a B.S.Ed. He flew helicopters in the U.S. Marine Corps from 1979 to 1985, including service in Grenada and Lebanon. He began his teaching career in 1985 on the Omaha Indian Reservation in Nebraska. He currently teaches tenth-, eleventh-, and twelfth-grade American history and eighth-grade English in Kimball, Nebraska, where he also serves as the district assessment coordinator. Teaching endorsements include history, English, social studies, political science, and assessment leadership. He is married with three children, all of whom have had the misfortune of being his students.

Pedro Noguera is a professor in the Steinhardt School of Education at New York University. Noguera's research specializes on the challenges confronting urban public schools. The author of numerous publications, his latest book, *City Schools and the American Dream: Reclaiming the Promise of Public Education* was published by Teachers College Press in 2003. Noguera was formerly an elected school board member in Berkeley, California. He is the father of four children who attend public schools in New York City.

Jeannie Oakes is Presidential Professor in Educational Equity and the director of the Institute for Democracy, Education, & Access (IDEA) and the All Campus Consortium on Research for Diversity (ACCORD) at UCLA. Dr. Oakes's research examines inequalities in U.S. schools and follows the progress of equity-minded reform. She is the author of seventeen scholarly books and monographs and more than one hundred published research reports, chapters, and articles. Her work addresses tracking and ability grouping, unequal distribution of resources and opportunities for education, and educators working for equity. She has received three awards from the American Educational Research Association (Early Career Award, Outstanding Research Article, and Outstanding Book), the National Association for Multicultural Education's Multicultural Research Award, and the Distinguished Achievement Award from the Educational Press Association of America. She is also the recipient of Southern Christian Leadership Conference's Ralph David Abernathy Award for Public Service and the World Cultural Council's Jose Vasconcelos World Award in Education.

Arturo Pacheco is the director of the Center for Research on Education Reform at the University of Texas at El Paso and the El Paso Electric Company Professor of Education Research. After twenty years as a faculty member and administrator at the University of California at Santa Cruz and Stanford University, he served for a decade as Dean of the College of Education (1992–2002). Pacheco is coauthor of *Centers of Pedagogy: New Structures for Educational Renewal* (2000) and a variety of articles and chapters on teacher education reform and higher education, including the 2000 AACTE Hunt Lecture, *Meeting the Challenge of High Quality Teacher Preparation: Why Higher Education Must Change*.

W. James Popham started his career as an English and social studies teacher, yearbook advisor, class sponsor, and unpaid tennis coach in a small Oregon high school. Later on, he taught courses in instructional methods for prospective teachers as well as courses in evaluation and measurement for graduate students at UCLA. At UCLA, he won several distinguished teaching awards and was recognized by *UCLA Today* as one of UCLA's top twenty professors of the twentieth century. In 1992, he took early retirement from UCLA upon learning that emeritus professors received free parking. Dr. Popham has authored more than twenty-five books, two hundred journal articles, fifty research reports, and one hundred and seventy-five papers presented before research societies. In 1978, Dr. Popham was elected president of the American Educational Research Association (AERA), where he was the founding editor of AERA's quarterly journal, *Educational Evaluation and Policy Analysis*. In 2002, the National Council on Measurement in Education presented him with its award for Career Contributions to Educational Measurement.

Vance Rawles was born in New York City twenty years ago. He attended Jacqueline Kennedy Onassis High School and Urban Academy before receiving his GED and currently is studying art at the Cooper Union. Vance also enjoys show tunes and singing off-key. He would like to be an actor, artist, cartoonist, or sculptor—and hopes he will be employed. Anyone with a good job is encouraged to get in touch.

Ken Rolling lives with his family in Evanston, IL. He is a parent of two public school graduates who are both now in college. He is executive director of Parents for Public Schools, a national network of parents who support public education and advocate for improving public schools for all children (www.parents4publicschools.com). From 1995 to 2002, he was executive director of the Chicago Annenberg Challenge.

Jane Ross currently serves as an assistant principal and lead mentor at a wonderfully diverse middle school in Austin, Texas. She has taught seventh-grade mathematics, was voted campus teacher of the year, and was a semifinalist for district teacher of the year. Ms. Ross earned her Ph.D. in education with a major in school improvement from Texas State University, San Marcos, where she recently accepted an adjunct position to teach a course on professional development in the educational administration department. Her areas of interest include culturally responsive education; new teacher development; sustainable parent and community involvement; sustainable educator commitment; curriculum, instruction, assessment, and professional development alignment; and teacher voice in educational policymaking.

Sophie Sa is the founding executive director of the Panasonic Foundation. The foundation has been dedicated to improving education in the United States from its inception. Since 1986, Panasonic's mission has been to help build the capacity of school districts in designing and implementing systemic reform efforts for the improvement of teaching and learning for all children.

Rather than make grants, the foundation enters into direct long-term partnership with districts to provide expertise on whole-system change through its network of education specialists. The foundation works only in districts where at least thirty percent of the students receive free lunch. Currently, it is in partnership with the school systems of Atlanta (GA), Columbus (OH), Corpus Christi (TX), Norfolk (VA), Norristown (PA), Norwalk-LaMirada (CA), Pasco County (FL), Racine (WI), and Santa Fe (NM).

Theodore R. Sizer is University Professor Emeritus at Brown University and currently Visiting Professor of Education at Harvard and Brandeis Universities. In 1984, he founded the Coalition of Essential Schools and has served as a teacher and principal in both public and private secondary schools. His books include *Horace's Compromise: The Dilemma of the American High School* and *The Students Are Watching: Schools and the Moral Contract*, authored with his wife, Nancy. He has four children, three children-in-law, and ten grandchildren.

Thomas Sobol is Christian A. Johnson Professor of Outstanding Educational Practice at Teachers College, Columbia University, where he teaches courses in educational policy and ethics, coordinates the program in educational administration, directs the inquiry doctoral program and the Superintendents Work Conference, and codirects the Future School Administrators Academy in collaboration with field practitioners. He served for sixteen years as Superintendent of Schools in Scarsdale, NY, and for eight years as Commissioner of Education in New York State. Nationally, he has chaired the board of the New Standards Project, served on the executive committee of the Council of Chief State School Officers, and cochaired the National Research Council's Committee on Education Finance: Equity, Adequacy, and Productivity. He is the author of *Your Child in School* and numerous articles in education publications. In 1996, Dr. Sobol received the Harvard Graduate School of Education Alumni Award for Outstanding Contributions to Education, and annually from 1997 to the present he has received awards from Teachers College for excellence in teaching.

Pam Solo, an internationally acclaimed proponent of grass-roots activism, is the founder and president of the Civil Society Institute, a nonprofit, nonpartisan organization dedicated to supporting and encouraging the involvement of community groups and individuals in the public life of the country. The institute is currently spearheading the Campaign to Put Learning Back in Public Education as part of its Results for America Campaign. Pam is the recipient of a MacArthur Prize Fellowship, is past president of the Social Venture Network (an alliance of five hundred CEOs committed to socially responsible business principles), and is the former executive director of Cultural Survival (a group that has helped indigenous groups in Central America achieve economic self-sufficiency). She was a consultant to the Multilateral Investment fund of the Inter-American Development Bank and a professional staff member of the House Armed Services Committee Panel on Burden-Sharing.

Mark W. Sorensen is the executive director of Little Singer Community School in Birdsprings, AZ, and the executive director and cofounder of the STAR School, a solar-powered charter school serving primarily Navajo students. Dr. Sorensen also is a member of the Tribal Task Force to create a Navajo Tribal Education Department and is the founding (and continuing) executive director of the Native American Grant Schools Association, which has grown from four tribally controlled schools in 1991 to twenty-nine grant and charter schools serving Indian students in five tribes. Sorensen has received numerous awards for his work in Indian education, including OIEP Principal of the Year (1993); the Alumni Head, Heart, and Hand Award for Community Service in the Navajo Nation (1998); and a Fellowship from the Open Society Institute in New York City for developing a manual for integrating traditional Navajo Peacemaking into Native American school discipline policies (1999). Mark is married with three children and lives on a solar-powered ranch near Flagstaff, AZ, with his wife, Kate, and his youngest son, Miles. **Derrick Attakai, Evalena Joey, Britta Mitchell, Melody Riggs, and Manuel Thompson** are former students who live on or near the Navajo reservation at Birdsprings, AZ.

Rachel B. Tompkins is president of the Rural School and Community Trust. She previously served as the Extension Professor for Community, Economic, and Workforce Development in the West Virginia University Extension Service. She has also served as adviser to West Virginia Governor Gaston Caperton, as executive director of the Children's Defense Fund, and as executive director of the Citizen's Council for Ohio Schools. She received her doctorate in administration, planning, and social policy from the Harvard Graduate School of Education. She also holds a bachelor's degree in biology from West Virginia University and a master's degree in public administration from Syracuse University's Maxwell School. Tompkins has chaired the Winthrop Rockefeller Foundation Board of Trustees, was founding chair of the West Virginia Commission for National and Community Service, and served as the vice chair of the Annenberg Rural Challenge Board of Trustees.

María Elena Torre is a doctoral candidate in the Social Personality Program at the Graduate Center of CUNY. Her research focuses on women and the criminal justice system, urban education, and youth activism. She is the research director of Critical Perspectives on the Gap (2002–present) and was research director and a coauthor of *Changing Minds: The Impact of College in Maximum Security Prison*. She has served as a consultant for city and state governments, community groups, and colleges interested in establishing college-in-prison programs such as those at San Quentin and Sing-Sing.

George H. Wood is principal of Federal Hocking High School, a rural school located in Stewart, OH, that serves some four hundred and fifty students. He was also the founding director of Wildwood Secondary School in Los Angeles, CA. Both schools are members of the Coalition of Essential Schools and have been recognized as leaders in their work of creating personalized high schools for engaged citizenship. Wood has been a professor of education at Ohio University, served as an elected school board member in Illinois, taught high school social studies, and was the founder of the Institute for Democracy in Education. He is married to Marcia Burchby, a kindergarten teacher, and they are the proud parents of two boys, Michael and John, and a foster son, Ivan Marshal, who serves in the U.S. Navy.